Genesis

A Novel

Gerald E. Forth

Genesis
©2019 Gerald E. Forth

Gerald E. Forth

P.O. Box 220

Healdsburg, CA 95448

forth.g@gmail.com

eBook: 978-1-7335461-0-2

Print: 978-1-7335461-1-9

Contents

Part One.. 1

Update...75

Part Two 77

Part Three...205

Aftermath...351

Part One

Not All Steps are Forward

-1-

Marseille, France

He could feel a tiny, warm drop of moisture slowly wiggle its way down the bridge of his nose. He knew it would be a mistake to stop what he was doing to wipe it away, but far riskier to allow it to spiral into the small nest of electronics he held in his hands. Slowly, and without moving his arms a millimeter, Jean-Claude leaned to his right and gently shook the droplet onto his shirtsleeve. He couldn't suppress the coming shudder. This was desperate work, several degrees beyond dangerous, and somehow exciting in a strange, carnal way.

The small mechanism he cradled in his hands had not been designed to blow up bodies, though it could easily launch his exposed limbs toward all points of the compass if it detonated now. Its reason for being—*la raison d'être*—was to disperse an invisible cloud of something deadly into the vital airspace above a large group of unsuspecting people. He didn't really care what the substance would be, only that he wouldn't be anywhere near it when this happened.

Jean-Claude didn't often think about how he had arrived at this place in life. He was the son of a career officer in the French Army and an English mother with ambitions that far exceeded her abilities. For reasons he rarely spoke of, he chose not to emulate either one. At school, his interests moved first toward history, through philosophy, and unexpectedly, into a fascination with disasters of the unnatural kind. He did not exhibit the curiosity of a boy who occasionally chopped the heads off frogs and lizards, just to see what would happen. For reasons even he could not explain, he grew unnaturally excited in the presence of genuine human suffering. No one who knew him could have guessed this secret. He lived two separate and remarkably balanced lives. Polite to an extreme to the authority figures in his life and a naturally capable student, Jean-Claude did nothing to displease anyone. He could smile, converse with anyone, and appear to be happy and well-adjusted. His other person, the one he guarded carefully behind that confident gaze, he shared with no one. Even in his own estimation he was a monster.

Today, he found himself in a tiny, squalid flat in Marseille, holding his life and those of perhaps thousands of others in his clammy hands. One more connection and he would be finished. He carefully transferred the object into his left hand and reached for the soldering gun with his right. One quick touch of the hot tip and the last wire was securely in place. Slowly, and with a care bordering on reverence, he positioned the device in a box lined with static-resistant foam. Then he took his first breath in what seemed like more than a minute.

Without any action on his part, the timer on the bomb suddenly snapped to life, flashing bright red, rapidly decreasing numerals beginning with 08:00. He gasped for breath, and then again, more urgently. *This can't be happening.* Jean-Claude's adrenaline-saturated brain could not make sense of what his eyes were seeing. The instructions for assembling the device said nothing about this possibility. However, one thing seemed certain. When the timer reached 00:00, he would be dead. His throat tightened; he could not swallow. He couldn't breathe. He seemed to be moving in slow motion. He could see his own messy end ticking down in a flash of red, and his brain said, *Run!* He hadn't quite achieved a standing position when the timer stopped itself at 04:00. It had obeyed a hidden command to reset itself to the four-minute mark, or so it seemed to Jean-Claude, and then it paused for the final directive to begin its relentless countdown. He felt a sudden release of endorphins.

***

In Tehran, a dissident by the name of Colonel Reza Tehrani had received the phone call he had been expecting, and perhaps also dreading. Once given, he realized that there would be no recall of this command. "Reza," the soft voice said, "it is time. All the pieces are now in place. Tell your boy to play his part. Do you understand?" Reza was so nervous that all he could manage was a squeaky affirmation.

Reza had found and recruited Jean-Claude, and many others like him, during his twenty-two years in the intelligence arm of the Revolutionary Guard. He specialized in discovering disenfranchised young men and women who were, sometimes without even knowing it, searching for something exceptional to give meaning to their lives. He didn't find it difficult to spot these special ones. They often also lacked the basic self-governing mechanisms that might protect them from becoming part of something dark and awful. To be honest, the process did not seem much different from recruiting someone to any normal job. It was a matter of matching temperament, skills, and the available opening. Even after a lifetime of recruiting young terrorists, it still distressed Reza how easily some people could be recruited to attack their own fellow citizens. He hoped the same process was not also going on in his own country.

He had discovered Jean-Claude quite by accident while he was on a visit in the South of France. He had flown to a friendly territory in Libya, and then had been whisked across the border to Algeria, from where he could fly unnoticed to Marseille. Reza's mission was to nose around the Arab sections of that uneasy city and make contacts for future development and exploitation. This sprawling city in southern France teemed with immigrants and had been one of his most productive markets. Even so, he never expected to find a white French citizen who would be receptive to his pitch, and so he had stumbled across Jean-Claude when he least expected it.

It had happened in a small café called La Jeunesse, one street removed from the Old Port. Jean-Claude was having an animated discussion with another youth who was loudly disagreeing with him on how to solve the racial issues facing the nation. When the topic moved to Israel, the other youth simply stood up, told Jean-Claude he was crazy, and walked away. Reza felt more than a little reluctant to walk over and introduce himself. However, he recognized something disturbing, and at the same time fascinating, about this young Frenchman. He sat down at his table, and a two-year relationship began. One would never consider this to be a friendship in the normal sense. Reza saw Jean-Claude as potentially useful, nothing more. The young man viewed it quite differently. He wasn't looking for a new life as a terrorist, he simply wanted a friend.

Reza had exercised unusual care in his development of Jean-Claude. As a white European, he didn't fit the model Reza had always used to identify candidates. The other problem with the young man was his obvious lack of mental stability. That wouldn't necessarily disqualify him, but it suggested to Reza that Jean-Claude might reach a point where he might not be controllable. Reza didn't intend to spend his time training and developing an agent who might go rogue, and possibly fail a mission by creating one of his own out of the circumstances. Reza understood that effective modern terrorism existed only because zealots would do exactly what they were told to do, when they were told to do it. It didn't involve a lot of deep thinking. *God loves you. He wants you to do this. Now pull the trigger.* The troubling issue with a person like Jean-Claude is that he still possessed the capacity for real independent thought. That much hadn't change despite his training.

Reza had a special program in mind for Jean-Claude, but first he needed to do a bit more due diligence. One day he asked him, "If I told you to do something, would you do it without questioning, even if it made no sense to you?"

Jean-Claude didn't hesitate. "Of course, I would. You are my friend. Friends do things for one another."

"It might end up being dangerous, or even something you would find morally difficult. Yes, morally difficult, possibly even wrong if looked at in a certain way. Could you do something I asked you to do even if your conscience did not agree?" He looked up and searched his face for the honest answer to his question.

Jean-Claude looked puzzled, like a young child might when asked if the sky was blue. He responded in the only way he knew. "Of course, I would do whatever you asked."

Reza smiled at the young recruit. "Thank you for being honest with me, and so loyal. You are truly my friend if you do as I ask. I think your Jesus said that too."

After several more visits to see him in Marseille, Reza decided to take the risky next step of inviting Jean-Claude to meet him in Algiers on holiday. The real destination would be a Libyan training camp in the ungoverned southern desert regions of that country, where he would learn communications, basic weapons handling, and bomb construction. Jean-Claude took to his studies with great enthusiasm, especially when guns or explosives were involved. He loved explosions, the louder the better, and even his hardened instructors were somewhat fearful for their own safety whenever he picked up a loaded weapon of any kind. Jean-Claude took too much satisfaction in destroying things. He admitted that he couldn't help himself.

Jean-Claude's training in Libya required fourteen weeks. For him, these were the happiest times of his entire life. He lived deep inside a region that no government controlled. His instructors filled each day with activities that to him were fun. He told his parents that he was working with a nongovernmental agency in the sub-Sahara, helping dig water wells for the local villages. This proved a relief to his father who had become increasingly convinced that his son would end up a welfare case or worse. Quite the opposite of what he told his father, that he was helping others: he had been learning how to kill with efficiency and without remorse.

The final ordeal, one designed to weed out possible moles and weak recruits, was to accompany local security forces on a raid of a small village where a large family group of some influence had refused to submit to the regional warlord. The attacking force included three potential graduates of the camp. The soldiers surrounded the family compound at about midnight. One armored vehicle crashed through the gates of the little fortified village. The attackers flooded in and began to methodically search every building, every room, killing all the men they found, and dragging the few survivors into the courtyard.

In all, about twenty people, the unlucky ones not shot during the initial assault, were clustered near the center of the village. Women and small children made up most of the captives. The women were weeping and pleading for the safety of their children. There were no men and only a few older boys among the survivors. The men had fought the invaders with courage but were outmatched in skills and weapons.

Each of the students now received a grisly assignment designed to test their loyalty. Jean-Claude took responsibility for the children. He would have preferred the women, but it really didn't matter that much to him. He followed his orders with precision. Within a few minutes, twelve bodies of small stature were laid out neatly on the sand for his instructors to view. It was not unlike how a cat might display its night's hunting for an approving master. Jean-Claude was not cruel in the completion of his task, only efficient—a single bullet to the top of each head. The other two hopeful graduates could not complete what they were ordered to do, and both were shot on the spot. The soldiers left one survivor from the village, a girl of twelve, who ran off to tell the remainder of the tribe what had happened on that sad night. That event had occurred exactly one year ago.

After returning to Marseille, Jean-Claude reenacted the massacre in his dreams many times, but he felt no real remorse. It was true that he had some lingering curiosity as to why he had obeyed without so much as a question. He didn't feel a need to rationalize or justify his actions, although he did wonder what sort of person this made him. However, the event had simply happened like most things in life. It was necessary for reasons made by someone higher than him, and it would have been what Reza would have wanted him to do. This settled the matter.

As a final test of his pupil's commitment, Reza visited Jean-Claude one more time, a month after his return. He gave him a handgun and the address of an Iranian refugee, a vocal dissident, who lived not far from the train station. Jean-Claude managed to corner the man and his family in their tiny apartment, but he couldn't force himself pull the trigger. He just stood there while the family ran out of the building, never to return. He felt he had failed his friend. He promised himself that he would never do that again. That he had not completed the contract did not seem to matter to Reza. He had another more important and urgent mission for his young protégée.

Perhaps Reza had become just a bit lazy, or a little overconfident. He had grown accustomed to using his personal cell phone to relay instructions to his small group of agents. He found it easier than searching for a working public phone in Tehran, and he was wary of the security services of his own country, who tried to intercept everything passing through the local phone system. He had Jean-Claude's number, as well as a few others, stored in the memory of his phone. This breach of security, if discovered, would have been severely punished by his agency, not to mention his outside employers. But here in his native country he felt untouchable. *Not even the Americans can hurt me here. And if not them, who else has the reach?* He smiled at his observation. He believed he was smarter than any of his opponents.

Jean-Claude could not be described as a typical 24/7 terrorist. He enjoyed the good things that life in France had to offer. For him, terrorism represented a way to get physically high, and a means of obtaining the friendship that life had not seen fit to grant him. It was well past one in the afternoon as he casually lunched at his favorite bistro down by the Old Port. Today, he was enjoying the brilliant blue sky and the flutter of the gulls overhead. He had finished the twelve-euro menu of the day and a second glass of a dry Provençal wine. His phone chirped twice and came to life.

"*Oui, c'est moi,*" he replied in response to the coded phrase that Reza spoke. During his training, he had been taught to respond with a variable numeric code based on the day of the week. It was a simple variation of his apartment address. Inexplicably, he couldn't remember it when he needed to. His eagerness to hear from his friend caused him to fail a basic rule of spy craft.

Reza had worked with a lot of amateurs. He frowned at his unadorned office wall, but he continued through the coded sequence. "Should I expect pleasant weather for my next visit?" he said after a pause of a few seconds.

Jean-Claude responded in English, "You can expect everything to be perfect." He had given the response that Reza hoped to receive. This meant that the device had been assembled and now required only its payload to be fully operational. Reza terminated the call without saying good-bye.

-2-

Libertyville, Illinois

Robert Chase had spent most of his adult life in the shadow lands of the necessary. This meant that sometimes his attempts to keep the bad guys from destroying the world overstepped conventional legal boundaries. He told himself that what he did was indispensable. He recognized that he might be overstating his importance, but it helped maintain his peace of mind when he viewed himself in the mirror of his own conscience. His special profession required focus and commitment above all things. His mantra was to never second-guess the suits who ran the shop . . . until they were wrong.

Chase had grown up in the small and safe northern Illinois town of Libertyville, a forty-minute train ride from downtown Chicago. In that peaceful place, everyone took for granted the sense of belonging that defined small-town life in America in the early 1970s. His father had been an army captain who went missing in Vietnam during the last year of that long, painful war. His unit had been overrun by North Vietnamese regulars during a punishing nighttime attack, and he simply disappeared. He remained "missing" for six long years until he was finally declared dead in a hasty cleanup of open cases at the end of the war.

Chase was far too young to have known his dad well. In fact, he hardly remembered him at all. His mother had been depressed and lonely for quite a while after she received the final letter from the army. Her personal way of dealing with the loss of her high school sweetheart was to try to replace him with as many other men as would have her. This left Chase to deal with his substantial young boy's grief in his own way. She finally married another former high school classmate, a mean-spirited man named McGonigle, and Chase found himself exiled from the house to live in a small storage room in the garage to make room for his new sisters. It wasn't fair, but then he didn't associate the concept of fairness with real life. He found a way to make this new arrangement work. He slept on a padded plywood board placed across the tops of the washer and dryer. It was more ironing board than bed. He learned to be self-sufficient, and he became skilled at reading the moods and intentions of others. It became a simple matter of survival.

His stepfather had developed a nasty habit of using Robert to relieve whatever stress or frustrations he carried home from his work as a midlevel civil servant. He was an unkind and weak man who saw Robert as an opportunity finally to dominate someone else. Chase soon learned to keep about twelve inches out of his reach, always. If McGonigle tried to take a swing at him for something, or for nothing, he could easily dodge the stroke without needing to run for his life. He could sense from subtle facial and body clues when a random punch was about to fly in his direction. If he had chosen to confront the older man, he could have intercepted his hand or fist in motion before it ever got near him. Robert was that quick and strong, even at the age of ten. He decided that he would save that for another day.

During the long, sweltering summer days when all activity, except for crazy insect dances in the steamy air, had been defeated by the heat, Robert would search out corn snakes in the cool of the woods, and test his reactions against theirs. The first few encounters were painful enough, and then he reached a breakthrough. He began to understand the little tells, the subtle motions or body positions that indicated a strike was imminent. He could not really move faster than the snakes; instead he was learning to outthink them.

One day, he crouched in front of a healthy four-footer he had aroused from a nap. The snake was coiled and angry, and Chase was trembling with fear and anticipation. He tempted the snake with his often-bitten left hand and readied his right to make the grab. He saw the reptile make a small, almost imperceptible twitch to the rear and then launch a blazingly fast move forward. His right hand was already in motion anticipating the attack. It wasn't much different than how a batter manages to catch up with a hundred-mile-an-hour fastball. He grabbed the snake about three inches behind its head and lifted the writhing creature over his head with a whoop of triumph. Anticipation became a skill that would serve him very well in his future career, but not with snakes, with dangerous people.

In high school, Robert exhibited exceptional ability in languages and history, less so in math and the sciences. He would certainly not have been mistaken for a jock. However, he had a certain animal quickness and natural physical strength that had not escaped the notice of his high school wrestling coach. Endowed with what appeared to be a well-cushioned body, Chase had taught himself the art of taking everyone by surprise.

He had weighed one-ninety on a barely six-foot frame in his senior year, placing him in the heavyweight class of wrestlers at his small school. His opponents typically weighed-in at more like two-twenty to two-thirty and were generally well-muscled. To a man, they thought that they would make quick work of this soft-looking boy. Chase always had other ideas. At the start of a match he would shuffle, without much apparent bad intent, to the center of the mat and smile at the other boy. And it wouldn't be just a friendly smile, but a big grin instead. At the referee's signal, he would immediately grapple for ways to use the obvious disadvantages in weight and strength to his own purposes.

In one match, the reigning state champion from nearby Lake Forest had charged forward like a bull, viselike hands locking firmly onto the back of his neck and right arm. Chase had never felt such raw power before or sensed such grim determination in a match. He understood that he needed to derail this train before it ran him down. He began to retreat toward the edge of the circle designating the area where both wrestlers must score their points. The other wrestler still had him in a tight grip, and Chase was feeling the pain more with each passing second. *This guy is a bull. I need to cross him up. If I don't, he's going to crush me.*

As he slowly gave ground up to his opponent, dragging him to where he wanted him, he suddenly reached across his body to grasp the boy's left arm. The bigger boy had not anticipated this move, and his delay in recognizing what was happening proved his undoing. Chase yanked the arm to the center, and across him, into an awkward and weak position as he made a quick dip to the left and lifted under the off-balance body of the heavier boy. Up he went, and then down hard onto the mat with Chase now on top. Two points were scored, but the loud pop from his opponent's collarbone was much more final. That was Robert Chase's last match. He really didn't enjoy hurting anyone.

After high school, he had attended the local junior college until he managed to earn his way into Northern Illinois University. He scored high on exams because of his exceptional memory, although he rarely handed in a homework assignment on time. He emphasized modern European languages, enjoyed attending the occasional football game, and avoided most things social. He wasn't shy in the traditional sense; he just preferred being alone. When he needed a social moment, he would sit in the student union and observe how the other students acted. He could call upon his memory whenever it served his needs; it was almost encyclopedic. He could immediately spot when a familiar student acted out in an unfamiliar way. He was privately dissecting a particularly interesting individual the day that his psychology professor sat down and began to recruit him to the darker side.

Professor Jonathan Edwards Hastings had had a talent for finding strong Midwestern young men and women who loved the idea of American-style freedom, and who had no idea what to do with their futures. He could eloquently describe a mission and a purpose far more exciting than lecture courses with two hundred students. At that moment, he had no fewer than twelve former protégées working for the less-visible agencies of the United States, Great Britain, and France.

Professor Hastings was a methodical recruiter. He acted as if he had all the time in the world to get to know his students and what they liked. Chase hadn't felt rushed. He did wonder why this professor spent so much time with certain students. For his part, Hastings noted several interesting qualities about Chase. He was deceptively athletic and strong. He had an intuitive sense of right and wrong. And he was socially flexible when it came to other cultures. Their many conversations invariably came back to why evil existed in the forms it did, and whether governments had a responsibility to stop bad actors wherever they might be.

"Robert, I have a hypothetical question for you: let's say that a country is good with the other grown-ups, you know . . . the international community. However, it consistently mistreats its own citizens and gets away with it. More than mistreats," he added, "they abuse and sometimes kill them. For a variety of reasons, the world community decides to live with this behavior, generally because it has bigger problems to deal with. And the citizens, the ones being oppressed, don't have much of a voice on the world stage. What do you think the United States should do about this?"

Chase didn't believe any government should possess unlimited power. He didn't believe nations had an unrestricted right to do whatever they wanted. Governments were designed to do the things that individual citizens couldn't do for themselves. He was deeply conflicted when asked how far he would go to stop someone who intended to hurt others. His views were still forming on the topic of his own personal use of force. What he often expressed to Hastings was more in the way of thinking out loud, and he felt safe doing so. For more than two years, the pair had met weekly to think and talk. And in Professor Hastings's unique way, to help Chase form a view of his own role in society that would eventually allow him to walk on both sides of the thin red line.

"Well, I don't have much information to work with, although I have some thoughts on the subject. Of course, my first reaction is to say that we should help them in some meaningful way. Squeeze the government with sanctions and try to support the opposition parties in elections. Send in the marines as a last resort. Oh, but none of that would actually work, would it?"

This sort of exchange went on day after day. Chase was changing, although he didn't understand yet by how much. Professor Hastings finally thought that Chase might be ready for the field; that is, if he could meet his standards. Before one of his hatchlings could leave the nest, each one had to complete their degree in an honest fashion. Robert Chase would be no exception. He graduated after four years, with mixed grades, but excelling in what he loved most: people watching. He returned to Libertyville a few days later and said his good-byes to his mom and McGonigle, telling them he had joined something like the Peace Corps, and then he disappeared. That was twenty-seven years ago.

-3-

Rural Virginia

Here he stood, at the tender age of twenty-two, in a white T-shirt, standard-issue fatigue pants, and dusty combat boots, in front of one of the meanest men he had ever imagined. He was in his third week of training at the CIA center known only as "The Farm." The instructor's given name was Marc LeBlanc, a short, wiry Cajun from the bayous southwest of New Orleans. To his recruits, he was simply and respectfully referred to as Top. He was not mean in any normal definition of the word; however, he was incredibly tough and focused. He had been a sergeant-major in the U.S. Army, retiring after thirty-four years of active service. He had barely survived two physically damaging tours in Vietnam and believed that his brand of hard training might help his young students survive in a much tougher world than he had faced.

Today's class was unarmed combat, and LeBlanc decided to make an example of a recruit named Chase. It was not a mean-spirited selection. He had already sized up this kid and decided that he wouldn't make it through to graduation. He had orders to cull through the group. Only the best would graduate and go on to field service with the Agency. He didn't think Chase had the right stuff to make it. It wasn't personal. It was an uninformed opinion and he had no idea how wrong it was.

Chase had a pretty good sense of how this exercise was going to end, and he was not looking forward to it. LeBlanc ordered him to take an aggressive stance and to try to take him down. Chase had done this move before, at least a hundred times. It was not an especially challenging task in his opinion. Before proceeding, however, he considered what might come next and how to handle it. He approached LeBlanc with apparent careless ease, both men circling in the sawdust pit. He made a slow, awkward lunge for the instructor's right forearm. He pulled his offering back at the last second to ready himself for the counterattack. Predictably, LeBlanc came directly at him to toss him on his college-degreed ass.

Chase had made this move before in wrestling matches, and he could see he was much quicker than LeBlanc. In fact, Robert Chase was faster of hand and body than most of the people on the earth. His mental checklist ticked off a brief set of thoughts: *retreat; let him think he has you; make him commit to an action; and then slam his ass to the ground.* This is exactly what happened. The surprised former sergeant-major fell hard into the sawdust and bounced back to his feet like a Super Ball, now with fire in his eyes.

"Chase," he bellowed. "Would you care to show me that little move again?"

This time, Robert played the role expected of him. He allowed the trainer to get him off-balance and took a soft tumble as LeBlanc swept his feet out from under him. A message had been sent and received.

"Where the hell did you learn to do that?" asked the instructor at the end of the class.

"I guess I got lucky, sir. Even a blind squirrel finds an acorn or two."

Lucky my ass, thought LeBlanc. *That was a professional and premeditated move. And dammit, you let me win the second match!* The point had been made on both sides, and the former army ranger took notice of this unusually quick and astute young recruit. Maybe he would make it through after all.

After graduation, exceptional individuals like Robert Chase were often invited for further training in other covert skills, including wet work, the disturbingly benign term used to indicate assignments that would result in the killing of other human beings. Chase received the only offer in his class for this unique instruction, but he declined and said that he preferred to find another way to defend his country. He understood at the time that this was likely a career-ending decision, but he didn't care. He really didn't like hurting people, any people.

However, he was lucky. His timing was good. The embarrassing takeover of the U.S. embassy in Tehran had just ended, and his country was looking for fresh ways to cope with what was changing in the world. The CIA was searching for new methods to counteract the unconventional forces that were rapidly emerging. Robert Chase became part of an experimental group of fifteen officers who would be trained to play an invisible yet vital role in protecting the unprotected. He liked how that sounded. It was exactly how he wanted to view himself.

The one enduring lesson from the ensuing training that made a lot of sense to the developing covert officer named Chase was that terrorists, anarchists, and just plain bad people didn't typically announce themselves when they entered the room. They were true zealots, often mentally unbalanced fanatics, who didn't possess the social checks and balances of normal people. They could kill anyone without thinking or caring. Sometimes they would willingly kill themselves in the process, without the slightest vibration of the chord of self-preservation that most of us depend on to keep us alive.

His first posting after graduation was Marseille, the sprawling port city in the South of France, a place he soon grew to love. There existed on that ancient continent an amazing collection of the best and the worst that humanity could invent. There were superb art galleries, antique buildings, great literature, and experiments in government that had radiated out to change the world. And it was also where, for centuries, countries had bludgeoned one another in endless, senseless warfare like punch-drunk fighters pummeling each other until they collapsed in the ring, both winless. The advent of the eurozone had begun to change that pattern, although no one really knew if it would hold together long enough to allow people to change as well. "This experiment might come back to bite all of Europe in its fat socialist ass one day," he wrote to Professor Hastings a few days after his arrival. "But I hope not."

-4-

Islamic Republic of Iran

In a carefully guarded part of central Tehran, a district that Reza was only rarely permitted to enter, a group of powerful men were planning to turn the world upside down. The current supreme leader of the Islamic Republic, Ayatollah Ahrimani, had been slowly turning a dull knife deep in the sides of the Israelis and the Americans for months with threats he would use Iran's newly completed nuclear weapons to reshape the region. Ahrimani knew the truth, however: Iran had only one functional warhead of barely fifty kilotons of explosive power. It could do considerable harm, but it wouldn't flatten an entire city, or win a war.

This apparent fact presented the ayatollah and the ruling council with a dilemma. If Iran used this weapon against its hated enemy Israel, it would never have the chance to make another. His own regime, and the Islamic nation itself, would not survive the devastating counterblows that the Zionists and their American master would deliver in return. Was it better to simply own it? To use it as a big stick to further Iran's agenda in the Middle East? The answers were not so clear. It also could be taken away by those same enemies.

"Ayatollah Ahrimani," began a grizzled cleric from the south. There were only men present. "You promised us that this new superweapon would make us forever safe from Israeli threats. Today, however, you seem much less confident. Why have you placed us in this dangerous position? Instead of being safe, it seems we are now a more attractive target than ever before."

Ahrimani glared at the man for several seconds while he allowed his anger to subside. "I have never proposed that having one weapon would be enough. If we use it now against the Zionists, we will be almost defenseless. The Israelis and the Americans would crush us, and that would be the end of our beloved republic, and the end of us."

The old cleric, sensing some new vulnerability, decided to press his attack. "You led us down this reckless path. Even a schoolboy would have considered this possibility, Ahrimani." His tone had now become more accusing and others in the council appeared ready to move in for the kill. They had put the ayatollah in power, and they could also remove him.

"My friends," he replied through clenched teeth, "we do not have enough material for a second bomb, not yet. We have few good options. We can hold onto this weapon and use it to reshape our region, but be aware that someone can also come in and steal it from us."

For the moment, Ahrimani felt he still was in a strong position. He understood that the generals in Tel Aviv were anxious to put an end to their political experiment with another preemptive strike. The new American president had been using all his influence to restrain them from such a region-changing action. The ayatollah understood both the strengths and weaknesses of his position. To be able to freely use this weapon against any enemy would require the ability to make or purchase a replacement. It was a matter of survival.

There was neither the time nor the fissile material available to build another weapon quickly enough. It was theoretically possible to buy a bomb from a handful of countries, but incredibly expensive. His intelligence service had already put out feelers to Pakistan, North Korea, and certain renegade elements inside the Russian Federation. The bidding would start at a price exceeding ten billion U.S. dollars. If a buyer appeared to be desperate it might reach thirty billion. Beyond the purchase price itself, the physical movement of a nuclear weapon, or any atomic material, for that matter, had become difficult. All the major nations, including Russia, were now monitoring shipments in and out of certain sensitive regions around the world to prevent the unplanned spread of this deadly technology. All the major powers seemed to understand that anything sold on the open market could also bounce back to be used against the seller. The rules of engagement had changed.

The inner circle of the Iranian leadership slowly reached agreement that they either must use this warhead, or someone would eventually fly in and take it away from them. It enraged the ayatollah that the big western countries, and Israel too, got to follow different rules. They could keep their arsenals and use them to threaten the smaller nations around the world; however, Iran was barred from such participation in big-boy diplomacy. He understood that the time left to him was growing short.

"My friends," he began, "Allah has graciously told me what He wishes us to do. It was at first a surprise even to me. It was not at all as I expected. Allah is all-knowing and wise. The mission that He has assigned us is to destroy one of the persecutors of His people. There are so many nations we might wish to discipline, but our first target must be Iraq. He promises another weapon that we might use on Israel later, if He so wills. Is there anyone present who feels otherwise?"

The logic of this proposed move would not escape any of them. Destroying an Iraqi city and then taking the country would not provoke an Israeli counterattack. It might even confuse them. It might buy him time to buy what he could not make.

Ahrimani waited several long minutes to allow the assembled clerics to whisper among themselves. Any one of them could challenge his power at any time, but that person had better judge his support well, or it would be his last official act on this earth. Finally, an old mullah from the western provinces stood up and bowed to Ahrimani. "Your wisdom exceeds our humble understanding combined, Ayatollah Ahrimani. We concur that your message is indeed from the great One above. We unanimously answer 'yes' to your proposal."

Few western intelligence analysts fully understood the animosity that all Iranian leaders felt toward Iraq. More than a million mostly young men had been sacrificed in the war started by Saddam Hussein in 1980. That struggle dragged on for eight long and bloody years, and the flower of Iran's youth was slaughtered by the tens of thousands as they attacked the massed tanks and the trained legions of the dictator. Eventually, Saddam declared victory and slipped back into Iraqi territory where he could torment his own Shia majority as a further insult to the Persian nation. Persians and Arabs have been enemies since the times of the Old Testament prophets. It was not about to change now. Iran now had, for a limited time, the ability to deal a death blow to the new democratic regime and spit in the faces of the offensive American unbelievers. The only remaining issue was how to deliver the weapon, but in a deniable way, in case things went wrong. The supreme leader thought he had the perfect solution.

***

In his office, a few miles away, Reza received an independent order to proceed with his private mission. He was completely unaware that his country was planning a stunning strike of its own. His instructions arrived in the form of a simple coded message in his email. He made sure that his mailbox received all manner of spam and legitimate messages as well, to make it difficult for the western security agencies to notice a suspicious pattern. He was certain that Mossad and the CIA both were aware of his activities. But neither of these agencies thought he was important enough to actually monitor. Reza was not considered to be a player of any significance. He was another close-to-retirement officer with few connections and no future. That would have been a correct assessment of Reza the Iranian officer. It was myopically short of the potential of Reza the free market zealot.

Now that he had been authorized to carry out the attack in France, all he needed to do was to deliver the bomb's payload to Jean-Claude along with final instructions for placement of the weapon. Reza was a committed Iranian citizen but the mission he was now carrying out did not come from his government or even from the leadership of the often-independent Revolutionary Guard. He was presently doing the bidding of a radical terrorist group based in Yemen, one that was pursuing goals that were not in conflict with those of his own country. Also, the money was attractive, and his share was already secure in a German bank account from which he could move it anywhere in the world. *Ah, the wonders of open banking and globalization. Will the West ever begin to understand how easy they are making my job? Probably not. It serves their purposes as well.*

His masters in Sana'a, Yemen had desperately been seeking a high-grade radioactive payload for the device Reza was having built, something dirty and frightening. To their disappointment, their Russian Federation contacts were unable to provide what was originally promised. The new Russia was becoming much more careful with nuclear material these days, in part due to financial incentives provided by the United States. As a replacement, they were able to procure a quantity of weaponized virus that had somehow been erased from the inventory of the former Soviet Union. A kilo of that material was now safely inside France in friendly hands. It was very, very deadly stuff.

The Marburg virus was an African hemorrhagic virus like Ebola. It normally incubated in a host for two to twenty days before causing a nearly complete breakdown of the victim's vascular system. Most victims simply bled to death from every organ, including the skin. The fatality rate for this strain had approached 90 percent in clinical trials held on condemned prisoners, carried out discretely and illegally in Russia. In its natural state, the virus was not typically spread by aerosol vectors; however, a Soviet program in the 1990s had not only genetically modified it to shorten the incubation time, but it had also created an effective aerosol version. A few micro-drops inhaled or ingested would result in a painful and certain death within a week. For the inventors of this new weapon, the Cold War had ended much too soon, but there was always hope that it would make a comeback.

Payment for the virus was now due and Reza understood all too well that his clients on both sides of the Russian border were not patient people. He normally used his cell phone for all secret banking transactions but moving so great a sum caused him to tremble. He hesitated and then closed his phone. His hands were shaking so violently that he couldn't even punch numbers onto the keypad. He went to his office computer and selected the web address of UBS in Zurich and made the transfer. He realized it could be a mistake, but the fear of failure drove him to do it anyway.

-5-

Tehran

Reza could not have fully known his error, although he did understand there was some degree of risk in what he was about. He was not being actively monitored by the American intelligence services; however, transmissions from the Revolutionary Guard offices in Tehran were. Two years earlier, the CIA had slipped a particularly stealthy worm into several networks in Iran, along with an American/Israeli virus called *Stuxnet* that had brought the Iranian nuclear program to a standstill for months. The other computer worm, *Orlando,* its code name in honor of the hometown of the kid who created it, buried itself deep inside a legitimate administrative email program used every day by the military and the Revolutionary Guard. To the average systems analyst it looked like a small bug-fix in an otherwise normal set of executable commands. The infected program itself was not classified, or an otherwise sensitive piece of software, and so it did not receive the same sort of attention that more critical software systems received after the Israeli incursion. *Orlando* waited patiently and listened for certain email conversations. It wiggled its ears and came to life when Reza began his transaction, and it swiftly went to work documenting the event. Then it quietly replicated itself and attached the new version to the transfer before it was sent. If it could successfully evade security and bury itself inside the UBS bank computer, it would be able to track the money to its destination as well.

***

In an everyday strip mall near Alexandria, Virginia, located next to a popular chain coffee shop, watch officer Katie Thompson was looking through the evening traffic coming from several carefully selected locations in Iran. This was exceedingly boring work, although every so often a message carried the right markers to light up the board. To almost anyone else, the message she had just read might be a routine banking transaction, some bureaucrat taking a slice of the people's money to finance a safe retirement in another land. But this transfer seemed to be different. It came from *Orlando,* which meant that it had been prescreened for relevance, and its footprints led to the front door of a company known to be run by former senior KGB officers. These renegades were suspected of having access to some seriously dangerous material. Every red light in Katie's head flashed at once. "Gotcha!" she shouted out to the empty room. Then she called her boss, a deputy director of intelligence at Langley.

"This is Thompson with a report, sir."

Reynolds Merrill smiled as the voice crackled out of the secure phone. He liked Katie a lot. It was not that sort of sick affection that older men of rank and privilege sometimes have for the young female up-and-comers. He liked her because she was beyond smart and the absolute best at her job. Earlier in the year she had noticed a set of seemingly harmless products being offered on eBay by a known Russian arms dealer hiding in the Far East under an assumed name. No one else on the team could quite grasp that the bids on some curiously configured electronics were cleverly disguised transactions of a particularly dangerous nature. Persistent and adept at seeing subtle word patterns, Katie won over the team, and an intervention was arranged. This dealer was now sweating out his future in a rat-infested prison in Thailand. Better yet, a shipment of Soviet-era shoulder-fired missiles was not going to end up killing

Americans in Afghanistan. "Well done," he whispered to himself as he relived the moment.

"Please continue," he said to allow Katie to make her report.

"Sir, we have a transaction of interest coming out of Tehran. It's not one of the usual suspects, and the destination has set off an alarm. The transfer of twenty-five million euros was initiated by a colonel in the Revolutionary Guard. He's not in a position to have access to such funds. He's not top management, and he's not on our watch list. The destination appears to be a German account controlled by a Russian national carrying the name of Viktor Ivanoff. I believe he is actually better known as Ivan Tischenko, the former KGB officer in charge of biochemical weapons for the southern sector."

Reynolds digested this information for a moment as he brought up the CIA file on Tischenko. His ulcer was beginning to burn. This man had once had custody over a vast stockpile of the most dangerous weapons. He had faded from public view more than a decade ago after the Russian police turned up the heat on this form of commerce. There had been the occasional rumor of offers to sell certain biological agents to the highest bidder, but the Russian government had intervened in each instance, and the threat faded away. *Why is he back now?* Then he mumbled a curse out loud.

"Sir, did you say something?" It came from the phone.

"No, I was just talking to the dog. What do you see in this, Katie?" He could hear her take a deep breath. She was unusually nervous, or excited. It was difficult to tell which when Katie was on a scent. She had a knack for finding trails others couldn't even imagine.

"Sir, this is definitely a deviation from the normal flow of money. I have bad feelings about this. Admittedly, this is a leap of faith, but please bear with me. I think the amount and the routing of the cash indicates this is part of a technology transfer."

Such a simple, careless fragment—a technology transfer. It represented one of the worst fears of modern man. It meant a weapon of serious mass destruction might be loose somewhere on the planet. Reynolds wanted to curl up and take a nap. He had spent his whole adult life trying to track down and prevent things like this from happening, and now he felt the sad, penetrating sense of failure. Now, no one except the bad guys had any idea of where, or what was ready to crash onto unsuspecting and innocent people. It was his worst nightmare.

"Thank you, Katie. You've done a good job tonight. Is there anything else of interest?"

Katie replied cautiously, "I think we have a name." Reynolds sat up at this statement. A name meant a hard lead and a chance.

"Katie, please call in your replacement and report to the situation room at the Bungalow in an hour."

As Katie rang off, a few threads of a plan were beginning to form within his mind. If they had an actual name, they could make a snatch, even in Tehran. He had the sort of people who could do it, who would do it.

The Bungalow was aptly named. It was a modest safe house in a convenient location in a suburban Alexandria neighborhood that was used as an occasional planning center and situation room. It was a well-cared-for home on a tree-lined street with a quiet little couple and their quiet little dog. It was a perfect cover. Graeme and Lydia were the owners of record. They were the opposite of the typical spy-novel couple. They talked often with their neighbors, watched pets for anyone, and seemed completely without guile. They were also very, very good at their business.

In this case, their business was analysis, and they worked for the part of the CIA no one ever discussed. Lydia had a day job running a small shipping supplies store a few blocks away, which left her free to come and go as needed. Graeme was a contributing writer, mostly dreaming up recipes for a couple of food magazines, which suited him just fine and required little actual travel. They entertained often, and nice-looking people were frequently seen coming up their walkway carrying a bottle of wine or what looked like a warm dish.

This evening, Reynolds Merrill arrived with a hastily purchased bottle of Syrah from a small producer in Healdsburg, California. It would end up in Graeme's expanding wine cellar, because wine would not be on the menu tonight. Katie arrived a few minutes later with a plastic container, no doubt containing some goodie for the evening celebration. In fact, the package that Katie carried held top-secret briefing materials for DDI Merrill. It wouldn't do to show up lugging a briefcase.

The basement of the Bungalow was a hardened, electronically secure communications center. Anything said or seen in the bunker was as carefully protected as if it had happened in CIA headquarters at Langley. Graeme remained upstairs in the kitchen to put on the show for the neighbors. Lydia would be the lead analyst for this operation, but Graeme was wearing a hard-wired earbud so that he could listen in. Merrill began in his typically deliberate fashion.

"Lydia, we have an intercept that indicates a possible transfer of technology from certain ex-Soviets to Iran. We're not sure what it might be. Katie has enough reason to believe that this transfer is not through official channels and may be an off-the-books operation. That concerns us on several levels."

As Katie picked up the briefing, Reynolds took a moment to admire how precisely and confidently she described the intercept and what she thought it meant. *This one is a true star,* he thought. Lydia was not quite so convinced by the evidence and began to pepper Katie with questions. In this business, they all understood it was important that every hypothesis have at least one critic.

"I get your points on the money movement. It's definitely a disturbance in the force, but . . ." Lydia had a habit of quoting from her favorite movies when she offered an opinion. "What makes you think that this isn't from the top? Could you be jumping over some of the facts to reach the conclusion you want?"

It's a good question, thought Katie, one she had been considering on the ride over from the shop. Reynolds quietly repositioned himself in his chair as he waited for her answer.

"The amount of money is significant—significant enough to point to the government," she began. "Still, there are inconsistencies that I can't resolve. Maybe you can help, Lydia. First, the sender is a relatively unknown colonel in the Guard who's never been connected with anything important. He's an unlikely player when it comes to executing orders from the top. Admittedly, he could be a sleeper. If so, we need to ask for whom? Second, Iran already has what they need in their own pantry, so why would they go outside to buy on the open market? Last point: *Orlando* has not been picking up the sort of traffic we usually see when an officially sanctioned event is being planned."

Lydia could see the threads, but she wasn't completely convinced. She allowed her dark eyes to rake over Katie a few times, to measure her commitment to her position, and then she turned and focused on her boss.

"Reynolds, I have some doubts, but I can't argue against the logic of the open-market purchase. It doesn't fit the pattern we expect from the leadership. It's a lot of cash, and it could buy some deadly stuff. If that's the plan, it will be something they don't have in their own arsenal, or something that's too well-monitored by us. I still can't see all the links, but I think we should talk to this colonel, and fast."

-6-

The CIA had been intercepting people of interest for years. It had been a dangerous and often sloppy business carried out by regular operatives and local hired help. People sometimes got killed unnecessarily, and foreign governments always seemed to be able to pin the action on the Americans. In the mid-1990s, the Agency decided to reassign this activity to a group of specialists who lived in the shadow world of the ultra-secret black budget, an appropriation that even most members of Congress couldn't access. This group of agents had no official operational name. Their file was assigned the code name LINEBACKER.

The members operated in small cells, just like the people they were charged with stopping. They were untraceable and paid only in cash. Not even the president could discover who was a part of this elite team. This was Robert Chase's new family. They were professional kidnappers with special talents. They were invisible, with certain characteristics and skills that enabled them to move freely throughout most of the world, and when requested, to snatch anyone, anywhere. They called it an intervention and they developed a proprietary language around their trade that almost anyone else would consider clinical. Chase was considered the best of the lot. He was blessed with a difficult-to-describe physical appearance, and he could change that with the slightest of adjustments to his face or his wardrobe. When witnesses to any of his bolder projects were asked for a description of the kidnapper, the most they could say was that it was a man, between twenty-five and sixty years of age, and of indeterminate height. Within the Agency, Chase was known to three people. One of those was a man he knew only as Control.

Chase also had a day job, a cover, as an insurance executive for an elite international firm with offices in New York, Paris, and Dubai. The firm had been financed and was still owned by the CIA through a maze of company structures that never quite pointed back to Langley. It wasn't unusual for him to be on location for a month or more at a time, purportedly to review coverage for international trade deals. When a significant international transaction was on the table, Chase might also appear on the scene and busy himself meeting with the negotiators. His appearance was friendly and nonthreatening, and his manner so restrained that foreign authorities rarely questioned his presence or his purpose. He could move freely and without notice. He always paid with cash and kept mostly to himself. That was, until he met Sam.

Samantha D'Aubrisson was born in Paris, educated mostly in the U.S., and had worked on both sides of the Atlantic until she finally settled into a comfortable position managing the three-star Hôtel d'Angleterre in the 5th arrondissement of Paris—the Left Bank. She was, like Chase, a person of a certain age who had never quite found someone interesting enough to capture her heart. Samantha considered herself attractive, most others would say beautiful, with luminous red-auburn hair, a fit body, and a smile that could melt an iceberg. However, she rarely bestowed that smile on anyone. She did her job and mostly kept her own company. She didn't really mind being alone, although when she thought about it from time to time, she would not have chosen it either.

She liked long books, small cafés, and unexpected conversations. Her favorite café, despite its prominence and popularity with tourists, was Les Deux Magots on Boulevard St. Germain. When she was seated there, she could feel the presence of the great thinkers, writers, and painters who had contemplated life from these very chairs in times past. Facing the busy boulevard, everything about life seemed to make sense. There was something deeply satisfying to her in the tradition of the French café, and the rite of sitting snuggly in a chair sipping a beverage, while the rest of Paris paraded past.

As destiny would have it, Robert Chase was in Paris on assignment in October of that year. He had successfully intervened in a project involving a former member of the Baader-Meinhof Gang, and after efficiently delivering the package to a private jet at a small airport outside of the city, he decided to treat himself to a careless walk about Paris. This was an extreme indulgence for him. He never did anything without a purpose. He loved the pulse of this city. Everything seemed more alive in Paris: eating, walking, and even breathing. He exited his time-worn hotel onto Rue de Rivoli, across from the Hôtel de Ville—the city hall—and strolled over the bridge to the tiny and exclusive Île St. Louis, and then across another leading to Île de la Cité.

Paris was dressed in its finest. The stately rows of plane trees glowed golden-yellow in the pale late-afternoon autumn light. The Cathedral of Notre-Dame stood guard, its fierce gray gargoyles ever alert to any intrusion from the underworld. A hint of a chill was in the air, which made walking an exceptional pleasure. Chase had originally intended to continue across the River Seine and make the slight uphill climb to the Luxembourg Gardens. Instead, something strong pulled him in a different direction. When these sudden impulses came to him, he was accustomed to yielding, and so he veered right toward Saint-Germain-des-Prés, a trendy area for shopping, strolling, and being seen. For whatever reasons, Chase hadn't been in a serious or informal relationship with a woman for at least two years, and he had grown to think of his loneliness as one of the downsides of his peculiar profession.

As he strolled past Les Deux Magots, unprepared for anything except a walk in his favorite city, his eyes met and then held on a bit too long with those of an attractive redhead sitting by herself, two tables back from the sidewalk. His training told him to walk on, but his feet would not readily obey. He found himself circling the long block, all the while telling himself that if she was still there he would find some way to meet her. His expectations weren't high although his heart was racing as it had not in years.

A few minutes later, he turned right again around the curved face of the café's outdoor seating. His heart skipped a couple of beats. She was still there casually observing the people strolling by. It was the sort of thing he would have done. He sat down at a small table next to hers. He couldn't think of anything to say. She turned, noticed that he was staring at her, and then she offered a rare, small smile. He returned it, entirely too eagerly, but it was the best he could muster on short notice.

He almost choked as he found himself saying out loud, "*Bonsoir madame. Paris has her best on this evening, n'est-ce pas?*" Although it was all in French, that's how he thought it sounded as it slipped out of his suddenly dry mouth. It was so corny that he wanted to slide under the table and keep crawling until a speeding truck ended his embarrassment out on the boulevard. Instead, he sat there as the woman examined him with a very slight look of puzzled amusement.

To his surprise, she spoke to him. "*Américan?*" He nodded his head and smiled weakly, but inside he was beginning to feel that the slow crawl into the traffic of the boulevard was beginning to look more attractive.

Two hours later they were still discussing—well, maybe some nearby would call it more than that—the respective merits of the American and European approaches to life, as they worked on a second bottle of wine. It would be the first of many liquid dinners as they came to be known. That meeting had been a couple of years ago, and he still felt a certain helpless yet warm feeling in her presence, as if they were excited teenagers meeting for the first time.

For Sam this was an unusual relationship as well. Chase was not like the other men she had known. He liked her—this much was obvious. But unlike the others, he had never pressured her for more physical intimacy than she desired. This was mostly the cheek kisses and hugs all friends gave each other. That was an unsolved puzzle for now. She thought she had given him enough silent signals of her desire for him, but for some reason he hadn't nibbled at the bait. Nonetheless, she felt an exceptional and deepening relationship with this quiet man. There was something unassuming and strong about him, and she loved how he preferred to listen to her rather than talk about himself. He was a deep pool, a man with even more secrets than she carried. This was a man she might be able to love for a long, long time. Chase felt the same toward her, though he would have put it in different words. There was something reassuring, compelling, and so lovely about Sam.

For the past two years, he had made sure he had reasons to be in Paris frequently, sometimes on business and more often because he could not bear to be without Sam's company for too long. He sensed that she cared for him, and he cared for her. His major stumbling block was how would he explain to her what he really did for a living? It seemed hopeless, and yet he still clung to the desire to be with her always. This sort of positive attitude was a quality that his employer valued greatly. Optimists and dreamers make the best intelligence officers. They quickly learn to adapt and find new ways to their objective. They don't tend to give up. This was Robert Chase in all respects.

Tonight, he found himself in a narrow coach seat on Air France flight #11 from New York to Paris. This wasn't going to be a social visit. He had been directed to Europe by Control for undisclosed reasons. He was pleased to be going back to France. *The funny thing about my business,* he mused as he looked out at the moon over the Atlantic, *is that it feels like I work for an individual and not a government. When he gives me an assignment, I don't know if it will prove to be important, or even if it will be the last one I ever receive.*

Of course, Chase understood that his true boss was a senior officer of the CIA, but this connection was tenuous and therefore disturbing. The Social Security number that appeared on the annual income tax return that was prepared for him wasn't the one he'd received when he worked as a teenager at the local market in Libertyville. He possessed a handful of passports, in different names and from countries he didn't call his own. And his assignments were passed along in text messages and encrypted email. He had been inside the sprawling CIA headquarters at Langley only once, and that had been more than two decades ago when he had been hired. He was permitted to contact only two persons in the entire world. For all practical purposes, he did not exist. Any funds provided by the Agency, including his salary, were either paid in cash or dropped into a Swiss account he couldn't access until he retired. It was almost as though they wanted him to be a ghost. It was unsettling at times. It was the excitement of the work and the sense of doing something good for his country and the world that kept him going. This time, hopefully, he would also be able to see Sam.

-7-

Paris

Chase hurried through passport control and past a couple of customs agents discussing the recent exploits of Paris Saint-Germain, the local powerhouse soccer team in the national league. He flipped on his Agency phone at the first opportunity. There were three urgent texts waiting for him. Two were cover messages sent by his nominal employer. The third contained instructions for the current rendezvous in Paris. He had an address and a password. He was to go to #22 Rue des Rosiers in the 3rd arrondissement and ring the bell for apartment number 2-C. He would be met.

Sometimes Chase's mind went off the rails in strange ways. When he was in Europe this usually involved food and drink. The Rue des Rosiers was the Parisian home of a particularly favorite food of his: the most genuine falafel this side of Beirut. He had been thinking of wrapping his mouth around a fat falafel pita sandwich, dripping with tangy white sauce and packed with pickled vegetables, ever since he landed at Charles de Gaulle Airport. His mouth was already watering. He convinced himself that it would be a sign of normalcy, and it would give him an extra few minutes to sweep the street outside to be certain that he wasn't being followed.

He finished his not-so-tiny snack and wiped his messy face with a couple of flimsy paper napkins. In the world of European fast food, this was perfection. He found the address a few doors down from where he had just eaten, rang the bell, and entered the courtyard to meet his contact. He listened as a matter-of-fact woman from the American embassy described the next project and handed him new passports, a thin file, and an envelope bursting with currency. He would depart for Dubai in a few hours to take custody of and accompany an Iranian prisoner.

Iran had never been a friendly place for any outsider, and the few assets that the CIA had managed to recruit there were reserved strictly for national emergencies. The proposed intervention did not seem to qualify. It had nothing to do with the interests of the United States so far as he could tell and seemed to be a favor to the French. He would have preferred to pass on the opportunity, but he didn't get to select his ops.

He made peace with the assignment and realized that he would have a few hours of downtime before his departure. He decided to call Sam. She wasn't expecting him, but he hoped she would be as eager to see him as he was to see her. They agreed to meet for an aperitif in about an hour. He told her he had flown over on a last-minute assignment and had a brief layover before departing for another country. He couldn't tell her the destination and he didn't like lying to her. Secrets—there were always secrets.

He would fly to Dubai late this evening to take part in the transfer of a prisoner to a destination he knew well, a joint CIA-Israeli interrogation center in the Sinai. The facility had been a busy place for the past few years as prisoners from Iraq and Afghanistan, men who would never see the inside of a courtroom, were processed and questioned. The staff liked to think that they did a pretty good job. Everyone who stopped over for a visit eventually talked.

Chase saw Samantha as she rounded the corner into the small plaza next to his customary hotel on the Rue de Rivoli. She simply took his breath away. No, wait—to be truthful—she took everyone's breath away. She was draped in the elegant European way with a large fine woolen wrap snugged about her shoulders against the late-afternoon chill. She wore a flash of color at her neck, and her magnificent hair luffed in the afternoon breeze. She flowed into the space like a rock band coming onstage, and

Chase was not the only one who stopped what he was doing to appreciate what she added to this moment in time.

Sam saw him, gave a little wave and a coy downward glance, and then came up to him for the customary two-cheek *bisou,* the French air kiss of greeting between friends. He inhaled the freshness of her skin and almost forgot to move to the other cheek to complete the greeting. Sam noticed the hesitation and enjoyed the long touching of their faces. As they sat at a small table under the shedding trees, neither could take their eyes off the other. *If true love really exists,* he thought, *it has Samantha's face and her smile.*

Two hours passed as though a few minutes, and it wasn't nearly enough time for either of them. Sam could sense that something important was on this man's mind, but what, she could not even guess. He wasn't answering her questions today. Falling leaves randomly decorated and then redecorated the white metal tabletop in the light breeze, and a feeling of potential loss such as she had never experienced before with this guy quivered through her. "Robert, is everything okay?"

Chase smiled a bit. He loved how she pronounced his name in the French manner. After a short pause, he looked at her like it might be the last time, ever, and said, *"Oui, ça va*—everything is fine." Then without a bit of his former hesitation, he leaned across the table and softly kissed her lips for the first time. Now, in the universe of all possible kisses, there are kisses and there are kisses. Some are a little too sloppy and urgent; some just tight dry lips meeting more of the same. Chase and Sam's first kiss was different. It was an intimate encounter of two lonely adults who, in their inner beings, needed one another.

Sam involuntarily gasped as a wave of excitement, warmth, and affection washed over her. Chase had a similar, but different reaction, and his body suddenly came alive. Both looked down as they leaned back into their chairs. Then they looked up at the same instant and regarded one another with big smiles. There was nothing more to say. Anyone watching the encounter would have remembered a remarkable woman with a not-so-memorable man. This was exactly how Chase would have wanted it.

"I need to depart in a few minutes. I think it will be a short trip, although I never really know."

Samantha tried a brave smile, and it painted unconvincingly across her anxious face. She knew so little about this man, yet she felt like she needed to hold him tightly, or he would simply evaporate into the evening darkness. She regained control over her emotions almost as quickly as she had lost it.

"Who are you really, Robert Chase? That is what I want from you when you return. I will accept nothing less. Now kiss me again . . . please."

As Robert Chase sat in his coach seat two hours later, he could still taste Samantha on his lips. He had said his good-byes and was now on his way to Dubai, and on an assignment that was somewhat out of character for him. He was going there as a minder, with a small role to play. It was as though he was the only available officer near the Middle East, so he got the job. This wasn't true in any way. He was the best that the Agency could muster, and he was outside of the normal chain of command, in case things got messy. There wouldn't be any congressional hearings if this project happened to fail. The Agency would quietly move Chase elsewhere, still under deep cover, and act as though nothing had happened. When he had asked his controller why he had been assigned this operation, he received a terse reply.

> Because you are so deniable. Don't be offended. The
> boss wanted someone there he could trust and who
> would never lead anyone back to us.

The CIA was about to expend one of its most valuable assets in Iran to kidnap Reza Tehrani, the man who had recruited Jean-Claude. The CIA had managed to recruit, and keep alive, very few well-placed Iranian citizens during the past two decades.

This officer was a colonel in the regular army, and he would be impossible to replace if compromised. His mission would be to lure the renegade Revolutionary Guard officer to a meeting, and then assist in his kidnapping. The hope was that they could also capture his phone and any other electronics he might be carrying and move him to a safe location outside the country. An interrogation team was already awaiting his arrival in the Israeli desert.

The challenges of this operation would be largely tactical. The most challenging task would be moving the man from tightly controlled Tehran to a neutral or nominally friendly territory where the fly-out could be staged. Tehran is in the north of that vast country, about two hundred kilometers from the Caspian Sea, and much too far from Dubai for that city to be useful in any way other than as a transfer point. Chase had reviewed the options and suggested that the safest exit directly out of Iran would be to the north, to a vessel he knew would be waiting in the Caspian. From there, the package could be transferred to a private plane in Azerbaijan or Turkmenistan and delivered to Tel Aviv via the Emirates.

The United States currently had few friends in the area; however, bags of cash or gold went a long way toward making new ones. The CIA had lots of both. As he worked through the planning, he understood more clearly that this was going to cost more than Langley had planned. In addition to the Iranian agent who would make the grab, they would also need a helicopter or other small aircraft to move the kidnapped man from Tehran and drop him near a repurposed freighter steaming slowly across the Caspian Sea. This transport needed to be already in Tehran, and this meant using up another irreplaceable asset, one that he could not command at the snap of his fingers. He would have to ask for more help. *Cha-ching, the price of this colonel has just gone up again.*

-8-

Dubai, UAE

Chase felt great empathy for the stresses and challenges facing their Iranian agent. This man was probably a person very much like himself. He lived in a hostile environment with two alert and highly suspicious military organizations, both of which harbored a deep fear of western threats. Even one misstep would mean that the opportunity would be lost, and the target would be beyond his reach, perhaps forever. Failure would also mean that the man trying to help them would probably die in a most unpleasant way, but this was what all covert agents everywhere signed up for.

This Iranian asset, Mirza was his given name, was the son of a former army general in the old shah's regime. Because of his bloodline and his demonstration of loyalty and bravery during the Iraqi war of aggression, he was now a senior field-grade officer in the regular army. He was aware of the existence of Colonel Reza Tehrani and had even spoken with him a few times at official gatherings. He was confident that he could create a plausible reason for them to meet in a neutral zone and away from prying eyes. The colonel was rumored to love money, which would make any story much easier to spin.

Mirza was also confident that he could immobilize Reza Tehrani and have him ready for transport. It was the transport part that worried him. Because of the constant threat of defections, all military aircraft, and most civilian fleets as well, were guarded by either the army or the Revolutionary Guard. It was possible to pry one loose, and hopefully it would be one that could still fly, but it would cost a lot. A helicopter would be best for this mission, one that was still in working order, a not insignificant challenge in present-day Iran.

Iran is a big country, security conscious, and very difficult to move in or out of unnoticed. The U.S. still maintained air assets in neighboring Afghanistan and farther away in the Gulf, but it would be impossible to fly all the way to Tehran, and back out again, without being noticed and intercepted. Greater limitations held for incursions from Iraq, the U.S. ally on the other flank. The heart of Iran was guarded by high mountain ranges on all sides and the air force, though greatly degraded by time and lack of spare parts, was still capable and ever looking outward for threats. *No,* thought Mirza, *the only hope was a desperate run toward the Caspian, away from the most credible air defenses.* As difficult as this might be, he thought that he could call in a long-standing family obligation to arrange the aircraft and the pilot.

Chase was pacing his room in Dubai like a caged big cat in a zoo. He had been forbidden to approach the U.S. embassy and risk his carefully constructed cover in hope of hearing the mission unfold in real time. The embassy personnel, even the CIA station members, wouldn't have recognized him in any case. And of course, Langley would never acknowledge that he existed, much less that he was here. He let that thought drop to the floor and die.

For the moment, all he knew was that the operation was on, and there was a CIA listening post floating twenty miles offshore from the seaside village of Chalus on the Caspian, waiting for the package. An ancient aircraft had been acquired for a one-way sprint through the mountain passes north of Tehran, and then over the sea to the drop zone. In Chase's most optimistic moments, he thought the chances of success were less than 20 percent. "All this for some washed-up colonel," he mumbled more than once out of frustration.

Mirza had arranged to meet Colonel Tehrani in a little-used corner of a former imperial air base, since rebuilt as Mehrabad International Airport. This hub handled most domestic flights but did not have quite the same elevated level of security as the newer Imam Khomeini International. Mirza had told Reza that he was taking a short helicopter ride to the north, and that he had a delicate matter of mutual interest to discuss. Reza, always alert for opportunities to add to his foreign cash reserves, assumed that Mirza was of the same mind. He thought it might be smuggling, although he was willing to move drugs as well. *What harm could there be in hearing the man out?* Besides, he was bored with Tehran and needed a diversion. He drove his own auto to the airfield, leaving his driver behind.

The two officers met in a small hangar on the military airbase that adjoined the civilian airport. After they exchanged greetings, and prior to the flight, Mirza served coffee in the Persian fashion. Reza loved this sign of respect and secretly hoped that it was a sign of something very good to come. The first couple of sweet sips were the last things he remembered until he was awake again, splashing and fighting for his life in icy water.

Mirza understood that in real life not everything goes according to plan. He had already succeeded beyond his hopes to have gotten to this point, although he felt that he was nowhere close to achieving actual success. Reza was now semiconscious and securely strapped into the aging Chinook helicopter, and they were making the best speed possible, only about a hundred and ten knots, as it climbed up the foothills of the Elburz Mountains north of Tehran. The pilot had planned to ascend out of the city at low altitude, hugging the main highway through the mountains, eventually veering off to pick up one of the steep, narrow valleys that descend rapidly to the coast. He hoped to avoid notice from air traffic control. The greatest risk was right now. If they could make it to the summit they would become invisible as they raced downhill to the sea, protected by the jagged ridges that fell away to the north. For the moment, they stood out like a wounded bird struggling to stay aloft. They would be an easy target for a fighter intercept or a missile if either were to be launched.

The Iranian air defense command was a confused but still dangerous entity. Mirza's slow-moving aircraft was noticed as soon as it circled out of the Tehran airspace and began its lumbering climb up the mountain slopes. It did not respond to identification calls from military air-traffic control, and no flight plan had been filed. Had the aircraft been incoming it would have immediately drawn a swarm of anti-aircraft missiles; however, tonight the officer on duty decided to scramble a single fighter, an aging American-made F-14A Tomcat left over from the shah's air force. The Tomcat climbed quickly on full burners, leaving behind a loud rumble and two bright jets of blue fire as it left its home field. It was an exhilarating climb-out for the pilot. Mostly, he was limited to short training missions to preserve what remained of this old aircraft. Tonight's flight was a treat.

"This is Guard Alpha 21, climbing out of four-zero for ten-zero. Please confirm heading and distance to target, over."

"Guard Alpha 21, this is Tehran control, climb and maintain flight level twelve-zero, heading three-three-zero. Your target is forty miles out and on the same heading. Do not, repeat, do not engage without authority, over."

"Guard Alpha 21, heading three-three-zero and twelve-zero, out."

The pilot didn't know what to look for as he surged up the slopes of the Elburz, only an unidentified aircraft and its heading. He passed the aging Chinook at Mach 0.9 almost without knowing it, and immediately slapped his aircraft into a sharp left turn and pulled back on the throttles to slow down on his second pass. He nearly blacked out from the building forces caused by the tight turn, and he fought for control of his aircraft.

His training had been a little light on this aspect of flying. His head cleared after a few frightening seconds. He flipped the switch for his air-to-air missiles to arm the birds and waited for the telltale growl that would indicate that they had locked onto a target. Still, he could see nothing except the faint lights on the highway coming out of Tehran. His aging attack radar was intermittently showing a signal and then fading out. The one thing he absolutely did not want to do was to launch a missile and next watch as a truck on the highway below flashed into flame. That would put an end to what little flying he got to do.

On his second pass, he overtook what he thought might be an aircraft below him, but he was still flying much too fast to make the intercept. He throttled back again to near stall speed, flaps fully extended, and executed a slower, wider descending turn. There it was. He had it. It was very slow, either a helicopter or small piston aircraft without lights, and it was nearing the crest of the first pass through the mountains. It had to be now or never. The pilot wondered: *is this a real threat, or a government official heading off for a long weekend on the beaches along the great inland sea?* He called in the intercept and requested instructions.

"Tehran control, Guard Alpha 21 . . . I have a visual on target. It appears to be small and slow, possibly a helicopter, traveling three-three-zero at less than one-two-zero knots."

Even at stall speed, he was once again closing too rapidly on the target. As a precaution, he selected a missile and waited for it to begin the low growl confirming it had locked on to the engine heat from the slower aircraft.

"Tehran control, Guard Alpha 21 requesting permission to engage target."

As the pilot held his finger over the launch switch awaiting permission to fire, he abruptly pulled up, went to full throttles, and narrowly missed planting himself and his aircraft into a hilltop that unexpectedly loomed in front of him.

Mirza and the pilot heard and then saw the Tomcat move past at great speed on its first pass. It was both impressive and frightening. They now believed that their desperate gamble had failed, and they would soon be dead. Without any defensive capability and lacking combat radar that could keep pace with the fighter's movements, they were like a tin can on a fence post. The fighter pilot couldn't miss.

They were nearing the point where they could evaporate into one of the narrow valleys falling away to the coast, although not quite close enough. The pilot dropped as close to the deck as he dared. Mirza bowed his head and asked Allah's forgiveness and mercy, not unlike what one of his Christian counterparts would himself do in a comparable situation. Only the name he assigned to God would be different. He waited for the end to come as he thought of his family.

Then, without warning, the fighter abruptly climbed away on full throttles. It shook the old helicopter as it passed overhead. The Chinook crested the summit and the pilot, without waiting for instructions, dove to the right into a narrow valley. The air force pilot reported back, in a spirit of self-preservation, that the craft appeared to have landed in the mountains before he could intercept it. It would be someone else's problem now. He banked the fighter back toward the glow of Tehran and safety. Then he smiled and took a deep breath. *It is a fine night to be flying.*

Mirza saw the lights of the coast first. He immediately went into motion, sealing Reza's phone in a watertight bag and taping it securely to his life vest. They would make a single approach to the ship—hesitate in a brief hover at about twenty feet above the water—and shove Reza into the waiting sea. It wouldn't be a pleasant drop for the colonel. After that, Mirza understood the decision that he and the pilot would need to make. Was there any hope of returning home as if nothing had happened? It would all depend on what the intercept pilot had reported back to Mehrabad. The moment they crossed the coastline the chopper pilot picked up a radio beacon from the waiting ship. They had less than fifteen minutes to decide the direction of their lives.

The pilot keyed his microphone first and said, "Sir, I am going to continue after the drop and dump this bird in Turkmenistan. I'm not going back. They will kill me."

Mirza had already made up his mind before the pilot began to speak. "I know a safe beach near Chalus. Can you drop me somewhere in the area?"

The pilot understood that this would mean turning back toward Iran and the risk that they would be seen as an incoming threat. However, at an altitude of fifty feet, if they didn't collide with a smuggler or someone else doing the same thing, it could probably be done. Besides, his family owed Mirza and his family a debt that demanded any sacrifice of him. For his part, Mirza decided to take the bus back to Tehran. It was a brave and patriotic move. He wasn't yet ready to give up on his country.

The CIA listening post floating in the Caspian Sea detected the approaching helicopter as soon as it cleared the mountains and began its race across the lowlands to the sea. The package they were about to receive needed to be in Dubai within a few hours with all cell phones or other electronics intact. Two former navy SEALs were already geared-up, ready to pluck the hapless prisoner from the water. A quick cruise to the east and a friendly helicopter would pick up the package and deliver it to a U.S. airbase in Afghanistan. Tomorrow morning this guy, whoever he was, would be meeting American and Israeli intelligence specialists, and singing like a little bird.

Reza splashed down about one hundred feet from the ship, and since he was still bound and gagged, he immediately assumed that he was being dropped in the ocean to drown. The splashdown was stunning and wet. Reza kicked with all his might to resurface. The water was cold, and he was barely awake. He thought he was about to die and panic flooded his brain. Suddenly, a set of strong arms grabbed him and began pulling him through the swells.

***

In Dubai, Robert Chase received an unexpected text message that simply read:

> Arrive Paris ASAP. We have some work
> for you there. Lafayette is asking for help.

He knew in general terms what this message meant. There was a person of interest to be located and followed somewhere in that great city. The DCRI, the French version of Homeland Security, Lafayette in this case, was asking for assistance. It was a curious request, although such joint projects did happen from time to time. Chase and his team were known in certain circles to be highly effective and very, very discrete. Sometimes it was all about deniability. He wouldn't know who his target was until later. He still had a long journey ahead of him. By the time he arrived back in France, Reza's phone would have been swept thoroughly for whatever it contained.

Chase received word of the successful acquisition of Reza Tehrani at about 20:00 hours local time. The package would be arriving from Afghanistan in a small charter jet at Dubai Airport in about five hours. Chase would take custody of the prisoner from a military escort and transfer the prisoner to a waiting Agency aircraft that had already filed a flight plan for Amman, Jordan. That flight would land short of the declared destination at a restricted airbase in the Israeli Sinai. Chase would accompany the prisoner only that far. He next stop would be Istanbul, where he could transfer to a commercial flight back to France. His goal was to remain dark—unknown and unfollowed—when he arrived back in Paris.

-9-

Marseille, France

The stop in Paris had been unexpectedly brief. One suspect had flamed out and another had taken his place. Chase didn't mind at all. He loved this city. He loved the fusion of cultures, the exotic aromas, and the staccato music of the countless languages, many from one slice of colonial Africa or another. He was strolling down the Rue Tapis Vert toward the Old Port, a spot first claimed by the Phoenicians, then the Greeks and Romans, and now émigrés from France's former colonies. Marseille was France's second-largest city, with nearly a million people, and was everything that Paris was not. Around him he could feel the clamor and friendly chaos of open commerce. It was wonderful. It was free enterprise in motion. The ancient street was becoming crowded as it neared the port, so Chase decided to duck into a less-traveled alley to find another way to his destination. He wanted to quickly reach the Quai des Belges and its vibrant fish market, and especially a little café called Ma Tante Marie that he had been thinking about as he landed this morning.

There was invariably the scent of danger in Marseille. It was barely a civilized city in the opinion of most in the Paris government, and savvy visitors were constantly alert for potential trouble. That went without saying for Chase. Awareness was his natural state of mind.

Chase saw the two young men even before they noticed him. They were lounging against a stucco wall by the rear door of a seedy café, smoking cigarettes. They had the careless manner of those looking for trouble. He'd observed this same scene play out in other big cities: New York, Philadelphia, and in Paris. The two exchanged a few words and then began to stroll in his direction, one behind the other, as though they were heading off to work. Chase sensed immediately that the right hand of the first in line held something that could hurt him, most likely a short, sharp blade to be used to immobilize him with quick thrusts into his upper or lower back. They didn't want to kill him, just take his money. It would be over in seconds. Chase didn't need trouble right now, but here it was in front of him, his for the taking.

As the first young man approached on his left, Chase put on his best Midwestern smile like an American tourist is expected to do. The boy looked away from his direct gaze, giving Chase the opening to lash out with his left arm to make hard contact with the windpipe of the passing would-be thief. It was a direct hit, he could feel the cartilage give way, and the youth fell to his knees clutching his throat and gasping for air. It was not a fatal blow, although Chase knew that it must be incredibly painful and frightening. He heard a metallic ring as a knife hit the cobblestones.

He turned immediately to the second young man, who by now was fumbling for his own knife. The two stared at each other, the boy in growing terror and Chase with a look of "do you feel lucky?" or his best imitation, burning across the three meters between them. "*Et bien?*" loosely translated as "what now?" came out of his mouth. The second youth hesitated, then turned and sprinted down the alley, leaving his fallen comrade behind.

This is a problem I don't want, thought Chase. *I can't be seen here, but if I leave now, this same kid will be robbing someone else in a couple of hours.* He made what he thought was the only responsible decision. He toppled the incapacitated youth over onto his back with his foot and quickly snapped his right forearm with a short, powerful heel stomp. The fallen assailant unleashed a cry of pain, followed by a string of curses as he struggled to hold his damaged arm close to his chest.

Chase looked down and said softly in French, "That hurt me as much as it did you." He took out the toss-away phone he had bought at the airport and called the French version of 911 as he walked away. The phone was now compromised and of no further use to him, so he wiped it clean and tossed it into a Dumpster at the end of the alleyway after removing and grinding the SIM card into the pavement.

***

Jean-Claude was still in Marseille. He had received instructions from an unknown caller earlier in the day. In a few minutes, he would acquire the payload for his small explosive device in a public park in the suburb of Marignane not far from the Marseille Provence Airport. He was deeply conflicted and nervous. He could smell his own dankness and every attempt he made to swallow met with resistance. This wasn't normal behavior for him. It was not so much an attack of conscience he was feeling, but one of complete anxiety. *What will happen to me if I fail or, for that matter, if I succeed?*

As he was sorting through his own issues, his contact sat down, deposited a small grocery sack between them, and glanced once more to make sure Jean-Claude was the intended recipient. Then he got up just as quickly as he had arrived and walked away. Jean-Claude's heart was racing. He had no idea of what was about to happen. He felt like throwing up. Then he did.

As he made his way back to central Marseille, Jean-Claude received a text message, and it wasn't from Reza. It was from an unknown number in Paris.

Tomorrow 16:00, Stade Velodrome, north end, top
row. Don't be late. I am watching you.

Jean-Claude looked up quickly and scanned the park. He could see only mothers and their young children.

Stade Velodrome was the major-league soccer stadium in the city and tomorrow afternoon his own professional football club,

Olympique de Marseille, would be taking the field in an exhibition match against a United States team. The stands, normally holding about thirty-five-thousand fans, were expanded for this special event. The prevailing winds this time of year would be light and from the north. *Whatever is in this package,* he thought, *it will cover all of us, even Olympique.*

***

Prior to arriving in Marseille, Robert Chase had mounted a fruitless two-day stakeout in Paris. Reza was proving to be a difficult patient in the little interrogation center in Israel. At least his captured cell phone provided a wealth of additional information. It was clear from message fragments identified and reclaimed from intercepts recorded by the French, that the intensity of traffic pointed to an agent or agents in that country. Two individuals came up as possible suspects: one, a Saudi banker residing in Paris; and the other, an occasional university student in the south. The banker, named Farid Al-Sharif, was immensely wealthy and well-connected, but he did not appear to have the radical inclinations that might make him want to blow up either himself or his wealth. Still, Chase had spent most of two frustrating days identifying his routine, his mistresses, and favored travel routes in case an intervention was ordered.

The other suspect, Jean-Claude Dumas, did not appear to have much more significance, except for the timing of one recent call. This one had escaped the ears of the DCRI, and it concerned everyone at the CIA. No one could answer the question: why would an Iranian Revolutionary Guard colonel have any legitimate reason to be in contact with Jean-Claude? And it was clear from phone records obtained from the French that this was not an isolated occurrence. Based on this evidence, Chase had been hastily dispatched from his empty stakeout in Paris to Marseille and told to track the young man and await further instructions.

After his scuffle in the alleyway, Chase had received a file that contained the information he needed to begin his search. He quickly set to work locating Jean-Claude's apartment, and it wasn't too long before he encountered the young man himself, nearly colliding with him outside his run-down building. Jean-Claude was returning home, apparently from the grocery store, for he carried a not-too-heavy plastic sack on one arm as he fumbled for his key. Chase took a careful look at him as they passed each other. Jean-Claude was slender, perhaps six feet in height, and not more than one hundred and fifty pounds. He looked much like the picture from his French identity card. He was not from the South of France, more likely the center, and had certain aristocratic facial characteristics. He was careless in manner, as a professional like Robert Chase measured other people. In other words, Jean-Claude would never see him coming.

When he received the order, Chase felt confident that he could take this boy and deliver him to a waiting car in a matter of seconds. For the moment, all he had to do was watch. Across the street was one of many cafés in the area. He first stopped at the tabac-newsstand next door and bought a local paper. He sat with his back to the wall of the café, facing Jean-Claude's building, and waited.

In the apartment, Jean-Claude trembled as he carefully lifted the package from the bag. It was a completely sealed container only about one kilo—two pounds—in weight and securely wrapped in a shiny foil-like substance. It looked like an oversized plastic water bottle, something a bike racer would use, but with molded space in the bottom where his explosive device was to be carefully inserted and taped in place.

His only instructions were to leave the parcel in the very upper seats of the stadium, then press the blue button to arm it and leave the area. He understood the part about leaving. He wanted nothing to do with what would happen once the timer ticked away its last four minutes. He carefully pulled out the box containing the assembled explosive device and a small messenger bag no different than the ones many young people carried. It had a false bottom that, once securely closed, would be nearly invisible during a routine check of bags at the stadium. A bottle of water and a sandwich on top would complete the disguise.

For some reason, perhaps it was his growing anxiety, Jean-Claude could not bring himself to arm the weapon right then. He was extremely agitated and needed to blow off nervous energy. He grabbed his keys and wallet and bolted down the stairs to the street and began walking briskly. A few dozen yards behind him was Chase, this time in European-style glasses and a light scarf hanging loosely around his neck. Chase was in no hurry to get any closer, so he would, now and then, cross the busy street and continue his watch from another vantage point. His target seemed to be unaware of his presence and appeared to be unwary in general.

Jean-Claude stopped at a noisy bar, peeked in, and then disappeared into the gloomy light. Smoking was officially forbidden in French bars these days; however, that didn't seem to move any of the patrons of this establishment to change their behavior. *This is good,* thought Chase, *very casual, no police.* He slipped inside and ordered a pastis, the anise-flavored favorite of the region served with ice water and, if one was lucky, a small bowl of olives. This time he received his drink and a saucer of greasy crisps—potato chips in America. It wasn't the Ritz. He sipped his drink and watched the soccer game on the television, its frantic commentary overruled by the animated chatter of the bar patrons.

Jean-Claude was talking with a young woman who seemed uninterested in whatever he was saying. Chase noticed that there were no obvious signs of affection between them, and the girl preferred to look away from him as he spoke, perhaps searching for better options. After more than an hour, the woman got up and left. Jean-Claude stared at his empty beer bottle and barely moved. There was something heavy resting on this boy's shoulders, observed his watcher. No one in the bar talked to him, and no one tried to engage him in any way. Even the server kept her distance. It was as though he had no friends at all.

***

Back in the Israeli desert, Reza had reached his breaking point. He had not slept or eaten in more than two days, and his interrogators were relentless. He was beginning to lose track of time and day, which he understood would signal the end of his ability to resist. He was about to become putty in their hands. He didn't know if he had succeeded or failed in his mission, nevertheless, he could take this treatment no longer. "Four seconds," he blurted out of nowhere after an unrelated question from the man across the table. Then he caught himself and resumed his silence.

"I am glad to hear you can speak, Reza. That's real progress. Now what is the significance of four seconds?"

The interrogator sat back in his chair to await a response. He had to wait a long time, for Reza's desire to speak ended as quickly as it began. Two hours later he spoke again and admitted that he had been running an agent in Marseille, and nothing more. He was so fatigued that he could not continue, so his captors allowed him exactly five minutes' sleep, and then they rudely shook him awake to begin once more.

Reza had entered an exhausted, dreamlike state. Visually, everything was spinning, everything seemed unnatural. Before long, he began to admit anything they suggested to him, but there was a pattern in the questioning that he could not pick up. They were slowly building an image of the real threat they were facing. The name of Jean-Claude resurfaced in the questioning repeatedly. It was clear from his reaction that this was Reza's man. Time was running out, and Reza wasn't yet completely broken. The team leader decided they should pick up this kid in

Marseille now. At this moment in time, no one in the room had any idea if an attack was imminent, or even if one was planned.

***

Chase had wished a quiet good night to Jean-Claude from across the street at about one A.M. after his apartment lights had been out for an hour. He had followed him from the bar and wanted to be sure that the boy was settled in for the night. Chase was tired too and knew he would need to be back in front of the apartment building not later than five A.M. the next morning. He was used to short hours, even welcoming the heightened sense of excitement they brought. He would sleep only two hours, then shower and be back on location long before the street sweepers started their daily chores. He was only monitoring the young man and no specific threat had been identified. He was awakened almost three hours later at his hotel; the text he had been expecting flashed onto the screen of his phone.

> Intervention approved—important—Old Port, pier 17,
> Dauphine NLT 10:00 tomorrow.

This young man would be going for an unplanned sea cruise with a couple of Agency interrogators. Chase's training now assumed control, and he began to go over his internal checklist. Then he called an old friend with a car who lived in Marseille. They would take the young man as he left in the morning for coffee. At least that was the plan.

***

Jean-Claude couldn't sleep. He tossed for several hours and checked the clock again; it read 3:30 A.M. He got up, dressed, and went to the table containing everything as he had left it yesterday. His purpose seemed more in focus now. He was less agitated, not as anxious. *I can do this.*

Before he proceeded with the delicate task ahead of him, he decided to call his parents and leave a message. He called his father's cell phone expecting to hear a recording. Instead, his father's sleepy voice answered after the third ring.

"*Oui,* Jacques Dumas."

Jean-Claude paused for a few seconds while his father repeatedly asked who was there. Finally, he replied, "Father, it's me . . . Jean-Claude. I wanted to leave you a message. I'm sorry if I woke you up."

"Is something wrong? We haven't heard from you in months. Are you still in Africa?"

"No, I'm back in France, Marseille to be exact. I'm thinking of returning to university soon, but I wasn't calling about that. I wanted to say hello and let you know I am well."

"If that is all, you might have waited until daylight to call. Your mother will be furious that she missed you. I can't wake her up now, it's much too early. Call back in the morning, Jean-Claude. Don't be so mysterious. Call back later."

Jean-Claude heard the line go dead as he whispered, "I love you, Father." He put his own phone down on the small table. He hit himself in the head with a cupped hand. *Why am I always so stupid to think he cares? Idiot! Imbecile! Well fuck you too very much, Father.*

After wiping his eyes with his shirtsleeve, he returned to his task. He carefully lifted the device he had assembled from its protective box and slowly slid it into its preformed niche, fearing that at any moment, it might explode. He gently pushed it into place and taped it securely with duct tape, leaving only the arming button and the display showing. He placed the completed bomb into the bottom of his messenger bag. It looked like it could rattle around in there and perhaps arm itself, so he wadded up old newspapers to cushion it on all sides. Then he secured the false bottom and closed the bag. He was mentally ready and hours early. He couldn't sit here and watch the minutes tick away. He needed to be in motion. One last look at the clock—it was 4:25 A.M.—Jean-Claude put on his jacket, grabbed his phone and keys, and walked out the door. Chase, even though he was thirty minutes ahead of his schedule, simply missed him by minutes.

By eight A.M., Chase began to worry. He needed to verify that Jean-Claude was still in his apartment, but he couldn't risk being seen up close, from three or four feet. He sent his driver Pierre to knock on the door and then make his apologies for waking the wrong party. As he returned to his car, he looked at Chase and simply shook his head.

As soon as Chase saw this signal he bolted up the steps and not so gently let himself inside with a shoulder to the cheap door. Nothing! There was an empty box, and a quick check of drawers revealed a few tools and a soldering gun. No Jean-Claude and nothing that could be construed as a threat. He immediately took out his phone and texted an emergency flash.

> Person of interest has fled. Need more information on other possible locations or acquaintances.

He sensed the spread of desperation in his mind. He had hoped that the prisoner in Israel would have provided more information by now. Without some sense of what Jean-Claude was about to do, even a man like Chase would be unable to stop him. He needed to know what, where, and when.

His only option, and not a good one at that, was to crisscross the neighborhood, checking cafés and bars in a desperate race to reacquire his target. He described the boy to Pierre, and the two spread out in search of him. *This was not how the mission was supposed to end. It must not end this way.*

***

Several miles to the south of the old town, the Stade Velodrome stands in the 8th arrondissement of the city of Marseille. It is a splendid venue for the highest level of professional soccer, and the local fans are as boisterous as any in the world. Every game was greeted by fans draped in team colors and large blue-and-white flags waving in the warm Mediterranean breezes. Today's game was highly anticipated by all, and the stands would be full and noisy. Jean-Claude sat on a bench along the Boulevard Michelet facing the grand stadium where his team would be playing the Americans in a few hours. *I love this place. I love this team. How did I get myself into this predicament? Stupid!* He was willing to kill people he didn't know, to make a declaration, maybe to prove something to his father, but he was having second thoughts about what it might mean for the reigning French national champions.

***

In Israel, Reza finally broke completely and pathetically. He begged for his life—he begged to save his hidden fortune. He did not plead for his victims. He spilled the frightening details of the planned bombing. The interrogators raced to the communications center to fire off warnings of the worst kind. They told the security services that paid their salaries that the target was indeed Marseille, the football stadium, and the weapon was already in the hands of the bomber. It was biological, and the detonation was set for today, during the second half of the soccer match. The start of play was less than two hours away.

Locating this deadly weapon could no longer to be left solely in the hands of a few covert operatives like Robert Chase. It was too late for patient, careful fieldwork. Merrill broadcast an urgent warning to the French security services, the French president, and to the president of the United States. There was now only one hour and forty-seven minutes left to halt this event and evacuate the stadium. On the slow clock of nation-to-nation communications, this would pass like one single second.

***

Jean-Claude had already joined the boisterous crowd as it swelled through the turnstiles and into the stadium itself. From the concourse, he could see the wash of bright green turf and flags already waving in the highly partisan crowd. The bag check was perfunctory—open it up—and let the regular security staff peek inside. The only objects the security guard saw in Jean-Claude's bag were a wrapped sandwich and a small bottle of Badoit. He waved him through and began a new search in the next bag.

Jean-Claude's regular seat was in the lower level, about midfield, and thirty rows back from the fence surrounding the pitch. He had received it as a gift from his father and he treasured it above all things in his life. He bought a beer, walked around, and finally went upstairs to see where he might leave his little surprise. *During the game,* he thought, *it will be safe to climb to the top of the stands without anyone paying attention to me. I can press the button and drop the bag behind a seat and leave. That will only give me four minutes to run for the exit. I'm not sure it will be enough time.*

He was also worried about trying to arm the device in the open once he reached the placement point. He considered stopping in a nearby restroom and arming it there. It would give him less time to escape, but it would reduce the risk that someone would notice him fumbling with the bag and then leaving it behind. This seemed to be a reasonable plan, although he had not fully decided what to do when a large roar from the crowd signaled that Olympique had taken the field. He went back to his seat and, for the moment, he was swept up in the spectacle that is European professional football.

The French internal security and antiterrorism agency, the DCRI, was very good at what it did. It was reported to be perhaps the most efficient agency of its type in the world except possibly for its counterpart in Israel. Word of the imminent plot was received from the Americans and pushed directly to the DCRI agency director with approximately one hour and twenty-five minutes remaining before the start of the match. Within minutes, and with the full support of the French president, the

Marseille police, the Police Nationale, and local elements of elite antiterrorism units (the GIGN) were alerted. By the time the first goal was scored by Olympique with fifteen minutes remaining in the first half, the streets around the stadium had been cordoned off and biological containment squads of the DCRI were only minutes away from the location. Still, a plan needed to be developed to empty the stadium, and no one knew exactly who had the authority to order such an action. In normal times, deciding jurisdiction between competing agencies had been known to take hours of discussion and more than a few urgent calls to Paris. With almost forty thousand people inside the stadium right now, an evacuation couldn't be completed in less than an hour. Any attempt to do it faster would certainly result in hundreds, if not thousands, of trampled bodies. The only real hope was to find Jean-Claude and neutralize him. It was their last chance.

At halftime, Jean-Claude got up and left his seat. He wouldn't be returning. Seeing his team perform so magnificently against the Americans, he had finally decided how he would handle his dilemma. He stopped at a bar in the concourse and asked for a beer, and after standing at a ledge for a few moments, he couldn't bring himself to drink it. He was now sweating profusely and hyperventilating. His vision was sparkling and distorted. He couldn't catch his breath even though he was panting like a dog. He felt like he might pass out.

He checked his watch. It was 3:50 and the crowd started to roar as both teams reentered the pitch. The concourse began to empty, leaving him still standing in the same spot. Jean-Claude was feeling sick, and so he made a dash toward the closest toilet, there on the ground floor. He barely made it into a stall before his insides convulsed, and he vomited loudly, to the laughter of several beefy young men who thought he was drunk. He closed the stall door and leaned against the wall for support. He could hardly move. *Why am I here? What is the point of all of this? What am I doing? Idiot!* As he was having this little internal conversation, two police officers entered the restroom. After a perfunctory search, they turned and left. They had been within ten feet of the man they were seeking, but they hadn't taken the time to check the stalls.

He steadied himself and looked at his watch again. It was time. It had to be now or never. Never wouldn't work. He couldn't disappoint Reza, his only friend. He would arm the bomb now and leave the bag here in the ground floor toilet where it would make a statement, but not kill everyone in the stadium. He could live with that. A few meaningless concessionaires and some drunks might die, but they would be an acceptable loss. He wanted to cause a disaster; however, he didn't want to be remembered as the fan who had wiped out the home team.

He fumbled with the latch on the bag and finally tore it open with a loud rip of Velcro. He tossed the sandwich and water bottle into the fouled toilet and unzipped the bottom compartment. The display on the device stared back at him as if daring him to do it. Hands trembling, Jean-Claude moved his index finger a bit closer to the arming button. He took several deep breaths, but all he could smell was his own vomit. In his mind, he raced through his planned retreat and even imagined, in a ridiculous self-serving moment, how he might act the hero and try to come back inside once the device went off, to rescue survivors. He had no clue what he was about to unleash.

At about the same moment, agents of the Police Nationale and tactical teams from the GIGN were flooding into the stadium grounds, fanning out in a frantic effort to find anyone who looked like Jean-Claude. It was an act born of desperation, although there was now no more time remaining. Any man carrying a bag was immediately stopped and roughly searched. Two squads of officers were dispatched to the upper seating areas and the remainder spread out throughout the lower stands.

Fans noticed the disturbances, and they stopped watching the game to see what the officers were doing. The decontamination units of the military had arrived at the stadium and were suiting up in their protective gear while the Marseille Police bomb squad brought out their dogs. Everything that could be done was being done. If the weapon detonated right now their efforts would not be nearly enough. It was a simple fact. The few who knew the nature of the bomb's payload understood how hopeless their position was. They soldiered on because it was what they were trained to do.

***

Robert Chase had been one of the last to hear of the target and the timing. He frantically called Pierre time and time again, and finally reached him on the sixth try.

"Our man is at the stadium. He's got a bomb, a bad bomb. Can we make it there in ten minutes?"

"That will not be possible. I can get you there in twenty if the roads are not blocked. The car is still in front of the apartment. I'll meet you there."

Chase sprinted across two busy avenues on his way back to Jean-Claude's apartment. As he turned the last corner Pierre saw him and gunned the small Renault down the narrow street, taking off the passenger door side-mirror in the process. Chase was not even in his seat before Pierre took off, tires squealing, to rejoin the major route that led in the direction of the Stade. Both men were sweating profusely in the cool air, Chase from his exertion, Pierre from his growing sense of panic. This was an impossible attempt to prevent the inevitable. Chase tried to fill in the gaps in what Pierre knew as the car raced past slower cars and through stoplights. There were no police anywhere until they neared the stadium.

"The Iranian finally broke," said Chase. "He gave the boy an unassembled bomb and then provided a biological payload. If it goes up, everyone in the stadium will be at risk. How could we have missed him?"

Pierre said nothing. He knew Chase, and that he was now in his own private hell. Nothing anyone could say would pull him out of that pit. Chase was a perfectionist. Against great odds, he had never failed to bring in his man, or woman. He had successfully blocked more than a few terrorist attempts and, if he was to be completely honest, he felt he was invincible. Now, for the sake of a couple of hours of restless sleep, he had lost his most important target ever. *If this bomb goes off, I will be responsible for whatever happens.* It was a crushing load for any human being to bear.

***

"Four seconds," that is what Reza had first said to his interrogators not so many hours ago. What he admitted was the truth, however cryptic it may have seemed at the time. The man who designed this bomb never intended that the unfortunate messenger, whomever fate happened to select, would survive to be a witness to anything or against anyone. Many worthy and holy people sacrificed their lives for the Islamic cause every day, and this misguided youth would be no different. He would not have the same reward that the faithful hoped for, but then again, his life and afterlife were of no concern to a true believer. Jean-Claude had been told that he would have time to arm the device and then leave safely. That was an unfortunate untruth. Sometimes even the devout were willing to lie when it suited their purposes. It was not four minutes that he saw on the display as he now pressed the button to arm the bomb. It would be a much briefer span.

Jean-Claude took another deep breath and started the timer with his thumb. It clicked as it engaged. Then he watched in disbelief as the display raced through the four remaining ticks and his world went black.

The seven ounces of high explosive in the device was meant to loft a billion droplets of the deadly virus into the air above the stadium crowd. Had it done so, it would have infected most of the unsuspecting fans and players who were directly downwind from the relatively small detonation. The number impacted could have been twenty-five thousand or more. Within forty-eight hours all except the most immune would begin to display symptoms of deadly hemorrhagic fever from this enhanced virus, and within four to ten days 90 percent would possibly be dead. At least that had been the plan.

Jean-Claude's change of heart had made a difference. He didn't have the time to understand this one important fact. He had, in his decision to leave the bomb in the lower-level toilets, saved his team, but he could not save himself. The initial force of the blast threw him backward, bursting through the closed door of the stall, and ten meters across the floor of the restroom. He impacted against the opposite tiled wall at a speed of about two hundred kilometers per hour and came to rest with multiple fragments of the small canister embedded in his abdomen, chest, and face. About one-half of the lethal fluid never became airborne and was now dripping down his lifeless body.

He undoubtedly died more quickly and more peacefully than would his victims. Certainly, tens of millions of virus droplets flashed across the room to the only exit point, and out into the concourse in a deadly fog of virus and smoke. On their journey, they coated the restroom floor and walls and condensed to a large degree in the cool concourse before reaching the seats. Several thousand fans and nearby stadium workers were immediately exposed to the deadly vapor. Even that number was far less than anyone could have hoped.

The retort of the detonation was noticeable, but not disturbingly loud in the stadium itself. It sounded more like the thump of a big ocean wave on the shore than a bomb. This prevented complete panic from erupting. Those in seats just off the concourse were impacted the most. The game was continuing, and many patrons in the affected area were beginning to get up and leave their seats as the cloud reached them. Police raced onto the playing field and spoke to the head referee. The match was stopped to the disapproving whistles of the unaware crowd. Bottles and other objects were beginning to fill the air.

Shortly, an announcement came over the loudspeaker: "Ladies and gentlemen, we ask for your patience. This match has been suspended by order of the Police Nationale due to a minor chemical explosion in the concession area. There is no reason to fear for your safety. We must all leave the Stade in an orderly manner. Please follow police directions to the exits and comply with their instructions completely. You will receive a complete refund of the price paid for your tickets. Thank you." That last bit of information probably prevented the riot that was already brewing.

Now only a mile from the stadium, Pierre and Chase saw a small plume of smoke begin its ascent out of the structure. They were too late. They drove through traffic for another minute in silence, before a police barricade forced them to halt. This was as close as they would ever get to the disaster.

"Pierre, you might as well turn around. This is as far as they will let us go. There's nothing more to be done. I am so sorry for what happened to your country today."

At each of the exits, the decontamination units were already setting up wash stations through which everyone in the stadium would be forced to walk. The crowd was growing noisy and unruly as they filed slowly toward the exits. Fights began to break out as slightly drunk bodies repeatedly collided with the slow pace of the retreat. On the concourse, biological countermeasures were already under way. The sharp smell of a solution of hypochlorite, common household bleach, was spreading everywhere, causing men and women alike to cover their noses with handkerchiefs or any item of clothing that would reach their faces. Teams of technicians, dressed in bright yellow hazmat suits and carrying backpack sprayers, fanned out around the explosion and doused every surface, every person as quickly as possible. It would not help those who had already inhaled the vaporized viral soup. For those who had not, it might prove to be a lifesaver.

A subsequent stage of the biochemical warfare plan developed by the GIGN involved large-area decontamination procedures. Once the toxin had been identified as a specific virus, the French Air Force was ordered to prepare tanker aircraft, to provide a more complete dosing of the now infected stadium. At an air base near Toulouse large propeller aircraft, normally used to fight the annual forest fires that periodically scorched the hills in the South of France, were loaded with hundreds of thousands of gallons of a diluted bleach solution. Everything visible from the air was about to be drenched with this antiviral wash, including everyone on the ground and in the open air.

This had only been a contingency plan until now, something possible, yet never really expected. The French government had been one of the first to understand that the porous borders of the eurozone, and the increase in radical militancy, might allow such an event to occur. They quietly planned for it and hoped that their security services would never allow it to happen. France and Germany were the only European nations with this level of planning. As yet, the United States had no comprehensive plan for such an event. That would be changing in a hurry.

Chase was devastated. He learned of what had happened at the stadium, first from the live news feeds, and later from details provided by Control at the Agency. He now understood how badly he had failed in what had seemed like such a routine intervention. He was crushed. This had happened on his watch. Even so, he understood that one thing he could not personally control was the information he relied on to do his job. That information came from others and often did not show up when he needed it, or in complete sentences. It was never like in the movies. Reza Tehrani had been their only source, and he gave up what he knew in fragments, and not nearly soon enough. Had he fully understood the hopelessness of his situation earlier, the

Iranian colonel might have confessed and saved his fortune and his life. Now both would be forfeited.

At the stadium, four hours of growing panic had passed since the blast had erupted out of the men's room. Everyone present had received at least a preliminary decontamination, and they were now milling around in a vast holding area in the approaches to the parking lot.

This was a recipe for a riot, and the nervous police guarding the crowd were feeling the situation slowly slipping beyond their control. The first major disturbance broke out around a vocal group of about twenty male fans who had come to the game together. They were all in the construction trades and not accustomed to having to follow anyone's orders. The most vocal of the group was a man identified only as Emile. His friends usually called him Roux because of his wiry red hair. He was short in stature, only five feet and six inches, but powerfully built, and capable of making much larger men back off when he was in the mood for a fight.

"We are all French citizens," he said. "They have no right to keep us here. I am leaving, and now."

Before he finished his last sentence, Roux began to push his way through the crowd and toward the closest perimeter barrier. Most of his companions came with him, and then to his surprise, he suddenly found he was leading a small army of men and women to freedom. Anyone who got in the way of this determined and growing throng was either shoved aside or to the ground. They were moving slowly and steadily toward barriers manned by army regulars. From the other side of one section of the fence, a squad of young soldiers, with loaded automatic weapons, was now facing at least several hundred of their countrymen, all determined to escape the quarantine. If they succeeded, the rest would follow, and the contained infection would become a plague.

The soldiers began to shout out for the crowd to stop, waving their free arms wildly. Some of the young men had tears in their eyes as their lieutenant ordered them to ready their weapons. At the command to fire, the squad leader, a sergeant only a couple of years older than his charges, took out the apparent leaders of the mob with precise, quick shots. Roux was killed instantly. Now the entire squad was firing short bursts of two or three rounds each at anyone who continued to approach the barrier. The crowd had pressed so close that the soldiers could see the individual hairs on the heads they were aiming at. Bodies were now piled three-feet deep in front of the barriers. Then, as quickly as the riot began, it ended. The survivors turned and pushed their way back into the crowd, and safety.

Medical personnel in gowns and masks cautiously moved into the no-man's land between the soldiers and the crowd, checking for the living. The dead would not be moved immediately, for fear of spreading the contagion beyond the containment zone. Unfortunately for the victims, the soldiers had been well-trained and were disciplined shooters. Eighty-seven lay dead and only seven came forward to have their wounds treated once the shooting stopped. There may have been more wounded, but they disappeared into the crowd, fearing for their lives. Everyone who had participated in this brief action was now in shock.

The thousands who had been contaminated by the blast still needed to be moved to a permanent quarantine area. One was hastily being established in an out-of-service section of the naval base at Toulon, and another near Montpellier. This would be a monumental task. Before anyone would be allowed to leave quarantine, they would have to be tested for the Marburg virus. This would not be possible for at least forty-eight hours, to allow the virus to begin to colonize the victims. French authorities and the World Health Organization estimated that perhaps one-third of the forty-five-thousand private citizens who were in the stadium at the time of the attack would need to be transported, fed, housed, and evaluated by medical personnel for up to three weeks, to ensure that the disease would not spread beyond its initial victims. Marburg was a highly infectious virus which was easily spread by person-to-person contact. Maintaining security was proving to be difficult with only two thousand local and national police on the scene. The president of the republic ordered the army to establish a tight perimeter along the boulevards framing the stadium, and to transport food, water, and sleeping bags for those trapped there. It was going to be a long, tense night. No living person would be permitted to leave the security zone, except in military custody. As darkness fell, seven lumbering aircraft finally left their holding patterns twelve thousand feet above Marseille and began slow drenching runs over the stadium area. The crowd quieted and, at least for a few moments, believed what they had been told.

***

In Tehran, the news of the terrorist attack stunned the Central Council. No one had any idea that one of their own countrymen, and a Revolutionary Guard officer at that, had been responsible. To these delusional men, it was another sign that Allah was about to strike down the nonbelievers. Caught up in the moment, they urged the ayatollah to proceed quickly with their plot to destroy Baghdad and reclaim Iraq. They did not intend to be upstaged for long by whatever ragtag terrorist group was responsible for this thing. The banker Al-Sharif had assured them that a replacement weapon could be purchased if they wished to proceed. Now the challenge would be getting it there unnoticed.

***

Chase was only now beginning to process how he felt about the loss of Jean-Claude and the magnitude of the attack. How could he have been so careless? It was wrong of him not to have set a watch over the boy throughout the night. He felt the loss of life in a very personal way. He vowed that this would never happen again on his watch. He needed to talk with Samantha in the worst way. There was little he could tell her, except perhaps that he had been in Marseille when it happened. His phone buzzed. There was a text message for him from his controller.

You are needed in Paris, ASAP.

There was more to do. He vowed to do it right this time.

Update

By the end of the quarantine, only 2,678 people were found to have been infected with the lethal Marburg virus set loose by Jean-Claude Dumas. Jean-Claude and two other men who were in the restroom died immediately from the blast. Of those infected, more than two hundred were of Central African birth who possessed a degree of natural immunity to the virus. They all survived, although not all easily. A total of eight hundred and seven men, women, and children perished from the disease, a remarkably small number given the mortality usually expected from hemorrhagic fever.

During the investigation that followed the attack, three factors were credited with the low death toll. First, and probably the most significant, was the decision by Jean-Claude to arm the bomb in the lower-floor restroom. Next, was the rapid response by the French emergency services, including the necessary and deadly decision to maintain a strict quarantine of the stadium. And the third was the questionable potency of the aging biological agent itself. Still, by any measure, it was a national and human disaster.

Colonel Reza Tehrani was relentlessly interrogated for another three weeks in Israel and then quietly transferred to French authorities. The consensus was that he had given up all his secrets. He stood trial for mass murder in Marseille and was convicted after a public trial that lasted eleven days. He did not speak one single word in his defense. The fortune he had so carefully gathered for two decades somehow went missing and was rumored to have provided a relief fund for the victims. If the guillotine had still been in use at this time, he would certainly have found his way onto its platform. Instead, he now serves a life sentence in seclusion in a prison in the middle of

France. His only visitors are intelligence officers. It is unlikely that he will ever be released. He still refuses to speak of the event to anyone.

Eight days after the attack, a U.S. reconnaissance drone aircraft, operating out of an American base in Yemen, identified an unusually large gathering of personnel at a training camp near Sana'a, one operated by the local branch of Al-Qaeda. The American president was fully briefed. Then, after consulting with the president of France, he authorized a three-stage attack that began with a sunset launch of six Tomahawk cruise missiles with high-explosive warheads, from a cruiser in the Arabian Sea. A second launch of twelve cruise missiles carrying antipersonnel warheads was timed twenty minutes later, with the clear intention of killing all survivors on the ground, a lesson learned from suicide bombers in Afghanistan. In the pause between the two strikes, two MQ-1 Predator drone aircraft operating overhead launched on and destroyed five vehicles attempting to flee the scene. Later reports by the Yemeni government put the death toll at one hundred and twenty suspected terrorists, including the mastermind who had planned the Marseille attack, and the three most senior leaders of Al-Qaeda in the Arabian Gulf.

In Paris, once word of the successful attack was released to the news outlets, a crowd of thousands of Frenchmen, many carrying small French and American flags, marched quietly around the Arc de Triomphe. In Washington, D.C., the same gesture was repeated the next evening around the Washington Monument. First in war, first in peace, these two nations had a long history.

The American president was quoted shortly afterward: "The United States will not cease to punish those terrorists, whether state-sponsored or independent, who attempt to harm our citizens or those of our allies. Be assured there is nowhere they can hide."

This was a warning that was not overlooked in Tehran.

Part Two

What Goes Around, Comes Around

-10-

France

Robert Chase returned to Paris by train, humbled and lost deep inside his private thoughts. It took a delay of two days before he could find his way out of the quarantine city of Marseille. The airport had been closed immediately after the terrorist attack for security and safety reasons. Even now, it was mobbed with frightened people trying to put some distance between themselves and the virus. All trains to all points were still crowded and reservations on the fast trains, the TGV, were unobtainable. Chase was content to shuttle first to Bordeaux and then through Brittany to Paris. He needed the time to process all that had happened. He couldn't shake the feeling that he was responsible for the attack. He had been proud and careless. This was a revelation to him. Chase the helper had proven to be helpless. This was not the person he wanted to be. He demanded redemption.

In Paris, Samantha was anxious and worried for Chase's safety. He had sent her a brief text telling her that he had been in Marseille at the time of the attack, and that he was safe. She could not eat, sit still, or sleep. The large French news outlets were giving nonstop play to this heinous attack on the French people. Fear was everywhere. Cell phone traffic was so heavy that many calls were dropped. The nation wept as one for those who had been infected with the virus. Right now, the ultimate death toll was unknown, nonetheless, the fear of the worst possible outcome kept the estimates in the thousands in the tabloids and on the broadcast news. Sam was worried about her sweet man. She felt guilty that she cared more about him than the thousands of her own countrymen who were at risk. Then again, she could not help how she felt.

Chase finally secured a train seat to Bordeaux and was about to begin the slow circuitous return to Paris. He tried to phone Sam several times and finally settled for a text message.

> I am safe. Taking the long way back to
> Paris. I need some time to think.

He realized that Sam could not begin to understand what he was dealing with, but it was the best he could do. He was processing things in his own way and when he finished he would be a different person. Robert Chase was a complicated man with a simple outlook on life. He accepted the existence of senseless evil and his unique role in helping to keep it in check. He never deluded himself into believing that it could be stopped entirely. Until now, he had maintained intact his original value structure that dictated, among other things, that some balance could be achieved. This latest act, and his failure to stop it, had shattered the fragile cover that protected who he thought he was and what his life meant. Perhaps it needed to be shattered. *If things have changed, then I must change too.*

***

The Saudi banker, Farid Al-Sharif, had departed Paris for the Saudi kingdom as soon as his part in the events of that day was completed. Although Chase could not have known it at the time, Al-Sharif had served as banker for several terrorist organizations. It was he who had been the conduit for the funds from Al-Qaeda in Yemen to Colonel Reza Tehrani. It was just business to Al-Sharif. For all he cared, the governments of the world could destroy one another, so long as Switzerland and Saudi Arabia survived. He was a brilliant student of world economies and experienced as few were in the stealth movement of money. He had no loyalties except to himself, and the few who knew him well would later say that he was morally deficient in those important qualities that separate man from the rest of the animal kingdom. His view of the world did not include Allah, God, or any other form of a supreme being. The "invisible hand" of the market was his deity and every outcome that was guided by his interpretation of Adam Smith's enduring economic theory must also be God's will. Whatever maximized his personal gain was good, and equally God's will. For the moment, this meant moving vast sums of money for whoever would pay his fee. And apparently, he learned from a recent urgent message, he now had a new customer.

***

Chase arrived at the Gare Montparnasse on the fast train from Rennes at 18:45 hours. As was his custom, he stopped at a kiosk near the station and bought a cheap phone and a thirty-euro SIM card. He paid cash. He inquired at his usual hotel on the Rue de Rivoli and the desk clerk welcomed him back to Paris. He told him that he had a fifth-floor single room for eighty-five euros per night, cash only. It would do. The room overlooked a little plaza and café between the hotel and the building next door. It was the same spot he had met Samantha on his last visit to the city. That seemed like a lifetime ago. He sent news of his arrival to Control by text message, and then he took a deep breath and called Sam.

Samantha's voice gushed with emotion. It was like standing under Niagara Falls in full cascade. Her questions hammered down on him. "How are you? I've been so worried. Were you near the attack? Are you okay? Why were you there? I need to see you . . . now!"

Chase waited her out. She had a million good reasons to be worried, and he decided he would not step in front of any of them. After he rang off with Samantha, he received a message from the boss.

Stay put, more soon. Glad you are safe.

He was pleased. The game was on. He could still find some degree of redemption.

***

Back in Alexandria, Virginia, watch-officer Katie Thompson had been working for several days trying to piece together a clearer picture of the threat from the abundant flow of information she had in front of her. More was coming in each hour. *Orlando* was intercepting and forwarding a great volume of email traffic, and in the process, was replicating itself and burrowing deeply into other systems within the Iranian government.

Communications within the military and the Guard were at an extremely high pitch. Something important had to be going on. Katie reported her limited analysis to Deputy Director Merrill, who in turn passed the information along to the director of the CIA. If the Iranian military was mobilizing, or preparing for something unexpected, he reasoned we should all be prepared. He reached for the phone and called the satellite operations center.

"This is Merrill. I need you to reposition our bird over Iran into a location where it can view everything from Tehran to the south, and east to the Iraqi border. Also, bring in extra analyst resources, now. Inform me immediately if any Guard or regular army units show signs of movement, or if the air force begins to reposition aircraft anywhere in the country. Please confirm my orders." The duty officer repeated his instructions verbatim.

Merrill put the phone down for the briefest of pauses, and then snatched it again to make one more call. This call was to the director of the CIA.

He began slowly. "Bill, we have a developing situation in Iran. *Orlando* has picked up heavy traffic within the military command. We're ninety percent sure something is in play, and we don't know much more than that. I've called in our eye in the sky, and I would like to be able to put more resources into the theatre, just in case."

The director of the CIA was William Saltonstall Hughes, an imposing man in physical dimensions, and a giant in the spy business. He was a New Englander, skeptical and questioning by nature, and skilled at coaxing more facts out of his followers than they knew they possessed.

"Reynolds, first an unrelated question: do you still think that the leadership was not involved in the Marseille incident? I'm wondering if we've missed anything."

After a slight pause, he replied, "We are pretty confident in our findings. The interrogation of the Guard colonel was thorough and conclusive, and we uncovered the money trail on both ends. It wasn't the mullahs."

"OK, I needed to hear you to say that. Tell me, now, what else do you need?"

Merrill ticked down his list. At the top were reconnaissance drone aircraft. Not only the big, visible ones reported in the major newspapers. He also wanted access to the new and highly classified mini and micro aircraft that no one could track. He got his wish.

For the past year, Iran had found some success tracking and downing the larger drones that the CIA and the military used for reconnaissance and attack. In one instance, the Iranian Air Force managed to block communications with an American stealth drone near the Afghanistan border, and then take control of it completely, landing it intact inside Iran. It was a considerable intelligence coup, and it made their Chinese benefactors happy as well. Two days after its capture, it had been loaded inside a Chinese military transport for a one-way journey to the homeland.

That bird contained the most sophisticated stealth technology America could build and now China owned it all. This embarrassing loss led the CIA to redouble its efforts to bring into service a new generation of tiny, almost invisible drones for its short-range intelligence work. Foremost in this new class of aircraft was the Mini Air Vehicle or MAV, a small-winged aircraft not much bigger than the models that enthusiasts fly all around the world. The only difference was that these aircraft carried bad intentions. In the words of a famous boxer, "Float like a butterfly; sting like a bee." The CIA had a number of these little warriors in its armory, and Reynolds Merrill had his eye on one special top-secret craft.

-11-

Farid Al-Sharif could not believe what he had just been told. He was accustomed to arms transactions of almost every kind, and he had participated as the money changer for many that were distasteful. This time he sat without moving for several minutes after receiving the new proposal. In Al-Sharif's view of the world, war was a given, like rainfall and sunshine, but to contemplate the permanent destruction of any nation was never part of his vision. It would be bad for business.

He could not comprehend a nuclear end to one of the Arab world's great cities. *Those Persian bastards. To settle a centuries-old grudge, they are willing to create a dead zone, Chernobyl times twenty, in the region of the world I love. Who is to say in which direction the fallout and the eventual slow, painful deaths will drift?* He hated the thought that this age-old bitterness could destroy an entire civilization. He wasn't sure he could be part of this.

The leadership council in Tehran had finally located a weapon to replace the one intended for Baghdad. The new civilian government in Pakistan was in desperate need of foreign currency and had indicated that it might be willing to sell one of its unneeded, older nuclear warheads, twenty kilotons of explosive power, to Iran for fifteen or twenty billion U.S. dollars. The weapon was more advanced than Iran's own homemade bomb, and it would be a substantial deterrent against any future aggression by Israel.

Iran was currently isolated from world financial markets and could not complete this deal without some outside help. They called in Farid Al-Sharif, reputed banker to the world's terror organizations. He would find a nation or organization willing to provide the bridge loan that would make this possible. No terrorist organization had that kind of cash. Only nations, or maybe the International Monetary Fund, possessed that sort of financial wherewithal, and the IMF was an unlikely investor in this project.

As he considered the problem, he realized that the nation that might benefit the most was China. The leaders in Beijing would never be in favor of a nuclear detonation anywhere in the world. But they might be persuaded otherwise if they could be guaranteed exclusive rights to develop the natural resources of the soon-to-be annexed Iranian province of Iraq. This meant oil, and China needed lots of it. For the right price, Al-Sharif thought that China might be induced to provide a small loan from its treasure trove of American dollars. It must be untraceable and deniable, and somehow the use of American money seemed fitting. Once the plan was presented to the ayatollah, he agreed.

It turns out that *Orlando,* the worm infecting Iran's computer network, had a twin named *Anaheim.* It was difficult to keep these things from reproducing once a government recognized their value. Like its sibling, *Anaheim* was a virus designed to burrow deeply into everyday communications software and tag along on messages of significance. It had been carefully planted inside the Pakistani defense establishment by an American contractor carrying an infected thumb drive in 2006. It had since spread to several critical systems in Pakistan, China, and ironically, back to the same U.S. contractor, who had yet to recognize it revealed his most secret messages to the CIA.

Anaheim had been a very productive source for the CIA. It was this worm that had first detected coded communications about a carefully protected compound in the center of a city in Pakistan that eventually produced the now-dead terrorist Osama bin Laden. Now, it was listening in on a flurry of messages between the government and the military. Things were not going well in

Pakistan. The military closely guarded all nukes, and although they had lost control over the new civilian government for the moment, they were not willing to let any of these weapons out of their direct control. The generals' greatest fear was that the radical Islamists in the government would use a weapon to attack India, thus provoking a final and unwinnable war with the powerful Hindu nation. The generals were Pakistanis above all else. They intended that their nation and their culture should survive.

***

In Beijing, General Secretary Xi Jintao had received the first message from his ambassador to Tehran with some suspicion. He understood that certain internal and external forces might benefit from leading him into an untenable position and then publicly embarrassing him. He had only recently ascended from the Standing Committee to the top position in the People's Republic of China. There were many rivals who might wish to see him disappear as quickly as he had appeared.

Xi was a practical man with training in economics and a long-held sense of China's destiny. He believed that China was now deserving of the American throne of world leadership. He didn't wish to do anything to complicate that ascendance. He understood that his role was multifaceted. China had many needs and his job was to meet them. He called his security chief to find out if this could be a trap. "I need to know if this is a genuine offer. If it isn't, unmask and arrest whoever is trying to destroy me."

Farid Al-Sharif received a second call. This was not an invitation, and it wasn't friendly. It was a threat. He took it seriously. Iran had sponsored assassination attempts in the United States, Saudi Arabia, and France in recent months. They were successful in three instances, resulting in the grisly deaths of twelve seemingly innocent people. He understood that their security people would not hesitate to kill family members, even young children, if the situation demanded it. Farid had three wives and seven children. In his own way, he loved them all. He couldn't bear to think they might be slaughtered if he refused the job.

He punched in the digits left for him in the message. He was told that the Chinese government had agreed with his proposal. *My proposal?*

China had agreed to loan twenty billion in American dollars to Pakistan for economic development and infrastructure upgrades. He would receive a commission of twenty-five million for his role as broker. Iran would receive unspecified benefits. Those were none of his concern. He thought he knew what it might mean. He was afraid to ask. He accepted the job, signed off the call, and wept.

-12-

Paris

A chilly late-autumn storm was buffeting most of northern France, and the gray, wet skies didn't do much for Chase's spirits. He had been in a holding pattern, the worst sort of purgatory for a covert operative of his caliber. For the past six days, he had been waiting for instructions, and none had arrived. He enjoyed seeing Samantha a couple of times; however, his recent experience in Marseille still weighed heavily on his heart. He was accustomed to success. He had almost had the boy in his arms and, still, he had escaped to do his terrible deed. This event rocked Chase's world. How had the bad guys won this one? He failed to see any positives in what had happened. Casualties, always bad even if a single human being, were low considering the nature of the attack. Nonetheless, he considered the fact that it had succeeded at all a personal failure. He wondered how useful he was now or would be in the future. Maybe this was why his bosses at Langley were suddenly shunning him.

He and Sam decided to meet for dinner at a newly opened Paris bistro in the 14th. This wasn't a typical night out for them, but Sam wanted to do something different and fun. She decided that this guy needed cheering up, and she wanted to get back to the real relationship, the one they had had before Marseille. The little bistro was named Les Pieds Noirs—The Black Feet—and it was a new eatery presenting some interesting takes on Algerian cuisine. The name of the place came from the colloquial term used by the Algerians for the French troopers, wearing black boots, who had subdued their nation.

The atmosphere was festive and loud by Parisian standards, and the food was better than good. Even so, both Chase and Sam sighed a few times, almost in unison, and looked in each other's eyes for a solution to the emotional chasm between them. The last mutual gaze, lasting a second or two, was the most complete conversation they had managed since his return from Marseille.

She glimpsed his extreme pain and some secrets he couldn't yet bear to share with her. He saw her unquestioning love for him, something he understood but didn't deserve. He realized at that instant that he must trust her with his life or not trust her at all. After coffee, he suggested they find a cab and return to the spot where it had all begun. They told the driver to take them to the old brasserie Les Deux Magots, on the Left Bank.

Chase had made the decision to open his heart to Samantha on his long trip back from Marseille. It was more difficult to do than he thought. It was against his training, his sense of duty, and his male pride. But it was the only way to resume life as he knew it. He chose life.

"I don't quite know where to begin," he began. "You once asked me who I really am. I couldn't answer you then, and I'm not sure I can give you a satisfactory answer now. My life is a little intricate. The best way for me to start is to say that I occupy two quite different worlds. I have a day job, after a fashion, and I am sort of a superhero the rest of the time."

Samantha laughed, snorted twice, and almost choked on her drink. Then she said, a bit louder than she intended, "*Say again?*"

"What I am about to tell you may never be repeated, not to anyone. I'm being serious now. Can you accept this?" Sam nodded her head and inched her hands across the table that separated them.

"This is going to sound a little crazy; sometimes I can't believe it myself. From time to time, I am asked to help save the world." Chase was still trying his own brand of humor to soften the impending impact of his double life, and he could see it wasn't working so well.

Sam stared blankly at him for at least fifteen seconds. She recognized there was an element of truth in that foolish statement. She was beginning to accept that this man she was learning to love really did have a double life, and that she existed only on one side or the other of that great divide inside him. Her heart began to beat faster, and she could feel the bitter taste of fear taking possession of her throat. She steadied herself for what might be coming next. She unconsciously pulled back from the table and folded her arms across her now chilly body.

"Robert, I think you are going to have to be a bit more explicit about that." It was in French, of course, which softened the tone but not the steely formality of the message itself.

He began telling her the unabridged version of his story at 10:45 P.M., still only late evening in Paris. When he finished it was after one A.M., and the waiter was beginning to look at his watch and wonder if these two were ever going to finish. Samantha had no words to express her astonishment. She tried to speak a few times, and she couldn't get past a gush of breath that sounded like she was, well, astonished.

After a few more moments of silence, she began to speak softly and deliberately. "So . . . if I'm hearing you right, everything you have told me about yourself has been untrue. And you told these lies because you wanted to protect me from some danger that you cannot divulge to me. Do you really think, Robert, that this little confession will make everything right again? I don't care if you're a spy or a schoolteacher. I want to understand how I will know when I can trust you?"

This last comment caught him by surprise. Chase didn't think of himself as a spy. He was a protector of sorts. He didn't hurt people; well, there had been rare exceptions, and he regretted those deeply. He considered his response carefully. Sam stared flatly at him. He had no way to read her emotions, but it was evident that she was already beginning to drift away from him.

He considered it a hopeful sign that she hadn't already gotten up and walked away.

He tried another approach. He decided to address the easy issue first. "Well, I work for certain people I can't name. Sometimes I intervene in exceptional circumstances to protect those who can't protect themselves. I'm not a spy. I try to do my part to make this imperfect world as safe as it can be."

Samantha began to push her chair back in preparation for departure, but he noticed she was not in a hurry. He was failing the test. Chase reached across for her hand, and for some reason, she allowed him to pick it up and hold it. There was warmth in this gesture, and this was obviously part of what she needed from him. This time he was speaking from his heart. "I am so sorry for hurting you. I didn't intend for this to happen, not at all. I am trapped in a world not of my own making. As feeble as you might think this attempt is, I am trying to let you into a place that has been shut tight for a long time. Please forgive me."

Samantha sat for several more minutes in silence, all the while her eyes were scanning and absorbing Chase's facial expressions. He could tell that she still wasn't pleased. He was so happy when she finally spoke.

"I'm not sure I fully understand what you are telling me. This is all very opaque. I want to believe you, but this aspect of you is all so unexpected, and incredible. When you began your story, I was secretly hoping that you were making another bad joke. I've known for some time that you were a person with secrets, probably many secrets. I can accept that for now. But I'm so hurt that you didn't tell me the truth earlier."

She let that last thought rest out in the open, as though it was flopping and writhing in agony on the tabletop between them, the spot where they both were looking. Chase wanted forgiveness and acceptance, and Sam wasn't ready to grant him either of those yet. When the amount of silence seemed right to her, she spoke again.

"We both have secrets, but I need you to promise me right now, that everything you tell me in the future will be true. It is the only way forward for us."

He looked her in the eyes and said with complete sincerity, "I do. I mean, I will." He meant it literally, as she had spoken it. To be fair, he wasn't already creating a reason to hide certain information from her. This was how his well-trained mind operated. He could change this, but it would take time. For now, whatever he chose to tell her would be completely true. But right now, and for reasons he couldn't even put into words, he had not yet decided whether he would be able to tell her all things.

***

This same day in Tehran, Ayatollah Ahrimani gave his consent to moving Iran's newly completed bomb toward the Iraqi capital. Everyone in the leadership understood that this would not be an easy task. A weapon like this could not be dropped into the trunk of a Mercedes and driven across the border. It weighed nearly half a ton and required a small army of technicians to prepare it for use. This project was such an important part of Iran's self-image that no less than a significant and capable military convoy could be trusted to protect it. The mullahs insisted on this. To an outside observer, especially to any of the terrorist groups that would have done anything to own this bomb, this approach would have seemed absurd. However, to the rulers of the new Persian Empire this was a national treasure that must be protected at all costs. It would have surprised the average American that the ruling mullahs were so conservative and excessively cautious. In real life, the ruling clergy were about as radical and adventurous as a block of ice.

The ever-trustworthy Revolutionary Guard was assigned the job of moving and protecting the weapon. The professional army could not be trusted with such a task. Someone in the ranks would inevitably ask why they were doing this, and what their orders were. The Guard had a different mission, and they could be depended upon to do exactly what the ayatollah demanded.

A convoy of trucks, including a full brigade of fifteen hundred of the best trained and most reliable soldiers would be selected to transport and guard the crate to the Iraqi border. Predictably, the ayatollah also insisted that a company of elite Guard soldiers, all in Iraqi uniforms, would accompany his precious cargo once it entered Iraq. The concept of stealth movement didn't rise to the top of his list of priorities. It would be hard to miss this parade as it moved westward.

The CIA satellite that had been repositioned over Iran immediately picked up movements of vehicles and troops in and around the Revolutionary Guard base near central Tehran. The analysts looking at the images had no idea what was going on, although to them, it looked like preparations for a large convoy. It certainly did not look like Iran was going to war.

More than five hundred miles away, at the U.S. Air Force Joint Special Operations Center in Kuwait, two reconnaissance birds were being readied for possible deployment. These were Reaper drones, the big sisters of the better-known Predator. These aircraft had been fitted with special pods that each would carry the new generation folding-wing MAVs, the mini-aircraft that could more easily evade Iranian air defense radars. They were capable of both reconnaissance and attack missions. The largest of these mini-warriors was the top-secret Raptor with its folding ten-foot wingspan, stealth technology, and an operating range of about one hundred miles. Raptor carried video and infrared sensors and an armaments package of six Spike missiles, the smallest guided missile in the world. Each Spike weighed only five pounds and yet was capable of locking onto a moving target and striking it up to a mile away. The Spike was designed to penetrate the interior of a vehicle and then detonate with devastating force. Each of the large Reapers carried two Raptor drones, plus other conventional ordnance. The final two pylons on each wing were reserved for advanced versions of the Maverick air-to-surface missile with an extended twenty-mile range. Once launched, the Mavericks would receive their initial targeting via a link with the little Raptor, eliminating the need to place the more expensive drone in harm's way. The heavy munitions would be loaded right before takeoff. For now, the aircraft were on one-hour standby.

***

In Washington, Reynolds Merrill was in the hot seat once again. The congressional oversight panel had been grilling him for two hours on classified operations, with a special emphasis on the CIA's intelligence-gathering efforts on possible chemical and biological warfare threats. This was to be expected after the attack in Marseille. As he waited for the next question, his mind wandered to the situation in Iran. *What are they up to now?* He made a mental note to call a meeting with Katie and his team of analysts to kick some ideas around.

"Director Merrill?" He jumped a little as the grating voice of the junior senator from Kentucky broke his trance. "Could I have your answer to my question? We have a busy agenda today."

Reynolds shook himself back to the present. He was annoyed by this process, and his response showed it. "Senator, I'm not sure I understand how you could have missed that key point in my briefing. I believe I've answered this same question already several times today. I can say it in a different way, but the answer will still be the same. What else can I tell you?" This day was not off to a good start, and he would certainly have to pay later for his abrupt response to the senator. He winced a bit at the thought of his likely penance. Last time he did something similar the senator filibustered the Agency's budget for a month.

-13-

For most of the day, Katie Thompson had been trying to piece together a meaningful pattern from the flood of communications from Iran that *Orlando* was capturing and forwarding to analysts at Langley. It was now clear that there was a limited mobilization of a single brigade from the Revolutionary Guard main base in Tehran, with no easy explanation for the movement. She understood that Guard units didn't typically take themselves out for a walk, just for fun. The mullahs liked to keep them close at hand for their own protection. The last time these troops had been called out in any numbers was during the civil unrest around the parliamentary elections about a year ago. Right now, there was no news coming out of Iran to indicate anything like that was happening. Katie was certain that the increased traffic indicated something of importance, but she didn't know what it might be.

A few hours later, Merrill reconvened the meeting with part of his team, including an analyst from satellite ops, Lydia from the Bungalow, and Katie all present in a room at Langley.

"People," began Reynolds, "our job is to make some sense of all this chatter. Peter, tell us what you and your team have been picking up on the ground."

Peter was a senior satellite image analyst, and he had been spending every minute poring over the new pictures from Tehran and everything to the west.

"There's no pattern that I can discern, and the only observable activity is in Tehran. "However," he paused, "we have seen a slight, and perhaps meaningful change in the type of vehicle traffic at the underground site near Qom."

The nuclear facility at Fordo, near the holy city of Qom, had been discovered in 2009 by CIA analysts, and it had been subsequently exposed by the western powers in the press and at the United Nations. From all appearances, this site was well disguised and heavily protected. It clearly had been built for only one purpose: to make something that Iran did not want the rest of the world to see. To these analysts it meant a bomb.

Peter continued, "We've observed thousands of big rigs arriving during the past two years, carrying materials and supplies for the complex. Last night, a military convoy consisting of six heavy trucks arrived unescorted. The vehicles entered the hardened part of the site and are still belowground. The mullahs have kept the military away from the internal workings of Qom until now—limited to guard duty. This is a change in pattern and those usually mean other related events will follow."

Before Merrill could lean in with a question, Katie added, "It will mean much more if any of the trucks leave with an escort. Have any ground units joined this little parade?" Merrill thought that this was a thought-provoking question. He decided to sit back and listen to the response.

***

Farid Al-Sharif was about to return to Paris from Saudi Arabia. With great personal misgivings, he had agreed to handle the money side of the transaction from one of the semiprivate banks in Beijing to a holding company in Pakistan. The money, if one could call electrons dancing across a silicon chip money, would all move with a few touches on a keyboard. Farid would negotiate the terms between the two parties, but his real role was to make the entire transaction look legitimate. The Chinese government made it clear that this loan could never, ever be revealed for what it really was. Its economy depended almost completely on the goodwill of, and extensive trade with, the

United States and the European Union. If word of what they were about to do ever leaked out, the resulting sanctions would certainly push China into a deep recession. This prospect frightened the members of the powerful Standing Committee of the politburo as nothing else could. Recession would bring more unemployment, and unemployment would lead to social unrest, the only real threat to their power.

Back at the shop, Katie Thompson continued to sift through the growing piles of communications provided by *Orlando*. There was too much incoming information to process, and what she had read was unclear. The worm was turning up lots of raw data; however, without a key it was mostly worthless. In desperation, she called her CIA counterpart who ran the analysis on the output from *Anaheim*.

Ron Tolar was an impressive man in both breadth of knowledge and intelligence. He was as fluent in Mandarin as the general secretary himself, although he readily admitted that the Chinese leader probably knew a few more ancient curses than he did. Ron loved his job. He would spend hours reading and rereading communications to be certain that he had picked up every nuance of the language used. His section was also responsible for Pakistani intercepts from *Anaheim*. His command of Urdu and Pashtun was not as great, and he always appreciated it when officials switched back to English, the old colonial language. This made things much easier, even with the British nuances as interpreted by the Pakistanis, and a couple of hundred years of idiomatic evolution. When Katie called, Tolar was piecing together a puzzle of his own, one he did not completely understand.

"Ron, I have a freaking mess over here, and Pakistan keeps coming up in conversations. I don't know what to make of it."

Ron replied, "Well, hello to you too, Katie. This must be the day for freaking messes because I have one all over my desk as well." Then he paused to see if Katie would give up her information for free. They both worked for the same agency, but information was the most valuable currency, and the first to find something new usually got the pat on the back.

"OK, I'll go first," he finally said to break the intentional silence on the other end of the line. He enjoyed their little game of chicken, and he usually won if he wasn't too eager to hear what she had found. Today he was unusually concerned about what he didn't know, and so he gave in to his own intense curiosity.

He began to speak rapidly, which to Katie meant that he was already on a pure-sugar diet. "The Chinese leadership, and I am talking top-shelf, is involved with what looks to be a really big transaction with Pakistan. It's a loan, no big deal, but they are using an outside broker, which is unusual, almost unprecedented. They never trust anyone except one of their own to handle the cash. As Lydia would say, 'This is a disturbance in the force.' I don't know what to make of it."

Katie waited to be sure he was done. It did not do to interrupt Tolar when he was on a roll. "How big of a loan is it?"

"I don't know yet. The People's Bank of China has put feelers into the Hong Kong market for the immediate liquidation of up to thirty billion dollars in U.S. treasuries. What makes this even more curious is that Hong Kong and Shanghai Bank, which is more European than Asian in character these days, has been engaged as an intermediary. This is too complicated even for the Chinese. I have a bad feeling about this."

Katie was racing to keep up with the banking talk. "Do you know who's on the other end of the transaction?"

"Sure," Ron quickly responded. "However, I don't know who he is. He's an Arab banker they are calling Al-Sharif."

Katie almost coughed up her last latte when she heard the name Al-Sharif. "I have a match on Al-Sharif from *Orlando,* and his last-known involvement was with Iran."

"Well, I guess the guy swings both ways," quipped Ron. It took only a few seconds for Tolar to start filling in the blanks. Katie could almost hear his mind working as he sorted data and followed the patterns. He was the sort of person who was rumored to do a crossword puzzle without ever picking up a pencil.

"What the hell does Iran have that China would want to buy other than oil? No, wait—reboot—what does Pakistan have that China might be willing to finance? Conversely, what does Iran want, that Pakistan has, and China might be agreeable to financing?" These questions came rapid-fire without any pause. Tolar had seen a vision, and Katie needed to hear him out. Abruptly, he terminated the call. "Katie, let me get back with you. I need to follow a thread, and right now."

As Katie hung up the phone, she already had a sense of what Tolar was starting to see. Pakistan had a weak, newly elected civilian government that had been starved for foreign currency ever since the U.S. Congress had cut off all aid after the last U.S. election. Pakistan had only one asset of any value to sell that might be worth $30 billion. If the military had been more in control, she might have guessed that China wanted to keep India on edge and the loan was for purchasing conventional arms. With the military temporarily out of the picture, there was only one thing that could possibly be worth so much. She dialed Reynolds Merrill even before she finished her own thought. She needed to be the first to tell him.

Merrill answered the secure phone and let Katie launch immediately into her analysis. "Sir, some of the pieces are starting to fit. I spoke with Tolar, and we have a match on a name. Do you remember the banker who was an occasional contact of the Guard colonel involved in the Marseille attack? His name is Al-Sharif, a Saudi with no known political affiliations. He's helping to broker a big three-way between Tehran, Islamabad, and Beijing." She paused for effect. "I think Iran is trying to buy a nuke."

Reynolds sat back in his chair and weighed all that he had heard. Iran already had at least one bomb of its own, and it was reasonable to assume that they were probably making more. *Why would they need another one right now?* A hundred possibilities shot through his head. *Are they going to war? Are they so insecure that they think they need even more firepower to keep the Israelis at bay?* This didn't make complete sense.

"Katie, thank you for the briefing; I need to leave you for the moment. I'll call you back as soon as I have a break in my schedule."

His next movement was to pick up the direct line to the director. "Bill, can I come up for a moment? This is urgent."

As Merrill took the elevator one flight up to his boss's office, he thought about what he was about to say and whether he could back it up. Normally, intelligence gathering and analysis were tedious efforts, and the outcomes were double- and triple-checked before any action was approved. He didn't believe there was time to follow that protocol right now. The gnomes would stay up all night verifying what he suspected, but this was a time for action.

He entered the director's office and was waved to a seat while Hughes finished a call. As he turned back to his visitor, he said, "Reynolds, I can see that I need to believe what you are about to say. I can always tell when you have the serious face on." Merrill smiled briefly and proceeded to outline the potential threat and the relatively slim support he had.

"Reynolds, if what you suspect is true, or even a good possibility, I need to see the president right now. How confident are you?"

This was not the time to rush what he had to say, so he took several extra seconds to frame his response. "Bill, right now I'm sixty percent. In a day or two that estimate might go up considerably. This situation is starting to deteriorate."

The director regarded Reynolds carefully as he considered his own reply. "That's good enough for me. Thank you. I need to make a call."

As Merrill left the office, he felt the crushing weight of the analysis he had delivered. In just minutes, the director of the CIA would be telling the president that Pakistan was about to deliver a live nuclear weapon to Iran for an unknown, and assumed to be hostile, purpose. He couldn't prove that the intent was belligerent quite yet, but the nature of the threat meant that there was little time to waste. *I have a lot of work to do and little time,* he thought as he raced down the stairs two at a time.

-14-

The intelligence community was struggling to build a verified and actionable scenario. What information it currently possessed could only be shared within the American services for the moment. Answers were needed and quickly. There was no time for consultation. The allies would have to wait until the president decided to let them inside the veil. An invisible wall silently went up between nations that usually cooperated closely with one another. The CIA analysts were moving through the mounds of communications extracts that *Orlando* and *Anaheim* were providing, but a clear picture of the threat had not yet been constructed. The president reportedly indicated that, if this suspicion proved to be true, it was a "go to war" issue. No one wanted to be the one to help pull that trigger, at least not yet.

Merrill returned to his office to reassemble his team. There must be something they were missing. He could feel it. While he waited for his analysts to join him, he made a call to a certain man with no official title who worked for him. It was time to identify the weak link and bring him in for questioning.

***

Robert Chase was beginning to enjoy his brief forced vacation. He'd been told to sit tight in Paris, and he was doing precisely that. In the meantime, there was no harm in enjoying a few pleasurable meals and spending time with Sam. She was warming to him again, and that made him feel better. The weather had turned seasonally cool, and Paris had no trouble keeping pace with the change in seasons. The leaves had already taken their final fling in the breezes and then let go for a fluttering dance to the streets. An unadorned beauty was revealed along every avenue. One could see everything that had been hidden since springtime. Chase was about to call Sam with a proposal to meet for dinner when his Agency phone woke him from his vacation. The text simply read:

> The banker returns today, SAA 6109, 17:45 CDG. Stay
> close, we need to talk to him.

So, the Saudi financier is coming back from Riyadh, and he is back in play.

***

Later that day, Farid Al-Sharif walked down the ramp from his Saudi Arabian Airlines flight. He bypassed EU Passport Control and French Immigration by showing diplomatic credentials and ducking out through a private exit reserved for the embassy crowd. His black Mercedes S550 and his driver were waiting curbside, outside baggage claim at Terminal 2C. Al-Sharif was delayed on the concourse by the milling around of a large tour group from China that stood between him and his freedom. He was so close to the group that he could smell everything about them: their slightly unwashed bodies; the food they had recently eaten; and the air they were breathing. He pulled out a silk handkerchief and pressed it close to his nose.

There must have been three hundred of them. Farid was not a patient man, nor could he tolerate most ethnic groups, even those from his homeland. He came from a proud past and thought most other humans were inferior to him. He had married into the house of Saud, the family—really a tribe—that supplied the thousands of civil servants and officials who ruled and administered the Saudi kingdom. His official duties were in the Ministry of Finance, and he carried diplomatic papers that identified him as a trade attaché to the Paris embassy. On the side, over the past twenty years, he had learned to convert his connections and his ability to move commercial deals forward into a personal fortune exceeding $10 billion. Even in the kingdom that was serious cash.

Chase knew that Al-Sharif would not be coming through customs with the gaggle of tourists recently off the big planes. He noticed the shiny black Mercedes idling at the curb and recognized it as Farid's ride. To be certain, he checked recent photos stored in his phone and quickly found the one he wanted: a clear shot of the license plate he had taken before leaving for Marseille. He walked close to the car, bent down unnoticed, and attached a small GPS transmitter about the size of a pack of chewing gum to the underside of the car near the rear bumper. *No sense losing him in traffic.*

Chase then strolled into the terminal holding a small handwritten sign reading MR. CHATSWORTH and stood off to the side of the main exit, close to an unmarked door. He was there mostly to read Al-Sharif's face and body language up close. He hoped no one named Chatsworth was looking for a ride this evening. Soon, the door opened, and Al-Sharif moved briskly across the concourse. He did not look happy and not in total control. This was a noticeable change from Chase's observations when he had trailed him a few weeks earlier. *This man has something troubling on his mind,* he thought. *He's not even aware of his surroundings. His face is grim, and the skin around his eyes looks strained.* It was not vintage Al-Sharif.

As the Saudi's car pulled into traffic, Chase got into the taxi line and waited his turn. There was no hurry. Al-Sharif would probably go first to the luxurious Hotel Georges V, the only place in Paris he lodged, to check-in and refresh himself. It was his pattern, and it was predictable. To make sure, Chase pulled out a tablet computer and activated an app. This wasn't the sort of thing one could buy on Amazon or in the Apple Store. It was a highly classified global positioning application with access to the invisible network of spy and defense satellites that orbited over every square inch of the earth that mattered to the United

States. It would show him where the car was with an accuracy of two meters, give or take a few centimeters. It was so precise that a micromissile guided by it could probably take out the passenger in the backseat of a limousine without the driver being aware of what had happened. He had never used it for this, not yet anyway.

Robert Chase understood how a man like Al-Sharif would act in normal circumstances. He had certain places he must be seen and in a certain fashion. Whatever transaction he was negotiating right now would lead him to a very small universe of locations. He was not an intelligence operative; he was a banker. He was not trying to hide; he was trying to be visible. He enjoyed the best restaurants when he was in Paris, and of course, the company of a select group of beautiful women.

One of the most striking inconsistencies of wealthy Saudi men was how easily they philandered and partied when away from home. A married Saudi woman could be punished severely for even inviting a male nonfamily member into her home. But her husband could fly to London or Paris or New York and bang anyone he wished, all without the threat of penalty. *What an interesting value system for an overtly religious society,* thought Chase. He knew that Al-Sharif had at least two female consorts living in Paris, because he had followed him the last time he was in the city. He didn't really care how the man lived his life, but these women were important to Chase because, eventually, he would contact one of them. He considered his options. *When he visits one of his girls, he normally goes alone. It will be the perfect time to extract him from his normal life and find out what he knows.*

-15-

Islamic Republic of Iran

The officials who had been tasked with moving the bomb into Iraq were smart and cautious people. They believed that they were the equal of any in the West. In the underground facility at Fordo, six heavy vehicles belonging to the Guard sat waiting for their loads. It was clear to the major-general who commanded this operation that the Americans must certainly be constantly monitoring most of Iran with their many spy satellites. *The Americans have no idea what is in progress,* he reasoned. He knew they did, however, understand that anything moving out of this highly secure underground factory had special significance. If he was to be successful in moving the weapon unnoticed to its staging point near the Iraqi border, he must make them follow one or more decoys. He hoped that they would take the bait.

He decided to send four separate convoys: one returning to Tehran; two toward different airbases in the south and southeast; and one final convoy to the west. The convoy back to Tehran would be escorted by a company of Guard soldiers in wheeled armored vehicles. They would do everything they could to be visible to the satellites, which mostly meant traveling by daylight. The two going to the south and east would have similar protection and would move at the maximum speed toward their destinations. The convoy with the weapon aboard would not depart until twenty-four hours after the first three, and it would contain only three trucks with no visible protection for the first part of the trip. This is the one he hoped would draw little or no attention from the Americans. Fifty miles after leaving Fordo, two full battalions of Revolutionary Guard mechanized infantry would rendezvous with the vehicles to escort them to the staging area. It was a solid plan. He expected success. His life depended on it.

***

At the White House, Secretary of Defense Branson was briefed by the president on the developing situation in a private meeting. Branson was a man of action, and he was backed by the generals of the Joint Chiefs of Staff. The military command had desperately wanted to remain in Iraq at the end of 2011 to continue pursuing the war against the insurgents. It was a great training ground for all the services, the ideal way to maintain their fitness while they waited for the next real war to come along. They had been overruled that time by the civilian government and by the wishes of the people. This decision did not sit well with the military leadership or with those in the defense industry. Branson now saw a unique set of circumstances that he could use to reengage the U.S. military in the region.

"Mr. President, we have been waiting for an opportunity like this to break Iran's balls and show them why we lead the world. We have several options already drawn up, any one of which could deal effectively with this threat. Our friends in Israel would love to help us. Give me the word and this thing is solved."

"Ken," the president began, "I don't want this to escalate into another war. We have precious few facts right now. We need to know what's being delivered and why. Sending in the air force won't get us any closer to that information."

"Mr. President, with all due respect, we can completely neutralize Iran's ability to deliver *any* weapon, *anywhere*. After that's been done, we can ask questions. It won't matter at that point what they had planned to do. We will have blasted them back to the Stone Age where they belong."

The president shifted uneasily in his chair, reached for a glass of water, and stared at his defense secretary with dark impassive eyes. "All I will authorize right now is movement of a carrier group into the northern Arabian Sea. Would that be the *Lincoln*?"

"Yes sir, the *Abraham Lincoln* and its strike group are in the area and can be on station within twenty-four hours."

"Good, let's do that, and nothing more. No shooting. Understood?" A quick nod from Branson was all he needed. He wasn't pleased, but he would do what he was told.

***

At the CIA's satellite intelligence center, analysts detected a movement of troops, only a battalion of about five hundred soldiers in strength, out of Tehran toward Qom, a distance of one hundred miles. Director Merrill was informed, and the watch continued. About three hours later the analysts confirmed that the soldiers had entered the gates of the complex at Fordo and were remaining aboveground, their vehicles arrayed as though they would be leaving again shortly. They didn't erect tents and were parked in three lines on the desert floor. It looked like something would happen soon.

About two hours after arriving, the three convoys began to move out, one at a time and in daylight. Each was joined by an additional truck from the facility itself, so the total number of trucks that had been observed entering the facility was matched by the number leaving. The first convoy appeared to be taking the long overland route to the air base at Zahedan, only fifteen miles from the Pakistani border. It had already been identified as a likely pickup point if Pakistan was involved. In addition to the two operational air squadrons stationed there, Zahedan was home to three batteries of medium-range Sahab-3 ballistic missiles. These missiles had the range to easily hit Tel Aviv and pretty much all the other capital cities in the region. The next convoy moved south-southwest in the direction of the Persian

Gulf and the air and naval base at Bushehr. From Bushehr, a weapon could be delivered to any number of Persian Gulf states by aircraft. These aircraft also had the range to threaten the U.S. fleet. This group of vehicles would be watched very carefully. The final group headed back toward Tehran.

***

DDI Merrill was briefed on the three convoys and possible destinations. This was obviously a shell game but one with a deadly serious outcome. *They don't know what we know,* he thought. *They are only being cautious. We don't need to respond immediately to these moves. If we wait them out, they may tip their hand.*

It was clear that they were planning to transport something important. If whatever it was had its birth at Fordo, it could only be a nuke. *How does this fit with the information we have about a big transaction with China? One convoy could be going to pick up the Pakistani warhead. Now, why all the others?* He needed more brainpower in the room. He called for a session at the Bungalow where he could escape the oppressive group-think atmosphere of CIA headquarters. The meet was set for 6:30 P.M., and as was the custom, everyone would arrive looking like they were coming to dinner.

The odd little group arrived a bit early, and each was carrying either a wine bottle or a small grocery bag. The team convened tonight included Katie Thompson; big Ron Tolar; Peter Jameson, an analyst with the satellite center; and Lydia. Each brought a unique perspective based on their sources of information, and Reynolds liked it this way. As usual, Merrill began with a briefing.

"Okay people, we have a dynamic situation. We have reliable information coming out of Islamabad, Beijing, and Tehran that suggests a nuclear weapons purchase, for what reason we don't know. It's a fact that Revolutionary Guard convoys, three in number, have departed the nuclear facility near Qom and are heading in different directions. Two are moving toward airfields within striking range of most of the Middle East; the third appears to be returning to Tehran. It's obvious that they think we are watching. The president is concerned and has ordered naval assets in the Arabian Sea to tighten up on Iran. Let me hear from you. What does this all mean?"

Katie looked around the room to see who wanted to speak first and then opened her mouth a second before Lydia. "Let's accept for this discussion that Iran has gone shopping for another nuclear weapon. We have been assuming for some time the success of its program. What if we have been wrong? They could have failed to produce a usable weapon for any number of reasons. What we are now seeing now might be plan B."

Lydia could not help herself. "It might not be as simple as that. These people don't think like we do. They could have an operational weapon . . . or even a few for that matter. We have no idea. The leadership tends toward caution and paranoia. This purchase could be nothing more than an expression of their need to feel completely safe. There are no indications in anything we've seen recently to suggest they are planning an action. They would never launch an attack of any kind without first putting their military on alert. Nowhere have we seen any evidence of this sort of mobilization and our precious little worms confirm this is the case. We're supposed to support our conclusions with fact. Show me something stronger or find another reason."

Katie squirmed with a prickle of annoyance at this direct attack; however, she decided not to fire back immediately at Lydia.

At this point, Tolar cleared his throat and saved the day. It was a sign he was ready to speak. The room quieted immediately.

"Iran is cut off from the international banking scene, right? Their oil production industry is falling apart from lack of parts and expertise. Revenues are down and aren't likely to improve anytime soon. They don't even have the ability to feed their own people. This might be nothing more than the mullahs trying to ease some of the domestic pressure with funds they can't get anywhere else. China is very cozy with Iran and has been for some time. My current assessment is that there is something valuable in this transaction for our friends in Beijing. Maybe we're not looking in the right direction."

Katie flashed a little smirk of friendly superiority at Tolar, and after the briefest of pauses, jumped all over his statement.

"If it was only food aid, why wouldn't China do it directly, for the entire world to see? They don't hide these sorts of programs. They like to look good. All indications are that this China-Iran connection is to be kept below the radar. They don't want the rest of the world to know what they are doing. The obvious question is: why not? I have my suspicions, and I think everyone in this room shares them." She glanced quickly at Lydia to confirm that she at least had her support. Seeing the nod of her head, Katie continued.

"On top of everything, there's something creepy about this Saudi banker. He shows up a few days before the attack in Marseille, and then he disappears as soon as everything hits the fan. Now his name comes alive in Pakistani and Chinese intercepts. There is no way that this guy is only a hardworking official of the Saudi government." She faced Merrill and asked, "Sir, is there any way for us to have an old-fashioned conversation with the banker when he returns to France?"

Merrill let the briefest smile escape before he replied. "I don't think the French would welcome our involvement. They don't always agree with our methods. Off the record, we have other ways to get what we want. Let me handle that part. Before you adjourn, we still need to find a plausible reason for the movements we've been observing at Fordo. Back to work, geniuses. I need more answers."

As he was driving back to his home in the Virginia countryside several hours later, Merrill was combing through the latest information his team had added to the discussion. There were too many pieces missing for any solid conclusions to be reached.

His present dilemma was that whatever Iran was doing might not wait until he had a perfectly clear picture. He was paid to make educated guesses about the intentions of hostile nations. Failure was not an option. He must bring the Saudi banker in from the cold. It might be premature, and it might piss off the French, but he could not think of another way to peek behind the curtain. He needed more timely information than he was receiving through normal channels. As soon as he arrived home he picked up the secure line and called the man with no job title. The banker needed a vacation, and there was a man in France who could handle the arrangements.

-16-

Central Paris

Chase received his updated mission instructions as he was strolling past the Hotel George V in Paris. Farid Al-Sharif had just emerged from the hotel entrance right in front of him and the banker was walking casually toward his car. He looked and smelled like he was going on a date, which meant that he would probably be stopping first in the exclusive shopping district around the Rue du Faubourg Saint-Honoré to pick up a gift. It was only ten easy blocks away, but Chase knew that men like Al-Sharif rarely walked anywhere.

As Chase passed the banker's car, he picked up something in his peripheral vision that immediately disturbed him. He turned his head slowly to his right to confirm what he had just sensed. He couldn't be sure. He had the strong feeling that someone was tracking him. Samantha had often teased him about his ability to detect an abnormality in the flow of people and things around him. It had been amusing at the time but not now. He saw a man across the street who had been strolling slowly along the sidewalk a few minutes ago, and who now was lingering a bit too long across from Chase and the departing Al-Sharif.

This hadn't happened to him before. After all, he was an invisible man and no one outside of the Agency knew who he was. His years of experience immediately took control of his actions. He stopped in his tracks, fumbled in his pockets looking for something he had obviously left in his room, and headed back toward the entrance to the hotel. He walked inside as though he lived here and turned toward the elaborate hotel bar.

He positioned himself where he could observe the lobby and waited. Nothing happened.

After about five minutes, Chase found a rear exit through the car park and moved in the shadows toward the front entrance. Again, there was nothing out of the ordinary. The mysterious man had disappeared. He took a moment to think about this before he emerged onto the main avenue. *If he's not following me, then Al-Sharif must be the target. This is going to complicate things. If he has a tail or even a personal security detail keeping a discrete distance, I am at risk. Trap or a coincidence?* He still had not read the previous text message from his controller.

Patient has appointment now.
Call for transport: 08 56 33 21 00.

This was unusual. He normally used Pierre or one of his own contacts when he was about to take custody of a suspect. His first thought was that he had been compromised, or worse, that Control had been hacked. He tapped out a code word to confirm the source of the message—liberty. The phone buzzed and the correct response—or death, glowed on his screen. He felt his entire body relax.

Chase walked toward the front of the hotel, looked around for anything or anyone unusual, and then grabbed the first taxi in line. He asked the driver, "A moment, please," as he flipped on his tablet and touched the tracking app icon.

"Please take me slowly toward Hermès in Faubourg Saint-Honoré. I am waiting for a call to tell me where to rendezvous with a young lady. You understand, right?"

It was delivered in near-perfect French, and the driver looked in the rearview mirror and winked at him. "I understand, monsieur."

The wait seemed unusually long. He smiled at what the driver was thinking—*this must be some woman.* A few minutes later the target vehicle started to move again. Chase waited another two minutes, watching the little screen all the time, and then he directed the driver to loop around and head toward the 16th arrondissement, an exclusive and beautiful quarter of the city, not far from the Eiffel Tower. The banker had used a hotel in this section of the city before. Chase knew this because he had followed him there.

Al-Sharif's car cruised around La Place Victor-Hugo and stopped in front of an expensive hotel a block away. The car hesitated there for less than fifteen seconds and then continued without the passenger. Chase witnessed the drop and had his driver stop three blocks past the hotel, in front of an elegant residence. He waited for the taxi to leave and then carefully made his way back toward the hotel, looking for any watchers or minders who may have followed the banker. A second later he saw one. A man had retreated partly into the shadow of a doorway to a residence. He was still too visible to be a professional. Chase turned and retraced his steps until he found a wineshop he had noticed near where he had been dropped off. He greeted the proprietor and purchased an expensive bottle of champagne. He walked back toward the hotel with this new treasure. As always, he paid cash, and he touched nothing in the store except for the bottle.

As he retraced his steps back to the hotel, he pulled a soft hat from his pocket like what a chauffeur might wear and put it on. He slowly approached the watcher, and then he noticed that he had a partner. He was parked barely a half a block from the hotel, motor off. It was evident, now that he was closer, that both men were Chinese and nicely dressed in a workaday sort of way. They were making only minimal efforts to not be seen. They looked like embassy staffers or midlevel managers in a bank. Chase still didn't know why they had Al-Sharif under surveillance. *Stay right where you are, guys, and everything will work out fine, for you and for me.* He crossed the avenue in a hurry, like someone on an urgent errand, and entered the hotel lobby.

"Bonsoir, monsieur," he greeted the desk clerk. "My boss arrived a few moments ago, and he sent me to fetch this." He held the attractive bottle in front of the man's approving eyes. "He told me he would have my job if I did not present him with this within ten minutes. As usual, he failed to tell me his room number."

The clerk's face tightened a bit. "Ah, monsieur, I can arrange to have it delivered to your employer right away. You needn't worry about it any longer."

Chase expected this response; the man was only doing his job. He also knew how to successfully push through this temporary barrier. His tone became more authoritative. "Monsieur Al-Sharif would not expect me to ask such a favor of you. He made it clear that I must deliver this personally. He is very careful about strangers, as you know."

The night clerk immediately recognized the name, and the assessment of the haughty Arab matched his own. Chase didn't give him even a second to think. He held out a crisp hundred-euro bill and continued to press his advantage.

"It would be a great favor to me. I will tell Mr. Al-Sharif how helpful you have been." The clerk's eyes were fixed on the banknote, but his sense of duty was not yet convinced.

Chase slowly began to retract the cash when the clerk stopped him by gently seizing it from his fingers. "Be sure to check out with me when you leave and be quick!" Chase flashed back the submissive smile of one used to taking orders, nodded, and took the slip of paper with the room number scribbled across it that was offered.

He took the elevator to the top floor, keying the pickup number into his phone as he went. A voice came on immediately and repeated the phone number, nothing else. Chase replied, "I am ready now." He gave the address of the hotel and the room number.

Before he got off the elevator, he quickly sent a text to Control.

The medical transport arrived barely twelve minutes later. The apparent leader of the two-person team told the desk clerk that Mr. Al-Sharif had suffered a seizure, nothing serious. He needed to be taken back to his hotel immediately where his personal physician was waiting to attend to him. He told the clerk that he already had been given the room number. He expected nothing less than his complete discretion. He did not offer a gratuity to the clerk, only a stern look that said, "stay out of our way." They pushed a wheelchair to the elevator and were gone.

Minutes earlier, Chase had appeared, uninvited, at the door to Al-Sharif's suite with the gift of champagne, now supposedly compliments of the hotel. Al-Sharif was momentarily angry at the intrusion, but Chase could hear his lovely companion trying to convince him that the bubbly always made her come harder. As soon as the door opened, Chase immobilized the surprised Al-Sharif with a quick spray of an ultrashort-acting anesthesia agent into his gaping mouth. He relaxed and fell into a soft heap with the assistance of Chase while the woman looked on in disbelief. He quickly put a finger to his lips, and the woman covered her mouth with both hands, lest she scream.

Chase did not attempt to approach her. He took a small auto-injector, similar to an EpiPen, out of a jacket pocket and popped it against Al-Sharif's upper thigh. The banker would sleep for at least an hour. While he and the woman waited in silence, he stood quietly, like he was riding an elevator with a stranger. The transport team knocked twice, and he opened the door for them. Al-Sharif was loaded into the chair, securely strapped in place, and the two attendants quickly wheeled him back toward the lobby. Before Chase left the suite, he spoke for the first time. "Wait twenty minutes and then leave. Farid will not be harmed. You can call him in a few days. Try this champagne while you're waiting. It's excellent." Then he left, wiping the bottle he had brought and the doorknob, inside and out with a discarded pair of lacy underwear. The entire operation had taken only fifteen minutes.

Chase rode the service elevator down to the ground floor and left by the delivery entrance. His phone buzzed as he walked across the parking area.

Can you deliver the Chinese too?
Call 08 44 21 33 01 for transport.

He wasn't happy with the unexpected request. He had just snatched a man in the hotel sixty meters away. The eyewitness to the affair would be coming out of the door in about twenty minutes and now someone wanted him to abduct two more men right out in the open air. This was unorthodox and dangerous. He texted back.

Difficult.

The immediate response was: try! Chase called the new number and gave detailed instructions including his location.

He was more nervous than usual as he waited. He was exposed, and he felt like everyone who drove by could read his mind. Finally, a taxi approached, dimmed its lights, and stopped next to the parked vehicle he had described to the pickup crew. The driver in the car glanced toward the taxi as Chase moved forward and immobilized his companion on the sidewalk with two quick pops to the man's solar plexus and back of the neck. The cabdriver rolled down his window as if to ask directions. The Chinese driver did the same and was hit with a small sedative dart in his neck, followed by a second. Both men were placed in the back of the taxi with a minder between them, largely to keep them upright when the car took a turn.

As the vehicle sped off Chase decided to call it a night. His part was done. He walked past the empty car in the direction of Place Victor-Hugo. He would continue walking five or six blocks more, enough to distance him from what had recently taken place, and then look for a taxi to take him back to his hotel.

-17-

Central Paris

Merrill learned of the successful snatch of the banker within the hour, and the unexpected acquisition of the two Chinese nationals. Control had field authority to improvise when needed, but this time he had managed to kidnap two members of the Chinese delegation in Paris. They were questioned briefly and then put to sleep again until a decision could be made on how to get them back to their embassy. They knew nothing at all. Their instructions had been to follow Al-Sharif and keep a record of where he went and take photos of everyone he met. This explanation was plausible to Merrill. The Chinese were cautious and meticulous in their planning. It stood to reason that they would want to make sure the proposed transaction, whatever it was, would not be a trap. He gave instructions to juice them up with a drug cocktail that would cause temporary confusion and memory loss and then to put them back in their car. Whatever they would recall in the morning wouldn't make much sense. If they cared to file a complaint, they would blame the French police. No English whatsoever had been spoken during their questioning.

***

The real center of attention was the banker Al-Sharif. He was placed in a windowless cellar in a noisy industrial part of the city, adjacent to a busy roadway. He was now fully awake, mostly alert, and still blindfolded. He was securely strapped to a strong chair that felt to him like it was anchored to the floor. He tried to tip it over but could not make it move even a centimeter. French music was playing in the background and he could smell the smoke from his captors' rough cigarettes. No one had spoken to him since he arrived. He had already assumed the worst. *I am in the hands of the thugs who threatened me. But why? I agreed to do what they asked. What more can they want from me?* He tried several times to engage in conversation with whoever was out there. He was ignored. It was the first stage in a rapid interrogation technique that had been developed in Afghanistan.

After four hours of silence, a voice asked him in Arabic if he would like some water. He replied, "Yes," and said he needed to urinate as well. He received only the water—poured quite rapidly down his throat. One more hour passed in silence, broken only by Al-Sharif's occasional cries for them to tell him what they wanted from him. He was becoming increasingly anxious and alarmed. The only other sound was the low music from the radio somewhere on the other side of the room. Abruptly, noisy footsteps approached him and the bands about his arms were released. He was stood up by two pairs of strong hands and dragged roughly across the room. His feet barely reached the floor. Without warning, his bladder lost control and he stood in his own wetness, humiliated. Right now, he was certain that his death was only minutes away.

His captors walked him farther across the room and led him into a small windowless cell. His hands were untied, and he was told to clean himself. Fresh clothes were laid on the bed, and he was given permission to take off his blindfold and change. Hope flooded back into his almost hopeless mind. He was left in the cell for four more hours, alone with his thoughts, as fear began to regain control. Then he was summoned before the inquisition, this time without blinders.

He was reseated in the original chair and this time he was not bound. He was free to use his arms and hands. They were important to conversation and his inquisitors wanted to observe all his responses, even the ones he might be unaware he was making. A bank of bright lights was aimed in his direction. He thought he could see at least three shadows beyond the lights. He could not tell if they were male or female, Arab or Western. The leader began speaking to him in fluent Arabic. By his accent, he made him out to be from the Emirates or perhaps Kuwait. He could not tell where precisely, but he was not Iranian or American.

"Farid Al-Sharif, this discussion can be as long or as short as you choose to make it. We know beyond all doubt of your involvement in a conspiracy that includes China, Pakistan, and the Iranian dogs. You can decide to help us, or you can decide to be destroyed with the rest of the miscreants as this unfortunate plan unravels. Everything is now your choice. You may live, or you may die. And I should advise you, time is not your friend." Then he waited patiently for Al-Sharif to speak.

He sat in silence for a few minutes. It felt like an hour to him. He could feel and hear his heart pounding like a bass drum. He was perspiring even in the icy room. He now understood what his captors wanted from him. He did not know exactly how much they knew, but it was evident that they knew enough. He had no loyalty to the principals in this transaction. *It was business. To hell with them all!* He feared most for his family and what might happen to them if he failed. He began to speak in a more halting fashion than normal. He was fishing for sympathy.

"My family has been threatened. I am a simple banker. I move money, create deals, nothing more. I am with the Saudi embassy. I demand to be able to contact my office."

More silence—just the boozy voice of a singer in the background to keep him company. It must have been a full fifteen minutes before one of the interrogators spoke again. "Farid, do you wish us to help you with these problems? We can, you know. In return, you must cleanse your conscience before Allah and before us. I think you understand what I mean."

Four hours later Farid finished his confession. His words provided a treasure trove of missing links that related to the money trails in at least four significant terrorist attacks. He described what he knew of the current Iranian plot, and he told them that he knew nothing of any troop and vehicle movements in central Iran. He had no knowledge of what would be bought with the twenty billion dollars being loaned by the Chinese. *This man is a gold mine,* thought the team leader, a former U.S. Air Force major and native Arabic speaker. There was one more bridge to be crossed, and he approached it cautiously.

"Al-Sharif, we appreciate your candor and in return, we will help you protect your family. However, your family will be the safest if you can continue to play your part in what is about to happen. You must not give the Iranians any reason to suspect you. We will protect you and your family. You must feed us the instructions you will be given. Can you agree to this solemn bargain?"

Al-Sharif was choking with emotion. He was so tired that he would have said anything at this point. "Yes, I agree. I give you my word on my children's lives. I will do it." He meant it at the time.

His first ordeal was over. It was now late afternoon the day after his abduction and Farid had been released by his captors. He felt free, but he wasn't. He would be watched until the deal went down and he was out of the country. He was dropped off wearing his borrowed clothes near the Hotel George V, the soiled trousers in a plastic bag in one hand, and his jacket folded over it. He went immediately to his room, sat in a chair, and wept uncontrollably. He was so emotionally exhausted. He had never realized before this how much he loved his family, and now he had made a deal to save them.

The interrogation process Farid went through was designed to induce a posttraumatic stress reaction that would reinforce the connection to his captors and to his promises to cooperate. The technique had been exceedingly successful on prisoners from the recent Middle East conflicts, so long as they could be immediately isolated from any other prisoner. Indeed, his captors had provided him with a way out and a way to prevent his family from becoming targets as well. It was not an empty promise. If Al-Sharif failed to fulfill his part of the bargain, the deal could be quickly canceled. For the moment, however, he would do what was expected of him. At least, that's how he felt.

-18-

At the Fordo nuclear research facility near Qom, the final convoy was preparing to emerge from the darkness and begin its journey westward. The group consisted of three heavy trucks. One was loaded with the six-hundred-kilogram weapon, more than half a ton, the first of its kind in Iranian history. A second truck contained the technicians who would arm the device and troubleshoot any problems that might arise. The third contained twelve extremely capable commandos from the Revolutionary Guard. These few men would be the only defenders of this national treasure until they joined with the two battalions of reinforcements near Arak. The three trucks pulled out of the underground facility after dark and made a leisurely turn onto the highway going west. The American satellites should be occupied elsewhere.

Three hours earlier, two battalions of Revolutionary Guard mechanized infantry had departed under cover of darkness from their base in central Tehran. The CIA satellite positioned over Iran captured this sortie and documented their route in a series of images that were immediately downloaded to the center at Langley. It was logged that a small mechanized column was moving southwest. The force was not large enough to cause concern, and certainly wasn't enough of a threat for the analysts to disturb the deputy director.

In Tehran, Ayatollah Ahrimani was growing restless. The transaction with the Pakistanis had not been concluded within the time frame he had expected, and he was becoming suspicious. *What if they simply kept the money and did not deliver the weapon? What recourse would I have? I can't go to war with them.* The Chinese would certainly side with the Pakistanis, and his single weapon would already be gone. Iran would be defenseless against the Israelis, and he would be tossed out by his own followers. Maybe this is exactly what they wanted to happen. He was prepared to call a halt to the project. The risk now seemed far too great. His aide knocked and came in.

"Sir, the banker contacted the Pakistanis. The price is acceptable, and the merchandise can be delivered to Zahedan within five days. They are waiting only for the money."

Ahrimani relaxed for a moment. He realized he should have been more trusting. This was Allah's work he was about, and Allah would ensure its success.

***

In the 16th arrondissement of Paris, the two Chinese diplomats were awakened by a loud tapping on their car window. It was already daylight, and a gendarme was indicating they should roll it down. The driver fumbled with the keys and finally got the power window to work. Immediately, he pushed his diplomatic passport toward the officer. His head hurt, and everything was so fuzzy. He felt sick to his stomach. The policeman was speaking to him in French and, for some reason, he could not fashion a response. It was as if all his language training was bottled up inside his brain and this important organ had turned to jelly. After a few minutes of one-sided conversation, the gendarme handed back the passport and waved his arm with considerable irritation to indicate they should leave. The driver wanted to comply although he wasn't sure he could manage even that simple maneuver in his present condition. He did it anyway, and the car lurched away from the curb and into traffic. When they got to the roundabout at the Place Victor-Hugo, the driver couldn't remember which way to go. He merged into traffic and made three circuits before exiting and immediately parking on the nearest street. The two men looked at each other one last time through bleary eyes, laid their heads back, and fell asleep. It would be hours before they would manage to return to the Chinese embassy and, even then, they could recall little of what had happened.

Farid Al-Sharif slept for a couple of hours after his release and was now ready to complete his duties with respect to the cash transfer. He called the HSBC office in Paris and made an appointment with the director of the bank for the following morning. He also called his contact at the National Bank of Pakistan, an old friend, and arranged to meet in the early afternoon of the same day. His part in this would be easy. He would add an air of legitimacy to the transaction. The Hong Kong Shanghai Banking Corporation was well known all over the world, with branches in all the major European cities. The bank was unaware of the nature of this transaction and was, quite frankly, extremely pleased to have been chosen by the People's Republic to handle one end of this loan. The managing director immediately assumed that all his efforts to woo the Chinese ambassador had finally paid off. He couldn't have been more wrong. The decision had been made in Beijing, and HSBC was selected only to help launder the funds.

Al-Sharif was still unsettled after his encounter last night. A little seller's remorse had crept in since he'd awakened. It wasn't quite enough to make him want to go back on the deal he had agreed to, but he was considering it. He decided to stay in the hotel this evening and not chance another misadventure. He didn't want to face the same woman he was with last night—too many questions would have to be answered—but he did want a woman. He picked up his phone and dialed Evangeline, another of his favorite companions in Paris. She didn't talk so much and her ways in bed, even in his still foggy memory, were enough to begin to arouse him. He agreed to meet her at eight o'clock in the hotel bar with dinner to follow. He rang the concierge on the house phone. "Please reserve a private table for two in Le Cinq, nine o'clock, thank you."

***

The satellite reconnaissance center at Langley was state of the art—the best that American tax dollars could buy. Images from a flock of satellites, both from the defense department and CIA, streamed in constantly, and were immediately transferred to the screens of the duty analysts who covered a geography. Peter Jameson was the senior analyst for Iran and he was pulling a double shift to be on top of whatever new data came in.

The latest set of images from the sector that included Qom and the towns to the west had popped onto his screen. He worked on one image that showed the two-battalion convoy moving southwest toward Arak and he then panned eastward to see what else was new. He stopped abruptly. A small group of trucks was moving to the west that he hadn't noticed an hour earlier. This interested him in no small way. He selected three different time sequences from the images of this area and then walked the convoy back to its origin. *My God, we missed this.* His throat went completely dry. He went back over the image sequence three more times. Then he called Merrill.

"Sir, we missed something small, but significant. The latest images of the area west of Qom show three heavy military trucks heading toward Arak. The two lonely battalions of Guard troops we've been tracking since they left Tehran central are moving in the same direction. I tracked the trucks back in time to Fordo. They departed twenty-four hours after the three main convoys left."

Merrill understood the significance of the information immediately. This was the diversion he'd feared might happen. Then he said, "Do you have any infrared views of what is in the trucks?"

"Sir, truck one is probably personnel, not many. Truck two shows driver and sidekick, the back is hot. It could be nuclear material that isn't well-shielded. The third vehicle looks like more personnel, and densely packed. My guess is a security detail."

The director paused again and then said, "Nice work, Peter. Stay on them and keep me informed."

***

Across the world, the new Pakistani president was meeting with the chief of the armed forces, and it was not going at all well.

"General Ali Khan, you will recall that in free elections the Pakistani people decided that civilian leaders, not the military, will rule our country." His already high-pitched voice cracked as he tried to be convincing and authoritative. "Your concerns have been noted, but I must now insist that you do as I have asked."

General Muhammad Ali Khan had been, not so very long ago, an up-and-coming one-star general in the army when many officers senior to him were summarily purged and exiled. The new civilian government had rapidly consolidated power, and now believed that the military had been pacified. The powerful military establishment and a parade of civilian governments in Pakistan had experienced a tenuous relationship during the past three decades. It was an accepted rule: whenever the army thought that the security of Pakistan was at risk, whether from external or internal threats, it had never hesitated to take power. Now it was different, or so the generals wished the citizens of Pakistan to believe.

The president had just presented General Ali Khan with a demand for the transfer of control of all nuclear weapons in their arsenal, along with the entire nuclear research and development command, to civilian hands. The president wanted this done immediately. General Ali Khan could not see this happening now, or ever.

"Mr. President," he began, "the security of our nation, today and in the future, rests on two strong pillars you must respect: that

Pakistan possesses such weapons of deterrence, and that we are able to protect them. Your government does not have the means to adequately secure these weapons against the many groups who might wish to steal them. This is the main problem with your proposal."

The meeting ended without resolution. The president was angry and felt powerless. *If the military would not give up the weapons, I cannot force it to comply.* He was president over everything except the army. The army ruled itself. He had a small personal militia that was loyal to him. Perhaps he could have his people steal one from the many hiding places the military used. But he knew immediately that this was not a realistic plan.

For his part, General Ali Khan left the meeting with great concerns. Something had changed, and he needed to understand why this weakling of a president had made such an unusual and urgent demand. He decided to pursue two independent lines of inquiry: the first would be to loyalists within the government; the second would be to his old military friend, General Tom Branch, the former commanding general of NATO forces in Afghanistan.

-19-

Paris

Farid Al-Sharif shifted nervously in his chair as he waited for the managing director of the HSBC. He was escorted into the ornate office by an attractive and businesslike young woman, where the managing director would formally welcome him. Business cards were exchanged, along with a few pleasantries and compliments. Finally, the managing director got down to business. "Monsieur Al-Sharif, we have drawn up the loan documents as requested. Officially, this loan will be between our bank and the National Bank of Pakistan. We understand that your role is to serve as the broker in this transaction."

Al-Sharif watched the middle-aged Frenchman as he continued to read a multitude of terms and conditions, emphasize disclaimers, and become completely absorbed in the minutiae of the loan. *He doesn't have any idea what he's participating in. Then again, neither do I.*

As the man droned on, Farid replayed the entire mental tape of how he had become involved and what important signals he may have missed along the way. His Iranian contacts had not explicitly told him of their plans for Baghdad, and then again, they probably didn't think that this was necessary. After all, he was known in certain circles for the company he kept. He was not sure what role he was playing on the larger stage. His instincts for self-preservation were stirring, and he began to tell himself that simply knowing about a planned terrorist incident didn't make him a criminal. *I am a banker, and I am doing only what bankers do. I'm not trained to make value judgments. I don't even have enough information to know where to begin. Perhaps my quick decision to cooperate the other night wasn't such a clever idea.*

Later the same day, Al-Sharif walked into the National Bank of Pakistan to a completely different reception than the one he had experienced earlier. He was immediately ushered into a room where not only the bank's general director stood, but also the Pakistani ambassador to France and another man he didn't recognize.

"Mr. Al-Sharif, thank you so much for coming. Permit me to introduce our ambassador, whom I believe you have met previously, His Excellency Salim Ali Khan." The two men shook hands and bowed slightly to each other. "Also, may I introduce Hussein Nasiri, a special envoy from the president of Pakistan." After introductions, the preliminaries began with tea and polite conversation, and questions about each family member and their well-being. These all took about an hour.

Finally, the ambassador nodded to Mr. Nasiri, giving him permission to begin discussing their mutual business. He spoke for about thirty minutes outlining in general terms a great technology transfer between China and Pakistan that would be funded by the Chinese loan. Al-Sharif smiled in agreement as the subject matter that a western businessman would say in five minutes, was expressed in carefully phrased statements and examples. This was all familiar to Al-Sharif, and he listened patiently. After all, he would receive $25 million for doing little else. No additional information was provided, but the conversation did confirm his growing suspicion that this transaction was being driven by Iran.

Al-Sharif left the bank after the formal documents were signed. His car delivered him back to the Hotel George V. It was a short distance and as soon as the car pulled away he received a call. A soft voice speaking Arabic instructed him to call a number as soon as he was back in his room. Al-Sharif had almost forgotten the terror of the other night and how he had begged for his life and those of his family members. He had almost talked himself into believing everything would be all right. He had performed his role as requested. He was still troubled by one thought: maybe he knew too much to be allowed to simply walk away.

Once he was safely in his room, he called the phone number he had been given, and proceeded to provide the voice on the other end with a complete debriefing of his day. He failed to share his concerns about the substance of the transaction, and he remained vague when questioned about Iran's plans. When he was pressed for more, he lied. He told the voice that Iran was planning a series of terrorist attacks to provide a pretense for armed intervention and occupation. He pulled that one out of thin air and was quite proud of his own cleverness. The call ended with an offer Al-Sharif was to consider with great care: he and his family could disappear into a relocation program where they would be protected until the regime in Tehran changed. It might be a couple of years, or it might be a lifetime. He needed to think about this. Everything was becoming very complicated.

-20-

Washington, D.C.

The mood in the capital had turned decidedly hawkish. Secretary of Defense Branson had been holding private meetings for the past three days with sympathetic members of Congress, expressing to them the viability and necessity of facing off with Iran. Rumors abounded, including the leading bit of misinformation that Iran was planning an imminent attack on Israel. When asked, Secretary Branson simply said, "We should be vigilant, a conflict like this is inevitable."

The president was having difficulty managing even those in his own party, some of whom were now advocating a preemptive attack on Iran. It hadn't been a year since the bulk of the troops had come home from the long campaigns in Iraq and Afghanistan. At times he felt like he was the only person in Washington who understood that the nation couldn't afford another punishing conflict like those. He didn't buy into the premise that war could solve geopolitical problems such as those in the Middle East. However, he was running short on time. He needed confirmation of Iran's intentions and he needed it quickly. He couldn't risk having Iran launch a nuclear weapon on any country, least of all on Israel. He called his chief of staff and arranged for a meeting the next morning with his intelligence advisors including the director of the CIA.

Merrill had called his work group on Iran together within an hour of his recent phone conversation with the director. This meeting would be at Langley and the expanded group included Katie Thompson, Tolar, Lydia from the Bungalow, Peter the senior analyst for Iran, and a political specialist who studied the leadership in Tehran. This might be their last chance to provide a meaningful analysis of the developing situation before Branson and his hawks wrested it out of their hands.

Once again, Merrill began with a point of view. "People, the director is meeting with the president tomorrow morning. The political situation is more unstable, and we need hard facts. The director and the president need our best analysis of the situation, and it must be right." *No pressure in that statement,* thought Katie. Merrill continued, "Our principal focus today needs to be on what Iran is doing, and with a special emphasis on why."

Peter Jameson was the first to offer new information. "We have satellite confirmation that the Guard convoy from Tehran has linked up with the three trucks we have been tracking from Fordo. They have configured the convoy into a protective posture, and the entire group is continuing to move west. The truck that I think is carrying the baby is in the middle, and forward elements are clearing the road for several miles ahead of the convoy. They're not letting anyone near whatever they are moving. This has to be the nuke."

Lydia spoke next. "I've been trying to reach another conclusion than the one that is so obvious. But I can't. Now the bigger question is: why would Iran move a nuclear device in the direction of Iraq? Are they planning to sell it to a terror group or are they intending to use it? It's really incomprehensible that they might sell something as important as this to anyone."

Tolar was unusually quiet. He felt that he had made a misstep at the last meeting, and he never liked repeating mistakes. He was still evaluating the new data the group was providing. Murphy, the specialist on Iran cleared his throat.

"The leadership in Tehran is conservative and very risk-averse, despite their rhetoric toward Israel. If they have a bomb, and they plan to use it, it will be for strategic advantage. They understand that they can't destroy Israel with one weapon, and I don't think it's likely that they will try. It would be suicidal.

Furthermore, they would never use it without having one or more backup weapons to ensure their survival."

For a moment, the group broke into three separate conversations, as some agreed with the summary and some did not. Reynolds brought the meeting back together with a sharp expletive.

"Work as a team! We have only a few hours before the president will be forced to let the dogs loose. Once again I'm asking you: what does Iran plan to do with this weapon?" Merrill sat back in his chair. The volume of his voice had increased to a near shout, and his own growing sense of panic troubled him.

For two hours more, the group ranged far and wide in their analysis. They agreed that there was enough evidence to believe the proposed China-Pakistan deal was a ruse to finance the transfer of a weapon to Iran. That could be managed as a separate diplomatic issue, and hopefully blocked before it happened. The immediate problem was a loose nuclear warhead that appeared to be moving toward Iraq. The consensus seemed to be that it was going to a terrorist group, but that idea fell apart almost as quickly as it was delivered.

Finally, Tolar took the floor. Now he was sure of his assessment. "Don't you see? The damn fools are going to destroy Baghdad. We've been assuming that target number one would always be Israel. We've been wrong this time, exceedingly wrong. Israel has been their enemy for only a few decades. Iraq has been a rival since forever. If they can destroy the seat of the Iraqi government, they can walk in anytime they choose and take the parts of the country they want. Whatever remains will become a tribal buffer zone. Our forces in the region are minimal and declining. We wouldn't be able to stop them alone, and our allies have neither the resources nor the will to help us. Imagine Iraq as a province in the new Persian Empire, and close-ally Syria protecting their southern flank."

The specialist on Iran piled on quickly, "I can see the mullahs accepting this proposition. It's the natural direction for expansion and most of Iraq is Shia, just like Iran. From this new position, they could strongly influence Turkey, Syria, and Lebanon to do whatever they want. They would control the countries that surround Israel and would become the dominant power in the region. This makes a lot of sense. It fits in so many ways."

Merrill could now see how bad this might become. He also understood how some elements in his own government, and in the press, might use it to push for immediate military action against Iran. His mind began to race. *By then, it will be too late. If central Baghdad is destroyed by a small nuclear blast, the entire region . . . no, the entire world will be thrown into an offensive posture. Once the first dog is out of the kennel, it will be too easy to let the rest out. Frayed nerves and pressure cause unintended consequences. Israel can be both predictable and unpredictable. They might launch the weapons they have on Iran and add in another country or two for good measure. Much of the region would be destroyed, the land contaminated for generations. The flow of oil to the West would cease.* He shuddered at how utterly cold his last thought seemed, even in the privacy of his own mind.

He shook himself out of this doomsday spiral. "Is there anything else we need to consider? This will all be going to the president in a few hours. Is anyone less than ninety percent on this conclusion?"

Tolar was the one to address this question. He was the expert on what was happening in China and, to a lesser degree, in Pakistan. Everyone in the room was listening as he began his assessment. "Both the Chinese and the Pakistanis can be warned off. They will live to fight another day. Well, maybe the Pakistani leadership won't, because there are others in Pakistan who will not want to see this transaction happen. Our relationship with the people who matter the most will remain intact. Our immediate problem is Iran. They are going to do this, unless we stop them. They won't realize that no one has their back until it's too late."

DDI Merrill looked at this exceptional group of thinkers and patriots. "Very well done, people!" Even Lydia smiled at this compliment. A "very well done" was like receiving the Medal of Honor for intelligence geeks.

-21-

Washington, D.C.

At nine A.M. the next day, director of the CIA William Hughes was ushered into the Oval Office. The chief of staff and the national security advisor were also present. Noticeably absent was the secretary of defense. The president stood up and walked over to greet the DCIA. Hughes had enormous respect for this man. He came into the job largely unprepared for the demands of being the leader of the free world. He had stumbled a bit out of the gate, and now, at the beginning of his second term, he was exhibiting remarkable courage, tenacity, and wisdom.

"Bill, I have a hell of a problem right now on how to deal with Iran. The Congress is looking for blood. I need your help. Tell me both what you know and don't know."

Hughes looked at his briefing notes, then back at the president. "Mr. President, if you will pardon my language, we have one hell of a fucking mess on our hands."

The president sat back, amused in a sense, because he had never heard the reverent gentleman from Massachusetts swear before. *Okay, this must be serious. You have my full attention, Director.*

Hughes got right to the point. "We can confirm that the new government in Islamabad has struck a deal to sell a nuclear warhead to Iran. It is a simple matter of money, not ideology. When Congress ended foreign and military aid to the civilian government last year, it set in motion a lot of unintended consequences. So, what's new—right? A further complication is that China seems to be a willing partner and is providing the financing."

Hughes continued to describe the alleged conspiracy with Iran that promised to deliver the bulk of Iraqi oil production to Chinese control, and perhaps some other advantages as well. He went on to confirm his earlier report that the Iranians appeared to be on the verge of an attack on Iraq that would alter the balance of power in the region. Once he finished, the president sat back and stretched his arms high in the air, then let them fall to his lap.

After a moment of silence, he asked, "Bill, do you have any recommendations to go along with this analysis?"

Hughes hesitated for a moment, mostly not to appear to be too rash. "Mr. President, it seems to me that we need both a diplomatic and a military option. I am confident that you and the secretary of state can get the Chinese to stand down. The new Pakistani government is shaky to begin with. It will be a difficult call whether to confront them, possibly bringing the military back into power, or to use a back door. With respect to Iran, we have adequate air assets already on alert to stop the convoy in its tracks. You realize that this will be viewed as an act of war. If we are going to go that far, maybe we should make a more definitive statement."

The president thought carefully about the last comments. The United States had enough military power in the region to prevent the bomb from moving to Iraq. A strike would not only end this crisis but would also silence his critics in Congress. It was a tempting option, but not for the right reasons.

"Bill, one more obvious question: do the Iranians really believe they can drive this bomb into Baghdad and blow up the government?"

"Yes, sir, that appears to be their plan. They don't have any air bases or ballistic missile capability between the convoy and the border. Whatever they plan to do with their nuke will involve driving it across the border or handing it off to someone else who will."

"Bill, thank you. This has helped a lot. You may arm your birds. Take no action without direct orders from me. I have a lot of bases to cover first."

A meeting of the National Security Council was called for the early afternoon. The Joint Chiefs of the military branches were included in the guest list. It was going to be a long day. Included in the meeting would be the newly appointed chief of staff of the army, General Thomas Branch, a former commander of NATO Forces, Afghanistan.

-22-

The final convoy from Fordo, currently expanded in size fifty-fold after meeting its escort at Arak, was nearing the point of no return. It was presently about ten kilometers from the little desert crossroads of Nasrabad and still inside Iran. When it reached the town, the commander had been instructed to halt and wait for final orders before crossing the Iraqi border near Khanaqin, northeast of Baghdad. From that point forward, the troops guarding the weapon would be slimmed down to look like a company-size unit of the Iraqi Army. The remainder of the two battalions currently guarding the convoy would remain in place as an emergency force to recover the weapon at the first sign of trouble. The Guard soldiers had no idea what they were protecting. They were told only that a small group would be permitted to enter Iraq and gain some measure of retribution for the insults faced by their Shia brethren there. That was enough of a reason to keep them all focused and alert.

It was now two days before the promised delivery date set by the Pakistanis. Ayatollah Ahrimani would not allow the convoy to proceed beyond its current position until that promise had been kept. He called in the president of the Islamic Republic and the chief of the armed forces. He told them that Iran was about to strike a blow against the murderer of Iran's young men. The armed forces were to go to a wartime alert status effective immediately. The army and the Revolutionary Guard should prepare themselves to occupy parts of Iraq. The general and the president simply looked at each other and shrugged their shoulders in unison. This was the first time they had been told anything about this operation.

Ahrimani was still highly suspicious of the Pakistanis and their real intentions. His ambassador to Islamabad had reported that the capital was restless. The military command, unaccustomed to being on the sidelines, was making itself more visible and the foreign press was beginning to hear rumors that another coup was possible. Ahrimani detested the secular Pakistani generals and their generally dismissive attitude toward his own military forces. *The generals have the power to stop this transfer at the last minute, especially that pompous bastard Khan. It is not wise to allow him to continue living.* He made a call to his chief of security and gave him urgent instructions. The offensive westernized general would need to be removed as a potential risk, and immediately.

The Iranian convoy reached their hold point near dusk, two days before the weapon was scheduled to be moved into Iraq. The two battalions immediately set up a security perimeter in a dry, rugged area framed by dry mountains. Mess tents were pitched, and latrines dug, but the soldiers were told to remain ready to move out on thirty minutes' notice. This meant sleeping on the ground or in their vehicles. The task force was protected by two Russian-made SA-22 mobile antiaircraft batteries with an effective range of twenty kilometers—about twelve miles. The radars and launch vehicles were set up and tested, with their backs against a slope of low, steep hills and their noses pointed south. If an attack came, the commander felt certain that it would be from Kuwait and not from Iraq. The Americans still had drone and other air assets there, and they had been using them to constantly probe Iran's defenses.

-23-

Islamabad, Pakistan

Quietly, General Ali Khan began to lay out his plot. He wasn't completely sure whom he could trust. His first order of business was to send out feelers to General Branch, whom he had met when he trained at the U.S. Army War College after the first Gulf War. They had both been lieutenant colonels at the time. Branch had commanded a tank battalion in the first Iraq war; Ali Khan had been assigned as an aide to the Pakistani general staff about the same time. They later became reacquainted when General Branch assumed command of all NATO forces in Afghanistan, about a year before the new government in Pakistan came to power. Branch was courageous, smart, and had a good listening ear. Ali Khan believed that they could have a frank conversation about Pakistan's future.

Within two hours of indicating his desire to speak with the new army chief of staff, General Branch called him back. Despite the increased political tension between the two governments, the two military commands tried to stay close. They had many objectives in common, and clear communications had previously prevented several friendly-fire incidents in their mutual war on terror.

"General Khan, I am so pleased to hear from you. Please tell me how your family is doing." General Branch was a quick study in the courtesies and the essential demonstrations of respect that made intercultural exchanges possible. Even if he had not been aware of these cultural necessities, he still would have done so because of his great personal and professional respect for the man.

General Khan began telling his story cautiously. He wanted to test Branch before he would be willing to lay out the entire situation in his country. People change; so do priorities. He needed to be certain that this was the same man he had known in the heat of battle. Ali Khan first outlined the rising tensions between the civilian government and the military. He knew that Branch already had a good understanding of the situation, but he wanted to be sure that the American general's perspective was sufficiently broad.

General Khan continued speaking for about twenty minutes while Branch listened patiently. Then Ali Khan changed the tone of the conversation by asking a question. "General, are there things that your government might ask of you—hypothetically speaking, of course—that you might not be able or willing to do?"

Branch thought he understood what the general was trying to say. He responded with a question of his own. "General Khan, you have raised an interesting and critical issue. I am curious: how would an officer under your command respond to a similar request?"

"Well . . . as in your military, we expect an officer to do his duty: first to obey orders, and a close second is to always be mindful of the best interests of Pakistan."

General Branch agreed. They spent another half-hour discussing—in general and hypothetical terms—what duty meant and how an officer might find loyalty to the government and loyalty to the nation at odds with each other. This social foreplay was necessary. Many Westerners could never get used to what they viewed as a waste of valuable time. General Branch wasn't one of those.

Branch had another appointment that was equally as important as this call, but he persevered. He could sense that there was something essential to be learned before the call was over. Finally, Ali Khan felt comfortable enough to share his secrets. He was concerned about two things: how the United States would respond if the civilian government was to be replaced, and his fear that one of their essential weapons was about to be transferred to another owner. The two spent another fifteen minutes discussing in general terms what each scenario might mean.

Branch needed to end the call to meet with the president and the National Security Council. He said, "General Khan, you have honored me by discussing these matters with such frankness. I know that you realize I must pass some of this information to others in my government. I cannot commit the United States to a position on either of these issues. However, I will do my best to represent your position faithfully and honestly. For your part, I know that you will take the right path for the sake of your country." When the two rang off, each understood the course the other would probably take.

General Branch immediately called the chairman of the Joint Chiefs and gave him a brief account of his conversation with his Pakistani counterpart. It was important to have the chairman well-informed and to give him time to consider options.

***

At the Iranian embassy in Islamabad, the station chief in charge of intelligence had received instructions from the head of the Ministry of Intelligence & National Security in Tehran. The sort of murder he was ordered to carry out was easy to arrange, especially in a violent society like the one that existed in modern-day Pakistan. He had a team of two Iranian thugs attached to the embassy, Ali and Saeed. They had killed before and would make quick work of this upstart general. He called them to his office and gave them the mission, including photos of General Ali Khan and his family members, and where his office and home were located. He instructed them to do it immediately. The two looked at him and grinned.

He gave orders for them to be issued Israeli-made Uzi-Pro submachine guns. These were modern, lightweight versions of the venerable weapon used by security forces around the globe. On full-automatic fire, one could empty a fifty-round magazine in less than two seconds. The guns had a limited useful range because of their short barrels, but Ali and Saeed planned to be almost in the general's lap before shooting him. They would follow his car to his home and execute him as he was walking to his front door. If they were lucky, his security detail would still be sitting in their car when it happened. If not, they would kill them as well. It didn't really matter. In the local traffic they would easily get away.

-24-

Washington, D.C.

The National Security Council met in the situation room at the White House at two P.M., Washington time. Present were the statutory members: the president and vice-president; the secretaries of state and defense; and advisors which included the chairman of the Joint Chiefs, the director of national intelligence, the director of the CIA, and General Branch as a special invitee. The president called the meeting to order and outlined the agenda.

"Ladies and gentlemen, our intelligence assets have been monitoring a developing situation involving Iran, Iraq, Pakistan, and China. It's not looking good. I have asked Director Hughes to provide the briefing. Please proceed, Bill."

The intelligence director leaned over the table a bit to be able to see everyone's face, and then he described in detail what they knew about the Iranian plot, and the apparent Pakistani and Chinese complicity. He concluded by saying, "So, you see this is complicated, and very delicate."

Hughes watched with interest as the secretary of state, Alice Bishop, just edged out Secretary of Defense Branson by a nose for next to speak. "If we can stop the weapon from getting to its destination, I think we can manage the other relationships without too much trouble. If we tell the Chinese what we know, they will back down with little hesitation and many denials. It sounds to me like they were being opportunistic rather than changing their fundamental position. We will need to provide a means for General Secretary Jintao to save face. The Pakistani situation is more problematic. That government will certainly fall, and the military will be back in power. I'm not sure that we will find this outcome acceptable."

Secretary Branson could barely wait for the secretary of state to finish. "Mr. President, just to provide some context: we have a *fucking nuclear weapon* on its way to Iraq! We have fifteen thousand American citizens attached to our embassy in Baghdad who will all die if this happens. There's a clear conspiracy between Pakistan and China to provide more nuclear firepower to Iran. This demands a strong military response. If ever there was a reason to make a clear statement, it is now!" As he finished this last statement, Hughes noticed that Branson's wild eyes practically challenged the president to come to any other conclusion.

The president held up his hand and invited the chairman of the Joint Chiefs to speak as to options. The chairman first wished to give General Branch a moment in the spotlight. Branch nodded and immediately began his briefing.

"Mr. President, based on a conversation I had an hour ago with General Ali Khan in Pakistan, I do not believe we can prevent a coup, no matter what we do. The civilian government has made a bad deal, and the military will make them pay for it. The army will not give up its weapons under any circumstances. The generals can see only one path in this crisis. It's the path they have followed countless times before. They know it well, and they are comfortable with it."

Secretary Bishop moved into an attack mode, something that, in Hughes's experience she could carry off better than anyone in the room. "Sir, we have worked for a decade to help pry Pakistan out of the hands of the military, and into those of an independent, freely elected civilian government. We must not let all of that hard work be destroyed."

"What sort of a half-assed, defeatist comment is that?" Branson sneered. "An act of war is about to be perpetrated on an ally of the United States, and on our own citizens in Iraq, and you suggest we continue to prop up the government that is making it possible? Am I hearing this right? What *bullshit!*"

"Most of us call it diplomacy," screamed Bishop in return, her neck veins bulging and spit flying out of her angry mouth.

The discussion went back and forth for two more hours. State and Defense were in their foxholes. The president was growing impatient. He asked the chairman of the Joint Chiefs for his assessment of the situation and for available military options.

"Mr. President, we have sufficient naval air assets on alert, in-theater, to be able to stop the convoy, and destroy it if you give the order. I am a little worried about what might happen if we hit that bomb with regular ordnance. It might detonate, or it might come apart and contaminate the whole area. We have less-destructive options available. In addition, I don't know what your position is on simply going in and taking the device away from them. If we decide to do that we will need to act soon."

The general paused to let the assembly catch up with him. "We are seeing signs of mobilization from all branches of the military, and we don't know what to make of that. We can do a lot of things, but time is not on our side. It seems to me that an ugly chain of events will occur once China and Pakistan drop out. The Iranians can be vengeful." On this last point, everyone, including Hughes, agreed.

The president stood and paced to the end of the table. Then he turned and spoke with an authority he hadn't shown while he was in listening mode. "As much as I would like to take away Iran's bomb, it would mean troops on the ground, maybe a lot of them. If we go in that direction, we will have losses that will have to be explained. We may start another Middle East war. I am not going to risk that."

"With respect to China, Secretary Bishop, I would like you to craft the strongest possible message to Secretary Jintao and deliver it to him immediately. Tell him what we know and say that Pakistani sources have provided all the details. They are telling us it was China that initiated this transaction. It's a half-lie, but it will give him something else to worry about. Plus, I don't want to compromise our flow of information coming out of China."

He walked around the table as he delivered his final order. "I would also like you to communicate to the Pakistani president that the Chinese have had a change of heart. Tell him we have uncovered his plans, and that I demand that he ceases immediately. If a nuclear weapon crosses his border anywhere, we will consider it an aggressive action against United States interests, and we will not rule out military options against his country."

The secretary of state started to object, then appeared to think better of it. She said, "Yes, sir."

"The situation in Iran is tricky," he continued. "The leadership deserves worse than we can give them right now. I don't intend to punish the Iranian people for the mistakes of a few wackos. I would like that convoy disabled, not destroyed. This job I am assigning to the CIA. They don't have the means to start a full-scale war, at least not that I know of. I want our carrier assets ready to strike if we can't get the job done with the drones. Furthermore, I think it is wise to move another carrier group into the region, in case we have misjudged Iranian intentions. Secretary Branson, you have my permission to work up an extraction plan for that warhead. We are not going to war, but we'd better be ready just in case."

The chairman of the Joint Chiefs spent another twenty minutes outlining what other assets should be readied in case things got out of hand. The president agreed, as did Secretary Branson. That was it. Hughes sat back in his chair and thought, *the nation is going to the brink once again in the Middle East.*

As the council members filed out of the room, the president asked General Branch to remain for a moment longer. He whispered something in his ear, and then said aloud for public consumption, "General, it is not in the best interests of the United States to have the military renege on its promise to permit and support a civilian government in Pakistan. Please convey my exact message to General Khan."

-25-

General Ali Khan spent the rest of his day in private conversations with current and recently exiled military leaders. The military had no faith in the civilian government, even less so after Ali Khan had recounted the demand for a handoff of the nuclear arsenal. He now sensed a clear unity of purpose. They would never allow their weapons to be exported to another country and certainly not to Iran. It was agreed that the military would assume control of the government the following night. They would make every attempt to make it bloodless, but there was some concern about the president's private militia and what it might do to prevent his overthrow.

General Ali Khan left his office late that night, nearly ten P.M. local time. His car was followed by his normal security detail of four men; however, as a precaution he had ordered a second detail to his house earlier in the day to keep watch over his family. He wasn't sure what the president might do in this situation, and he didn't want to take any chances. As the two cars left his office, a red motorbike with a driver and a passenger took up the pursuit. Traffic was always light this time of the night, and the trip was quick. If the two assassins had not wanted to enjoy watching their target die up close and personal, they could have successfully made the hit right there on the roadway. It would have been relatively easy to drive past the two vehicles and unleash a swarm of 9mm rounds into both. Instead, they waited and followed a couple of hundred yards behind the second car.

Ali and Saeed had not done an earlier drive-by of the general's home to see how it was laid out, or where the general might be disembarking from his car. They'd discussed it but ran out of time in the day. They had been street thugs in Tehran, with no formal security training of any kind, so their preoperation prep was mostly about getting comfortable with their weapons. Like so many homes in Islamabad, Ali Khan's house featured an enclosed outdoor courtyard protected by a strong gate. The two government cars turned left, off the main road, and went directly into the courtyard without slowing. Ali made a snap decision and motored through the still open gate. He shouted over his shoulder to Saeed that he should prepare to shoot.

Ali steered the bike through the tall opening immediately after the second car. Saeed had been planning to fire from the right side, but Ali turned to the right, away from the cars, leaving the now exposed Uzi machine gun facing the wrong direction. He quickly raised the weapon over his head and down to the left, to bring it to bear on the group of men moving rapidly toward the front door of the house. Saeed fired off two undisciplined bursts of perhaps ten rounds each, hitting the huddle of men where he assumed the general would be. Bodies tumbled, and shouts rang out. He was about to empty the remainder of the magazine into the mass of bodies when he was hit with a burst of fire from the security detail that had arrived earlier in the day. Two snipers had positioned themselves in a protective posture on the compound wall and had their weapons ready when the general arrived. Saeed was dead before he realized he had been shot. Ali instinctively gunned the motorbike and tried a sliding turn to make his escape. Saeed's body flew off the seat and hit the ground with a soft thud. Ali never completed that turn. He was tackled by a security guard as the motorbike dug for traction in the loose gravel. He would now face some of the most painful interrogation techniques on earth. The plot would no longer be a secret.

General Ali Khan was not injured in the assassination attempt. His bodyguards absorbed the rounds meant for him; two were dead and a third was badly wounded. The general was spattered with fresh blood and this made him look even more fierce than he already was. He sprinted into his home to see to the safety of his family. They were frightened but not injured. A terrible rage arose inside him, exiting as a primal scream. The visceral demand for retribution was like nothing he had ever experienced before. For a few minutes he wanted only blood, and he would start with the president, who had surely ordered this attempt on his life.

An hour later, after the initial interrogation of Ali had been completed, General Ali Khan was informed that the shooters were Iranians and that they were attached to the Islamabad embassy. *Fine, I can take care of that in due time.* He called his chief of security and whispered a few instructions. The Iranian intelligence chief would be snatched at the first opportunity, never to see his homeland again. The other assassin, Ali, he ordered held in a prison cell for another purpose.

Ali Khan had a great deal of work to do before he launched the coup the next day. However, he couldn't focus. The events of the past two hours were too fresh in his memory. He had many calls to make and loyalties to test. He was about to make his first contact when General Branch called him once again.

"General Khan, I need to speak with you on a secure line. It is urgent."

Ali Khan knew that this would be a plea for restraint, but he could not refuse his friend a chance to make his case. He recited a private number and waited. The phone buzzed, and the two men began a careful dialogue that slowly crawled its way to the heart of the issue. Ali Khan described the assassination attempt to Branch although he did not reveal the nationality of the attackers. "If you were in my position, General, how would you react?"

Branch listened more than he spoke until the conversation was nearing the end. "General Khan, I am so thankful that the gunmen missed you. I am sincerely sorry for the loss of your men. You have many reasons to be angry. My advice is not to let that anger destroy all that you, and other courageous men, have worked so hard to achieve. Pakistan needs a freely elected civilian government if it is to take its rightful place among the great nations of the world. If the generals move to retake power, it will set your country back a generation. My president has asked me to pass along a private message to you: 'Please find a way to protect the civilian government from an overthrow. If you must sacrifice one lamb to achieve this, so be it.'"

A new plan was forming in Ali Khan's mind as soon as he terminated the call. He hastily retraced his steps with the officers he had met with or called earlier in the day. The exiled generals demanded to come home. They would have none of the nonsense they were now hearing from Ali Khan. He persisted; they wavered. The current cadre of officers agreed with his new assessment. If the president could be forced to resign, they would agree to continue working with the new civilian government. If he didn't resign, they would stand with the purged generals. *Resignation would be a nice outcome,* he thought, *but difficult to achieve without military force.* Ali Khan decided on a different course. He called his chief of security and had another lengthy conversation.

-26-

The Indian Ocean

The USS *Carl Vinson*, a Nimitz-class aircraft carrier, was newly returned from San Diego to its duty station in the Indian Ocean. It led a strike group that included two guided missile cruisers and a complement of smaller antisubmarine and antiaircraft ships, one attack submarine, and assorted supply ships. The secretary of defense had just ordered the strike group to proceed northerly toward the Persian Gulf, and to establish a new duty station off the coast of Pakistan, about two hundred miles behind the *Abe Lincoln* carrier group. Secretary Branson was feeling his oats. He had two carrier strike groups in position, ready to kick some Iranian ass and do some serious damage. For the moment, he forgot that he was not the commander-in-chief.

The USS *Abraham Lincoln* had arrived on station twenty-four hours earlier and was already flying recon missions to within twenty miles of the Iranian coast. The commander of the strike group, Rear Admiral Davis, intended to let them know he was here and active. He gave strict orders not to engage Iranian vessels or aircraft, unless they were perceived to be threats to either the carrier group or to the aircraft flying the missions. What exactly would "constitute a threat" would be left up to the pilots. Around the clock, the admiral kept two flights of F/A-18 Hornets in the air, with another flight ready to launch immediately in case of trouble. He was not the sort of leader to take any chances with his command.

***

In Kuwait, two CIA-owned Reaper drones were loaded with heavy weapons and the first aircraft was launched. The Reaper would be easy prey if it strayed into Iran's airspace, so the flight controller back in the United States flew it ten miles inside of the Iraqi border on its way to spy on the convoy. He gradually climbed the aircraft to twenty-five thousand feet and waited for the Reaper to reach its target location. Once there, it would fly a predetermined holding pattern, always maintaining at least ten miles distance from the Iranian border. It could remain on station for about thirty hours before being replaced by its twin.

The Iranian Air Defense Command noticed the air traffic off their southern coast as well as the single aircraft flying north. The duty officer immediately called his superior, who in turn called his.

"We have what appears to be a drone flying mostly northerly, inside Iraq, destination unknown. It is probably reconnaissance. What can only be carrier-based aircraft, two flights of two each, are probing but not approaching close enough to be a concern." Iranian forces had already been put on alert, so it would be an easy call to launch a flight to confront any possible intruder.

"Colonel, I am going to call Bushehr and tell them to put two fighter aircraft in the air, to let the carrier know we see it. I am less concerned about the drone. If it is reconnaissance, we will deal with it if it strays into our territory. There are no important military assets in the area. It seems the Americans are wasting their time, as usual."

The Reaper reached its assigned station and began making lazy loops across the sky. The controller received an order to launch the first Raptor mini-drone, and a second pilot/controller took charge of the little bird as it dropped free, wings extended to all of ten feet, and its engines came alive. The Raptor had been programmed to the coordinates of the stalled convoy about thirty-five miles away. Its primary mission was to provide images of what was on the ground, although it also carried quite a sting of its own. It took the little aircraft about twenty minutes to acquire the convoy and begin transmitting images and infrared information back to the Reaper. The pilot put the Raptor into a pattern about a mile from the convoy, at an altitude of five thousand feet. From that distance, it looked like a big condor riding the air currents. The drone's motor was too silent to be heard by the Iranian soldiers, but its profile was large enough for the antiaircraft radar to pick up a weak intermittent signal. The commander of the SA-22 battery looked at the screen and was confused by the indistinct image he saw. It was too small to be anything he recognized, so he climbed out of the vehicle to take a look with his field glasses. It was a tiny aircraft, certainly a drone. It was circling and did not appear to be a threat to this group of vehicles. He called his superior for further instructions.

***

Back at ground control, the images of the convoy had been received and were immediately forwarded to the analysts at Langley. They confirmed that this appeared to be the same formation they had been tracking. The challenge was to identify which trucks came from the facility at Qom and which were Guard vehicles from Tehran. Satellite images showed three vehicles parked with a security zone of at least one hundred meters around them. The Raptor's images came from a different angle, and it was proving difficult to match the two aspects. The little aircraft had a limited fuel supply, so time was important. Peter Jameson was working with two other analysts, but even so progress was slow.

"I think I have them," one analyst shouted. "There, immediately below the two SA-22s. I make three trucks, different markings than the others, definitely in their own space. If I had more time I could tell you how many guards are there and what they had for breakfast."

Peter called DDI Merrill. "We have confirmed identification of the vehicles. We are within range. Are we free to engage?"

Merrill paused only briefly, as was his habit, and said, "You are weapons-free. I have presidential approval. Launch at will."

The ground controller confirmed the launch command and then went through the procedure for locking the little Spike missiles, one at a time, onto the three target vehicles. For good measure, he targeted another on the lone active radar for the SA-22 battery. Spike was a fire-and-forget missile designed for engaging moving targets. This should be a piece of cake. He took the Raptor out of its pattern and pointed its nose in the direction of the convoy. Four missiles were launched, two seconds apart, from a range of just less than a mile. As they were streaking toward their targets, the pilot of the tiny aircraft prepared to lock his two remaining missiles onto whatever else looked interesting. The little Spikes were traveling at more than one thousand feet per second, with the sound of their rocket motors trailing by a second or so. They reached their targets in five ticks. Each was aimed at the engine compartment of one of the trucks. As each missile struck, it penetrated the truck body and detonated right on top of the motor. Hoods and other assorted metal pieces suddenly went flying. These trucks wouldn't be going anywhere anytime soon.

The pilot selected the mobile antiaircraft vehicles for the final two missiles and launched them quickly. He instructed the Raptor to climb and make a pass directly over the burning vehicles. The little drone took the requested images, transmitted them, and finished its mission. It turned toward the west and the Iraqi border. With its remaining fuel, the pilot gained as much altitude as possible, saluted the monitor in front of him, and then initiated the self-destruct sequence. The few remaining pieces of the drone would fall over a five-mile swath and be of no use to anyone who found them.

The Reaper that had released the Raptor also carried four advanced Maverick missiles. The Maverick was designed primarily as an antitank missile. This newer version had an effective range of twenty miles. The order was given to launch on the command vehicle and to destroy completely the damaged SA-22 launchers in case a follow-on strike by the navy was needed. To engage these targets, the controller needed to change the course and altitude of the drone. He brought the Reaper through a wide descending turn and pointed it at the Iranian border. The Reaper descended to ten thousand feet and was approaching the ten-mile point from the frontier. The SA-22s had lost one radar, but the second one flashed to life and began tracking the incoming threat.

The two opposing weapons systems, the Mavericks and the SA-22 missiles, were now within the effective range of each other. It would be like a gunfight in the Old West, but who would be the first to shoot?

The Reaper pilot now had good coordinates for his targets from the satellite center, and he prepared to launch the four missiles. The SA-22 commander was still waiting for instructions from his superior in Tehran. The Reaper fired first. The Mavericks stormed off their rails and were at maximum velocity in seconds. The SA-22 radar picked up the four incoming missiles and the commander launched in self-defense. He was uncertain which targets to lock onto. In the heat of the moment, he chose the incoming missiles, which were the immediate threats to his position. He launched six SAMs and hoped for the best.

The Mavericks were incoming at seven hundred miles per hour and each had the profile of a spiraling football when viewed from the front. They took all of forty seconds to reach their targets. The U.S. controller watched as all but one of the SAMs sailed past the wave of incoming missiles. One appeared to detonate and took out a single Maverick. The three remaining U.S. missiles hit their targets with devastating force. The video pickup showed Guard soldiers running in all directions and firing their weapons in a general panic. It took them ten minutes to realize that the attack was over. The Reaper launched its second Raptor to fully document the carnage, and then it turned and climbed back into its lazy orbit over Iraq.

On the USS *Vinson*, Admiral Davis received an order to prepare ten cruise missiles with antipersonnel warheads for possible launch. He was given the coordinates of the convoy that had just been attacked by the drones. He transmitted the orders to fire control on the missile cruiser, USS *Princeton,* and told them to prepare the birds and hold for further orders. *Only the president can make this call.*

-27-

Washington, D.C. Department of State

United States Secretary of State Alice Bishop had finished drafting her messages to the Chinese general secretary and to the Pakistani president. Her intention was to force a stop to the hostile actions approved by both, and to not so subtly place the blame for the leaks squarely on the other party. She planned to speak to each leader in person on the telephone, and she wanted to provide a clear context for her calls: to put both leaders in the right state of mind. She had met each within the past year and felt she understood their needs and how they might respond to her approach. To Xi Jintao she wrote:

Mr. General Secretary,

In the interests of peace and harmony between our two nations, which I know you sincerely seek, I feel it is my duty to inform you that we have received the most troubling report from sources inside the Pakistani government. Certain reliable parties have asserted that the People's Republic of China has attempted to purchase a weapon of devastating force for delivery to Iran. Our president is most troubled by this allegation, and he is certain that there must be some falsehood in this report. You and I should speak directly about this matter promptly. May I suggest a phone conversation within the next two hours?

As soon as she finished the first letter, she drafted a second to the new president of Pakistan:

> Mr. President,
>
> We have received troubling news from sources inside the People's Republic of China that indicate your country intends to deliver a weapon of mass destruction to the government of Iran. Should this be true, it would be considered an aggressive and provocative act against the United States of America. The world community would also consider such a transfer to be a danger to world peace. May I suggest that we have an urgent telephone conversation to defuse this situation? I am prepared to discuss this anytime; however, I urge you to schedule the call within the next two hours.

Secretary Bishop was certain that both leaders would respond to their individual messages promptly. The Chinese general secretary would pile denial on top of denial. He would assure her that China was a responsible power and remind her of how China had been working recently to curb North Korea's nuclear program. The Pakistani president was a little more difficult to predict. He would most certainly deny the allegation and, to protect the civilian government he led, he might not cancel the transfer in time. With enough pressure, he would surely cave; however, she knew he was not a decisive man and time was of the essence.

True to form, it was Chairman Xi Jintao who responded first. The call between the two would take place within an hour. The general secretary wished for his ambassador to Washington to be present in person, and he asked if Secretary Bishop would consent to this. She agreed, all the time thinking it would make the communication much easier, for the ambassador had been educated in the United States and understood the American mind.

The call came in precisely on time. "Madame Secretary, when I received your message I was utterly shocked by its content." The Chinese leader obviously intended to do damage control and wanted to be first to speak.

"I have no knowledge of such a plan, nor do my generals. We have gone on record as being against the proliferation of nuclear weapons at the United Nations, have we not? I want to give you my personal assurances that China has no interest in seeing something like this happen."

Alice Bishop waited patiently for this first tide of denials to ebb, then she carefully and firmly outlined her country's position.

"Mr. Chairman, it pleases me greatly to hear you say this. You can appreciate our great concern at hearing such an allegation. If such a thing should ever happen, it would completely undermine the relationship between our two nations, a relationship that I know you and my president are committed to building. It may be that the Pakistani government has misunderstood a communication from a functionary in your government. May I be completely assured that this miscommunication will be resolved?"

At this question, Xi Jintao asked if his ambassador, now present in the room with Secretary Bishop, might be allowed to convey the position of his government. Ambassador Xiadan had only a few minutes earlier been given his instructions. He was ready to speak, but he also was visibly nervous.

"Madame Secretary, my government deeply regrets that this misinformation has caused distress in our otherwise excellent relationship with the United States. Chairman Xi has asked me to make completely clear to you that China has not, and will not, participate in any such adventures. If anyone in the government is found to have held any discussions with Pakistan, they will be punished."

As she listened, Secretary Bishop understood the reality of the situation. If anything about this aborted plan should happen to appear in the Western press, it would require a human sacrifice. An out-of-favor general, or a less-than-enthusiastic supporter of Xi Jintao, would be tried and executed. It wouldn't be fair, but it was the way that their system worked. She was being presented with an unspoken quid pro quo, and it was not negotiable. If the U.S. government stuffed this story and made it go away, she was being assured that the threat would also go away without any further harm being done. It was up to her to decide whether a somewhat innocent human being would need to die as a scapegoat. *It's a hell of a way to run the world.*

"Mr. Chairman, Mr. Ambassador, thank you for your help in this important matter. I think that we can contain this between our two governments. We have no desire on our part to see this information made public. I will convey to the president your concern and what we have agreed here today. Thank you."

When she finished the call, she thanked Ambassador Xiadan for his help, and the two held a private two-minute conversation. He departed, and she then turned to the matter of Pakistan.

The Pakistani president came on the line about an hour later, and Secretary Bishop was not in a mood to let him blather on about the injustice of this accusation. There were no pleasantries.

"Mr. President, there is deep concern in my government that Pakistan is about to make a serious misstep that will turn world sentiment against you. We know of plans, confirmed plans, for the transfer of a weapon from your nuclear arsenal to Iran. Such a transfer would be unacceptable to the United States and to the rest of the world. My president has asked me to call you personally and demand your help in preventing this from happening."

The Pakistani president was not confident in his position. Alice Bishop immediately sensed his hand caught in the cookie jar, and this made her less sure of the outcome. He began to speak.

"Madame Secretary, the people and the government of Pakistan resent the tone of your message and this call. It would be against our national interests to allow Iran to dip into our arsenal of weapons. There is no great love between our nations. The Chinese government has misled you for their own reasons, and you are falling into their trap. Pakistan has had no such dealings with Iran."

Well, she thought, *I guess we accomplished one of our goals. These two countries won't be sitting at the same table for a while.*

"Mr. President, I understand that national priorities can sometimes cause the truth to become a casualty. The United States is asking for your personal assurance that no weapon of mass destruction has been, or will be, delivered to Iran. Our president has made it clear that if such a thing were to happen, it would be considered an aggressive action toward the United States and would draw an appropriate response."

"Secretary Bishop, am I to take this as a threat?"

She let this question hang in the air for a minute. "Let's just say, Mr. President, that you should be more worried about forces within your own country than what my country might do. Certain people will not tolerate what has been alleged to happen, and we will be forced to encourage them to that end. You have worked long and tirelessly for a freely elected civilian government and this is what you have put at risk. My personal advice to you is to choose wisely."

The line was quiet again as the Pakistani leader considered his options. He finally responded to this challenge. "Madame Secretary, you have my personal assurance that this thing will not happen." In his heart, he already knew it would be impossible to pull it off anyway. *To hell with the Iranians.*

"Thank you, Mr. President. As always, you show your wisdom and your commitment to the security of your nation." Alice hung up the phone and called the president of the United States for a victory lap and a high-five over the telephone.

-28-

Tehran, Islamic Republic of Iran

The United States urgently needed a direct communication channel to the leadership in Tehran. It had to be someone who could gain immediate access to the right person, and who could also be convincing. The honor fell to the embassy of the Netherlands in Tehran. The Dutch ambassador received instructions from his government to deliver an urgent message to Ayatollah Ahrimani on behalf of the United States. It was couched in proper diplomatic talk, but the essence of the message was that a certain convoy must be recalled, or it would be destroyed. Ahrimani was livid with anger when he received it. He vowed all manner of retribution against the messenger and those behind it. He was growing frustrated. His contact with Pakistan had grown cold. He wondered once again of the wisdom of trusting the Pakistanis. They were more Western than Muslim in his mind. The United States still had enormous influence over its military, and this had been a constant risk to his project from the beginning.

After the first raid on the convoy, word about what had happened filtered back slowly through the chain of command. It was difficult for the officers along this chain to comprehend fully what they were hearing. And passing the unwelcome news along was not without risk. The field officers didn't know what the convoy was doing in that remote area or what it carried. An attack on such a small force made no sense and, at first, the assumption was that it had been carried out by dissidents. It took more than four hours for the full details to filter back to Tehran. It had been a missile attack from one or more unknown aircraft.

Ayatollah Ahrimani did not receive the news with good humor. He was truly between a rock and a hard place. This national treasure, this one-of-a-kind weapon, was now stranded in a remote section of Iran. The Americans knew exactly where it was and were threatening to destroy it. If they wished to, they could helicopter in and steal it. Then all their secrets would be laid out in front of the American intelligence services. He could not see a way to continue the ill-fated mission to the Iraqi capital. He was boxed in and he could do nothing other than capitulate. His anger raged against anyone who approached him for the next two hours. He imagined many ways to punish those who had betrayed him, but he had a more pressing need. The bomb needed to be safely retrieved. He called in his aide and gave the order to retreat. This galled him to no end. Amid his rage, he called his security chief and gave orders to erase the trail of evidence leading back to him.

The convoy had been badly damaged by the drone attacks. More than one hundred of the vehicles were still operational, but no one on location had the authority to move the precious cargo out of its original truck. Another request went back up the line to Tehran. It was a comedy of errors, but it was the way that the military-to-clergy-to-military chain of command worked.

Satellite imagery being captured in the United States about the same time revealed that the convoy had not moved and was still close to the frontier. This led to a vigorous debate at the Pentagon as to the intentions of the Iranians. Perhaps there was another delivery system that had been missed. The failure of the convoy to retreat led some to believe that the attack might still be on. Secretary of Defense Branson made the decision to pull the *Vinson* strike group farther north and to put both carrier groups on the highest alert. He ordered the chairman of the Joint Chiefs and the commander of U.S. Naval Forces Central Command to prepare a plan for possible air strikes on selected targets inside Iran. The objectives would be the complete destruction of the damaged convoy carrying the nuclear weapon and its birthing place, Qom. He fudged a little when he told the chairman that the president had authorized the higher level of alert and the prestrike planning. The secretary of defense was part of the national command structure and authorized to make this call. If he received orders to launch a mission, the chairman would want the president to deliver that order to him personally. He didn't trust the secretary of defense and penetrating Iranian airspace would be costly in men and machines, but mostly, he thought with sadness, in men. Machines didn't have families.

The USS *Vinson* and the USS *Abraham Lincoln* were combined into a task force under the command of Rear Admiral Davis, now on board the *Vinson*. He put two more flights of F/A-18 Hornets into the sky armed with HARM antiradiation missiles, from the *Abe Lincoln,* which was closer to the Iranian shoreline. The pilots were instructed to probe as close as twelve miles from the coastline and to be alert for Iranian surface-to-air missile batteries tracking them. If engaged, they were given permission to fire.

The flight leader was an aggressive lieutenant commander with the nickname "Bruiser," and a reputation to match. He led his flight in a straight-on approach at six thousand feet toward a known Iranian antiaircraft position. To any defense command in the world, it would look like an attack. As he passed through the twelve-mile mark at five hundred knots, the Iranians lit up their attack radars as a warning and quickly called their superiors for instructions. Bruiser took the routine warning as an imminent threat to his flight and ordered two HARM missiles launched on the offending radar. It was all over in thirty seconds. The panicked Iranian air defense crew ran from their doomed vehicle only seconds before the missiles hit. Things were rapidly getting out of hand.

The admiral called for current satellite images, and his team of planners began to plot an attack strategy, including tactics to neutralize all known antiaircraft positions along this section of the coast. The facility at Fordo represented a significant challenge to any navy strike force. The air force was better armed and had more suitable aircraft for such an attack. The navy could blanket the area with Tomahawks, destroying everything on the surface, but the bunker-busting bombs needed for the destruction of the underground city were not carried on these ships. The air force had a presence at Ali Al Salem Air Base in Kuwait, but no combat aircraft other than drones were stationed there. The closest air base with heavy bomb delivery capability was in Turkey, and there wasn't time to receive permission from the Turks to use their airspace. It looked like the navy would be on its own this time.

Secretary Branson was convinced that he was right about the situation. He believed that the Iranians were reckless enough to proceed, and the lack of movement of the damaged convoy was all the proof he needed. He decided to go around the CIA and instead use the Pentagon's intelligence capabilities to gain the updated information he needed. There were enough true believers in the necessity of ridding the world of this Iranian government to allow him to cover his tracks. He reviewed the targeting for the mission with the chairman of the Joint Chiefs. The plan didn't promise nearly enough destruction for his taste. He demanded more targets, more aircraft. This was making the chairman nervous. He understood the risks of going to war, even a little war, with only two carrier strike groups. There was no air force support and no way to extract downed crews safely from the deep-inland area of hostilities. This was all making him doubt the legitimacy of his orders.

-29-

Pakistan

In Islamabad, General Khan finally hammered out a consensus with the other generals. His role would be to inform the president that he must resign. Ali Khan understood how difficult this might be, so he secretly selected plan B instead. He still had the recently captured and merely slightly-tortured Iranian assassin Ali in custody. He was given one, and only one way to save his miserable life. If he didn't agree, he was told he would be stripped of his skin and fed alive to dogs. Even to a stupid street hood like Ali, the first option sounded much better.

The president was scheduled to appear at a celebration around midmorning. The ceremony would mark the opening of a new school that was the fulfillment of a promise to provide more educational opportunities for young women from the countryside. The location was barely twenty kilometers from the capital, and he would be transported by car and guarded by an elite army platoon with a small cadre of his own militia as personal bodyguards. In total there would be twenty-five armed soldiers, and his vehicle was hardened as well. He felt that he would be safe and well-protected.

The arrival at the school was uneventful, and the crowd was officially enthusiastic. The president spoke eloquently of his plans to use this fine facility as a model for the whole country. Local dignitaries shook his hand and mothers and daughters pressed close to him. Ali was in the crowd as well. His instructions were simple. He was to wait until the moment of departure. The president would be moving toward his car, and his security detail would have lowered its guard a bit. Ali would step out and deliver his full magazine of bullets into the president and his guards. He thought he could handle the small group of personal bodyguards, although the presence of the army troubled him. He still hoped that he might somehow be able to escape and return home to Iran.

The president concluded his appearance and began to walk the fifty or so meters back toward his waiting car. The crowd applauded and continued to press forward, reducing the distance from them to the departing presidential party. His bodyguards were alert but not overly so. Ali began his final approach through the throng of onlookers. He was suddenly aware that the army was nowhere in sight. The army platoon had retreated about one hundred meters from the president's car and had carefully put itself away from the expected line of fire. Their vehicles were still aligned as if in a convoy. Everything looked normal.

Ali waited until the president and his entourage were about ten meters from the limousine. They were close enough to the safety of the vehicle to feel secure. One of the bodyguards was already opening the car door for the president. Ali pushed through the last layer of onlookers and into a kneeling firing position. He had an unobstructed line of sight. He fired repeated short bursts from his embassy-supplied Uzi. It was all over in less than five seconds. The president and his four bodyguards lay bleeding on the dry, stony earth. His personal secretary was wounded, but not critically. The army did not move to intervene, except for a lone rifleman perched on top of an armored vehicle who promptly dispatched Ali to his maker with a single shot through the head. The bullet exited Ali's brain at high velocity and harmlessly gouged a small hole in the sand, exactly where the sniper had intended. It was a textbook execution. It was expedient for one man to die that the nation might be saved. That prediction did not include the unfortunate Iranian young man named Ali. He was a casualty of a much larger struggle that he never fully understood. He was, nonetheless, dead.

General Khan was informed immediately of the shocking death of the president. He called the prime minister immediately to tell him of the assassination, and to pledge the support of the military for the civilian government and the next president. He also released to the foreign and in-country press similar commitments as chief of the armed forces. He finally took time to relax. This had turned out much better than he'd thought it would only last night. He realized how much he appreciated the advice he had received from his American friend. It helped to keep an open mind.

-30-

Peter Jameson at the CIA's satellite imaging center was the first to suspect something was going off the rails. The two carrier groups in the Arabian Sea were moving into a posture that suggested hostilities were imminent. Supply vessels made their final visits to the carriers and the other warships. Then the support ships were pulled back, well away from the ships of the line. The normal peacetime positioning of the antisubmarine ships, the destroyers and the frigates, changed and patrol activity seemed heightened. The cruisers moved away from the carriers and into screening positions where their antiaircraft and antimissile defenses could be better used to protect the big boats. He knew this pattern. It was like what had happened before Gulf War II. He decided to go out on a limb and call Merrill.

"Sir, this is Jameson. I have kind of strange question to ask. Are we about to strike Iran?"

Reynolds Merrill sat upright in his chair. "Peter, tell me what has prompted you to ask this question."

"Well, I have been keeping an eye on the two carrier groups for the past day or so, and it appears to me that they are moving into an offensive posture. They are not in normal patrol formation. It's not consistent with the last briefing you provided the team. I thought you should know."

"Has there been any change in the position of the Iranian convoy?"

"No, sir, it's still sitting there. The fires are out, but there has been no attempt to move the baby, or any signs that they plan to move anything anytime soon. I've been expecting a relief column to come to the rescue. Nothing has moved so far."

Merrill thanked Jameson for his update and immediately called the director. "Bill, has the president ordered any action toward Iran other than the drone strike? The reason for the question is that satellite images seem to suggest the two carrier groups are going offensive."

The DCIA did not allow his voice to show his alarm, but he was concerned. Branson was known to have a propensity for action first, with apologies to follow. "Reynolds, this is news to me too. Can you see if your listeners are getting anything of concern from *Orlando*? To me, it appears that the Iranian leadership is still trying to figure out what hit them. They generally don't make quick decisions."

Merrill called the shop to speak with Katie. He trusted her sense of unfolding events more than most. "Katie, can you tell me if things are beginning to unravel in Tehran? I'm interested in any communications concerning the convoy."

"Sir, we have a lot of raw communications but nothing to indicate any major movements. The leadership seems stunned, and the army has not yet been included in most of what I am seeing. They won't be using email for what comes next. The military, including the Guard, has their own secure communications network for their command structure. I think the satellite boys will be able to provide a more complete picture of what is really happening on the ground."

"Katie, I understand all that. I need your informed opinion of what is happening."

"Well, sir, I think the clergy will take more time to make a move than we generally think they should. The ayatollah will have to retrieve the weapon and put it back in its hole. This may take more time to accomplish than we might anticipate. The army will be livid when they learn of this adventure, and the clergy will need time to talk them down. Everything takes time in their system. This is where we are at risk of doing something impulsive. If I had my hands on the controls, I think I would sit tight and let them do what they must do. We have the military assets to visit considerable destruction on them whenever we choose. They know this. We also can see in real-time everything they are doing. They know that too. I don't think we should be in too much of a hurry to go to war."

Merrill couldn't help but smile. Katie had just expressed in her own inimitable way what he believed to be the right course for the United States of America. "Thank you, Katie. It is always a pleasure to work with you." He signed off and called the director.

"Bill, it seems that part of our team has lined up a bit offside. I can confirm that the navy is getting a bit aggressive along the Iranian coast, and I am not sure that's what the president ordered. My opinion on the situation is that we need to give the leadership in Iran time to cool down and take their nuke back home. I know I'm taking a chance here, but I think we are going to win this battle if we don't get too crazy."

Hughes had reached the same conclusion before the call. He thanked his faithful deputy and called the chairman of the Joint Chiefs. Admiral James Mendenhall was a thoughtful military officer with no political aspirations. He already had reservations of his own on the upgraded alert status.

Hughes spoke first. "Admiral, my agency doesn't usually keep track of the navy, but our bird is monitoring the area and feeding us lots of images. The two carrier groups on station off Iran look like they are about to go to war. You and I were both in the same meeting with the president. Did you hear something that I didn't?"

This posed a difficult dilemma for the chairman. He reported to the secretary of defense in the national command structure, but the president, and no one else, was the commander-in-chief. He held a great deal of respect for the DCIA; however, it was awkward for him to open the window between the military and the intelligence agency too wide.

"Bill, the two carrier groups are on alert, but they should not be in an offensive posture at this moment. Would you be willing to share your satellite intel with us so that we can see what you see?"

A digital file was delivered to the office of the chairman minutes later. Admiral Mendenhall instructed his intelligence staff to give it a thorough review and report to him as soon as possible. The analysts manning the center took one look and confirmed that the *Vinson* and *Lincoln* strike groups were not in normal patrol formation. Something was about to go wrong.

Admiral Mendenhall debated with himself how to handle this delicate situation. He had served his country for thirty-four years with great distinction, and he didn't intend to end his military service in a major-league screwup. In his other role as chief of naval operations, he called the commander of the Central Command who controlled the 5th Fleet and all navy assets in the Middle East and the Indian Ocean. It was nighttime in that zone, but the commander took this call without complaint.

"Admiral" he began, "this is a little out of the ordinary. Please bear with me. The situation in Iran is delicate, and we don't want to provoke an incident that might lead to an unintended outcome. It would be advisable to instruct Admiral Davis to resume normal patrol activities and withdraw from his current position. He's too damn close to the Iranian coast. I will handle the civilian side of this." The commander agreed. The order would go out to the fleet immediately. Now came the hard part.

The chairman of the Joint Chiefs could go directly to the president on any military matter at any time. That was in theory. What made this difficult was that Secretary Branson was his direct superior in the normal chain of command. Branson had clearly exceeded his authority and appeared to have issued orders that conflicted with those of the president. If Admiral Mendenhall went to the White House with the evidence he had gathered, there would be a certain amount of deniability by Branson. The secretary had a bad habit of airing his disappointment with this president in clandestine meetings with certain disgruntled members of Congress. In the admiral's opinion, the United States didn't need a public shouting match between the secretary of defense and the man who had appointed him. He would have to deal with this in another way. It was somewhat distasteful to him to do this. *But hell,* he reasoned, *it's only politics.*

Admiral Mendenhall retrieved a small thumb drive from his safe and inserted it into his laptop. He chose not to view the material again. The drive contained a fairly complete digital record of the defense secretary's proclivity to bang anyone wearing a skirt, including one that was rumored not to be a she. His list of conquests and supporting photos included women provided by defense contractors and one lady known to the intelligence agencies to be a covert Russian agent. This evidence had been entrusted to the admiral a year earlier by a disgruntled defense contractor CEO who, despite all his own under-the-table and on-the-mattress offerings, had lost an important contract with DOD. He compiled this information to force his rejected bid back into the running and had then lost his nerve. Instead, he entrusted it to his former roommate from his days at Annapolis. Admiral Mendenhall never thought he would need to play this card. Now he could see no other option. He sent a quick email, along with the file, to someone he knew in the press.

The *New York Times* published the story the next day. It was front-page news. The *Times* elected to publish only one photo, and it was of Branson lunching a little too close to a certain lovely woman attached to the Russian embassy. The next day, the photo in the follow-up story was of an angry Ken Branson departing the White House after what would be his last visit to the Oval Office. Within a week, he resigned.

-31-

Paris

Farid Al-Sharif completed his second visit to the National Bank of Pakistan, during which formal apologies were expressed by all parties present. He was informed that the loan from China to Pakistan had been aborted for political reasons, and the Pakistani nationals in the bank spoke of deep concern about what would happen next in their country following the assassination of their president. It was being widely reported that an Iranian hit man was responsible for the murder, something that the military finally confirmed. It was also reported that the security chief for the Iranian embassy had disappeared soon after the killing, and it was presumed that he had ordered it and was in hiding. The truth of the matter was that the man had been snatched by the Pakistani security service and General Khan would be his judge and jury once the interrogation ended. As the general had promised himself, this man would never see his homeland again.

Al-Sharif went back to his hotel after the meeting. He opened the door to his room and noticed the light on the house phone flashing. There was a voice mail message for him: "Farid, this is your protector. It is time to decide. I will call you. Be ready." In his genuine relief that the Pakistan-Iran deal had fallen apart, he had conveniently forgotten his promise. In a naïve sort of way, he had been hoping that the "no harm—no foul" rule would apply in this case. He had badly miscalculated. At this moment he was in more danger than he had been at any time in his life. He was a link in the chain of evidence leading back to Iran, one that was already in the process of being erased. The order had been issued, and his executioners were now in Paris searching for him. In typical fashion, his family had also been targeted. The ayatollah declared that Al-Sharif's memory be extinguished from the face of the earth. Nothing less would satisfy his rage at being betrayed.

The call came an hour later. The soft Arabic voice reminded him of their mutual promises. "Farid Al-Sharif, we have precious little time with which to work. If you wish to save your family and yourself, it must be now. We have a team of rescue specialists within minutes of your family at this very moment. You must choose."

Al-Sharif knew he was caught between a life of privilege and his desire to protect his family. He didn't believe that the Iranians would dare to harm him. After all, he was potentially useful to them, and they were a practical people. He wanted to remain free, but at the same time, he did not wish to take any risks with his children and his wives. "Can you not just protect my family and leave me free to assist you in the future?"

The soft voice sighed heavily and replied, "That will be impossible even if we wished for that outcome. They will eventually come for you too. We know them better than you do. Without you, we will not be able to protect your loved ones. It must be the whole deal or none."

Farid was sweating profusely in the cool room. Everything he had worked for could now be lost. What good was wealth if one was forced to live an anonymous middle-class existence on an island somewhere? His internal struggle went on for several minutes. The soft voice said nothing more. Reluctantly, Al-Sharif consented to his exile. The voice assured him that his family would be extracted within the hour, and he would be brought in shortly thereafter.

"You will be met by a man tomorrow morning in front of the National Bank of Pakistan, eleven A.M. sharp. You will know him because he will know you, and he will nod and smile. He is not Arab; however, he is among the most trustworthy of men. He will introduce himself as Chase. Go with him. Until then, do not go out in public, do not answer even a knock at your door."

Robert Chase received instructions to lead Farid Al-Sharif in from the cold. It would happen on October 31, the Day of Tormented Souls. The meeting location was set for under the colonnade in front of the National Bank of Pakistan on the Avenue des Champs-Élysées. It was very public and separated from passing traffic by a wide pedestrian walkway. It seemed as safe as any place in Paris.

Chase had recently received a new assignment and was eager to get on with it. He viewed this meeting as babysitting, and he wasn't pleased to be delegated the job. For once he wouldn't have to find and trail a potential target. Al-Sharif would be standing there waiting for him. Chase would lead him to a safe house outside of the city, where he would be processed and questioned before being transported to meet his family in Morocco. Once there, he would be hidden away in a small city with enough security to protect him until, if ever, it was safe enough to return to his country. He would be living in a walled villa with the latest electronic security features. So long as he did not leave the compound, he would be safe.

Chase had the remainder of the day to himself. He was preparing to leave for Germany the day after tomorrow where he would begin a search for an elusive person of interest. There would still be time for dinner with Sam later.

-32-

In a dimly lit coffeehouse in Frankfurt, Andreas Nilsen crouched behind the small screen of his laptop. He could have been about thirty years old, plus or minus five, with slightly dirty, almost-blond hair tufted under a knitted cap. He could have been a student or maybe a Euro-vagabond living on savings, with a little help from the goodness of his fellow man. Andreas's true name was Anders and he was Norwegian rather than German. He was perhaps the world's premier hacker, and he specialized in the electronic burglary of big, complicated systems. He led a loosely organized international group of young men and women who always signed their handiwork with the phrase: *Publicus Lux Lucis,* PLL for short. It meant "open to the light." Their mission was to break into corporations, intelligence agencies, and their governments until there were no more secrets.

This evening Andreas was completely absorbed by a system that did not seem to belong to anyone. The site address had been posted on a bulletin board by an American student at Cal Tech, who had come across it while fishing around classified U.S. government sites about a year ago. He and his friends had attempted to breach it numerous times, but could never find a way in. In true egalitarian fashion, the undergrad then posted it on the dark web and asked for feedback if anyone ever got through the security and inside where all the goodies were. It was the sort of challenge Andreas loved. The fact that it might belong to the American government made it even more delicious. He felt certain he could crack it eventually. It was only a matter of time and computing power. He had lots of both.

He was distracted by the arrival of a young woman, Rebekka Odegaard, a fellow Norwegian and current traveling companion. Bekka was stunningly beautiful. Her hair, like his, was blond, but impressively so. It was positively golden in hue and cut to brush her shoulders. Her eyes were sea blue and bright—alive—and almost mischievous. Her skin was pale and perfect. When she smiled, it seemed as though the stars had come out to play. Her beauty aside, Rebekka was brilliant and able to keep pace with Andreas in almost everything he did. They made the sort of unlikely couple that one could see anywhere in America or Europe these days: a beautiful young woman and a slightly scruffy companion.

The PLL had recently made a big score. A member of the team had broken through security at a major Italian bank and done a "hack and extract" that yielded a bonanza in information, including about a thousand account number and password combinations. Within two hours, using this information, he completely scrambled all thousand accounts with a blizzard of intrabank transfers. The hacker even had time to send external bank wires to his favorite charities in the total amount of one and a half million euros. If the hacking itself was not a serious crime in the eyes of the public, this last caper was too much. Money mattered. The group had finally reached the front page of Interpol's most-wanted persons' list, right next to Hans Stumpf, a wacko white nationalist who, in the recent past, had blown up a bus full of children. This was going to bring them more attention than they really wanted, but it mattered little. They still felt invisible and invincible.

Katie Thompson was on the receiving end of Andreas's probes on this night. She was manning the CIA's listening post that kept track of the feed from one of the two worms the CIA had long ago buried in selected Asian governments. Her system was receiving an extraordinary number of requests for access, not unlike a denial of service attack. Earlier, she alerted the tech group responsible for maintaining and protecting the system. Eric Smith was the lead systems analyst, and he was busy ensuring that the system security was holding. At the same time, he was doing his own tracking to try and identify the source of the attack. He understood that the inquiries would not be coming directly from one computer to his. They were undoubtedly being routed through a labyrinth of pathways using computers that had been hijacked from unsuspecting owners.

Katie called Deputy Director Merrill to inform him of the problems at the center. The attack effectively stopped the flow of information from *Orlando,* and if this continued, it would be a serious blow to their efforts to understand how the Iranians were working to resolve their problem. When she reached Merrill, he was in the middle of his own crisis.

"Thanks, Katie. We have experienced a series of attacks today, and we are still assessing the damages. It looks like one system was breached although it is too early to know if anything was extracted."

Merrill was very concerned, but he tried not to let Katie feel his anxiety. The system that failed contained highly classified information about CIA assets and informants in Asia. The data about China was a special worry. If these attacks continued the CIA would be out of business. A lot of good men and women might also be dead.

-33-

Tehran

After a delay of almost twenty-four hours, the Revolutionary Guard finally sent a relief battalion with medical aid and additional trucks to their stranded comrades near the Iraqi border. This time it was the regular army and not the Guard who took control of the scene and secured the weapon. Peter Jameson was watching the whole thing from six hundred miles above the earth. He reported the transfer of the bomb to a new vehicle and the reforming of the convoy back in the direction of Qom.

"They left behind the destroyed vehicles," he noted. "On the next satellite pass it looked like everything of value had already been stripped. On the next pass all I could see were burnt tires and broken glass."

"And the convoy?" asked Merrill.

"I tracked it back to Fordo. I think we can declare mission accomplished."

"I agree with your assessment, though I am always reluctant to use those exact words. Well done, Peter."

In Tehran, Ahrimani was embarrassed and angry. The other mullahs were restless, but also appeared to be relieved that they still had their national treasure intact. Word had been received from Islamabad concerning the assassination of the Pakistani president by an Iranian attached to the embassy there. The disappearance of the station chief for intelligence and security was also troubling. In their conclave, the mullahs were not shy about expressing their displeasure. Ayatollah Mohammad Azizi was the first to speak.

"Ayatollah Ahrimani, it appears that we have some reckless adventurers among us." His gaze was fixed on Ahrimani. "I understand why we chose this course of action and I supported it, but I don't think you have adequately explained why it failed. What steps do you intend to take now?"

This was the first time Ahrimani had been seriously challenged since he ascended to the position of the supreme leader. He understood that these men could unseat him just as easily and raise another to his position. However, he still wielded enormous power.

"My friends, this failure was entirely the fault of the weakling in Pakistan. He turned his back on us, and now he has been dealt with, and our honor has been restored. I have ordered the weapon returned to Qom, and the Saudi banker will soon be punished as well. We shall still rule Iraq in due time. We must be patient and allow Allah to lead us."

If there was any grumbling among the mullahs, it was kept inside each of their carefully draped heads. When the name of Allah was invoked, it was wise to avoid any direct criticism. Azizi listened respectfully and then bowed slightly to the supreme leader to indicate his complete agreement, at least for now.

-34-

Paris

Robert Chase and Samantha enjoyed a rare, wonderful evening together. After dinner, on a whim, they jumped aboard a *bateau mouche* for a late-night cruise under the bridges of Paris. It was very late when he finally walked her by the Musée d'Orsay and back to her room at the Hôtel d'Angleterre. One warm kiss led to two, then three even warmer than those before it, but Robert wanted to woo her the right way, and this was not the time or place.

"I have to work tomorrow morning, and then I am over to Frankfurt for a little while. Can we resume this in about a week?"

"What sort of work?" she teased him. "In the entire time I have known you I have never seen you do anything except eat, drink, and take walks with me. I am beginning to wonder if you even have a job."

He responded to this comment perhaps a bit defensively. "You know I work. I also know how to have fun. This is the fun part. I hope that this is all you will ever have to see me do."

Sam pouted a little. She wanted this relationship to move to the next level. And she was more than a little aroused by their sixty-second embrace standing upright on the cobblestones in front of her hotel. "I want more of the fun part, Robert. See to it that you keep your promise."

Chase walked back to his hotel, crossing the Seine by way of the bridges at Île de la Cité. He was in a buoyant mood. *This is the place I most feel alive. My life is here, now and always.*

He awoke early the next day to patchy clouds and the expectation of finishing a long mission. He'd been in France for the past forty-five days. During that time, he had attempted to stop a terrorist in Marseille, and now he was about to accompany a man, whose role in history was to help terrorists finance their activities, to a safe life in another land. Chase thought about the many victims of men like Farid, and it galled him to be put in this position. Still, this was the life he had chosen. He shook off his funk and went out into the streets, letting his nose guide him to a good coffee and a brioche.

By 10:30 A.M., Chase was already in position. He had arrived on foot to the place where he would meet Al-Sharif and then carefully walked both sides of the Champs-Élysées near the bank to be sure that there would be no complications. There were no unexpected utility trucks or parked vans. No one walking by the bank seemed to have any interest in what lay behind the locked doors. He settled himself into a chair at a café about a block north of the bank and waited.

Farid Al-Sharif had arranged to be admitted to the rear door of the National Bank of Pakistan about ten minutes before he would meet the man called Chase. During the night, he had transferred the more liquid portion of his portfolio into places where he could access it easily if he ever decided to run away from his protectors. He felt good this morning. Things weren't so bad after all. His family was safe in Morocco—he had verified this himself in a phone call—and he would be there too in a short time. But he also had been a little careless. Not believing that he was in any imminent danger, he took no precautions to disguise where he was going.

Samantha had an appointment with a close friend this same day. They were to meet at a little bistro not too far from the Hotel George V, so she took the Paris Métro to the stop only a few steps from the hotel. She walked briskly to the top of the stairs, exited the station, and headed south along the Champs-Élysées. As she glanced ahead she could not believe her eyes. There was

Robert about a hundred meters in front of her, walking toward her. He wasn't looking in her direction. His eyes were fixed on a tall man in a nice suit who had just emerged from a nearby building with ornate double doors. She smiled and waved, but Chase didn't see her. He was moving toward the other man, and his attention was now very focused. It was evident that they had planned to meet. She was fascinated to see him in his element. He looked so confident and so handsome. *What the hell,* she decided, and quickened her pace to close the distance between them. *I want to say hello to you, Robert Chase.*

Neither Chase nor Samantha noticed the car that slowly cruised by and then stopped at curbside, something that no true Parisian other than a taxi driver would do on this busy avenue. A flash of movement caught Chase's eye, and he instinctively turned toward the interruption. He and Farid were now about ten feet apart and Samantha was only now entering his field of vision. It was one of those moments when everything happens in slow motion, at least in hindsight. Chase saw Samantha and then he saw the shooters. It was far too late for him to do anything to protect himself or anyone else. Two gunmen were now on the curb with automatic weapons already leveled, and they wasted no time in engaging their target. They weren't good marksmen, not that it would matter in this case. They fired dozens of high-velocity rounds in the direction of the banker and quickly climbed back into their car. The entire episode took less than twenty seconds.

Instantly, Chase realized that he and Samantha were in the line of fire. She was hit midstride and fell forward with a look of surprise on her face. She never stopped looking at his face as she fell hard onto the pavement and bounced once. He felt more than one searing hit on his own body and knew he too was in trouble. Al-Sharif took the brunt of the attack and was leaning back against the doors to the bank. Chase realized he was facedown on the pavement. The increasing pain was starting to carry him away. He lifted his head for as long as he could to look across to where Sam had fallen. All he could see was bright red blood beginning to pool on the ground, and a vacant stare.

Part Three

A Random Walk

-35-

Paris the Left Bank

At exactly three-thirty in the afternoon, with low, heavy clouds scudding across the gray skies of Paris, Robert Chase approached the small chapel in the former abbey directly across from Les Deux Magots. He had been walking for the past hour trying to bring his emotions under control and failing for much of the time. He felt like he was finally ready to face what he must do. This little church of Saint-Germain-des-Prés was best known as the resting place of René Descartes, the famed French philosopher and mathematician. Now it would become, for Chase, a place of remembrance of a different sort. He still limped slightly from the bullet that had gone through his thigh, but the true pain was chiseled onto his heart.

He pushed open the heavy wooden door and entered the nearly empty chapel to the aroma of spent incense and beeswax candles. Then he saw her. She was arrayed in cream silk against the backdrop of the cold hard stone. Her face looked so pale. His eyes filled with tears. Slowly, a few others drifted into the church. Reynolds Merrill had come over to support Chase. It was Merrill who had first recruited him to this strange life he now led. Alone in a pew toward the back slumped a man Chase didn't know by face. He only knew that this man was the voice on the other end of the phone, the author of so many texts over the years. Control had come as well. In all, there were six people here for Robert Chase.

Chase stood at the back of the church for a few minutes. Then he took a deep breath and started toward the front. The few souls present turned to look at him as he moved slowly forward.

As he walked, he understood that he could never let his life be the same again. He owed her more than that. He looked toward Samantha one more time; she looked back . . . and this time she smiled. He was visibly nervous, and he was exceptionally happy. This quiet, unsanctioned ceremony was their version of a wedding day. It was not a typical marriage celebration. A nonexistent man with half a dozen passports and a top-secret covert job couldn't exactly apply for a marriage license at the Hôtel de Ville.

Today, both Samantha and Chase understood that they were following a tradition as old as mankind. In the presence of their adopted families, in his case the few people who genuinely loved them, the couple was preparing to make lifelong promises to each other that would bind them more permanently than any legal or religious ceremony could ever do. As he reached Samantha, he held out his hand, and she accepted it. Their vows were brief. There was no priest or minister to announce the new Mr. and Mrs. Chase. In fact, that name had already been permanently retired by the Agency. Tears flowed freely down both of their faces as they alternated between speaking and listening. Two individuals became one and the deal was sealed with a long soft kiss.

As the small party emerged from the chapel, two waiters in formal attire braved the heavy traffic and crossed the boulevard from Les Deux Magots to the front of the church. They each carried a tray, one with a magnum of champagne with the classic pale orange label, the other with exactly twelve flutes. As they poured the bubbly there on the wide sidewalk, motorists honked, and passersby clapped their approval. Sam and Chase toasted each one in return.

The Paris newspapers had briefly reported the sad story of a Parisian woman and an American businessman who were caught in the crossfire during a bloody assassination of a Saudi banker. The American had died according to informed sources. In true CIA fashion, no names were mentioned.

Samantha and Robert spent their wedding night together in a safe apartment adjacent to the Bois de Boulogne, not too far from central Paris. Their first sexual adventure was a blend of pleasure and pain. They both had wounds that had not yet fully healed, and their chamber was soon filled with the sounds of passion and occasional notes of discomfort, as a sensitive spot was touched or stretched.

Chase slowly slipped Samantha's soft, short robe off her shoulders and let it slip to the floor. She was more beautiful than he had imagined. He first gazed at the two angry scars, one on her upper chest and the other on the left side below her ribs. He regretted the pain she had endured because of him. Her breasts were round and warm to the touch, and he took them gently in his hands, and kissed them each in turn. He looked up and smiled into her expanding grin. She pushed him gently onto the bed and kissed each of his two wounds, one on his chest and the other on his upper thigh, near his hip. She was mildly surprised by the lean, muscular body that he had managed to hide beneath his often-frumpy clothes. She ran her hands along his abdomen, up over his chest, until they met behind his neck. She kissed him gently. Then she slid on top of him and kissed him the way she had dreamed of doing for quite some time.

-36-

Paris

While Samantha was healing in the hospital, Chase had decided to never again put her in a position where she could lose her life for simply being near him. Sam had caught two heavy 7.62-millimeter slugs in her torso. Big-game animals being hunted in the wild had died from less. The first slug passed through her upper left chest, missing vital organs, and had passed beneath her clavicle, leaving a larger hole as it exited. The surgeons patched that up as best as they could, but the muscle damage was significant and would take time to fully heal. The second bullet hit her below her ribs. Two inches in another direction and it would have missed her completely. That bullet didn't hit her lung but snagged a bit of the small intestine, requiring emergency surgery and a long hospital stay. When she recovered enough to talk to Chase, she told him that the first sensation of being shot felt like running into a closed door in the dark. That was before the intense pain started to register. She remembered him reaching for her from his own fallen position; then everything went black.

To understand Robert Chase at this time of his life, one would need to understand that he didn't necessarily believe that he inhabited a violent world. Very few were the times that he felt it necessary to hurt another person, either to protect himself or someone else, during his long and active career with the CIA. The event on the Champs-Élysées was not what he was used to, and it deeply offended his sense of who he thought he was. He was having trouble processing the whole event. He felt that his superiors had exposed him unnecessarily to danger. If this was the dawning of a brave new world of clandestine work, he wanted none of it. But what else could he do? For the past twenty years his identity was whatever the CIA decided it would be. Robert Chase officially died on that day on the streets of Paris. His betters had made that decision for him, and it would be irrevocable. His file had been marked "died in the service" and tucked away in a box somewhere at Langley. During many sleepless nights after the shooting, he often wondered if this had been their way of forcing him ever deeper inside the Agency, with no way out.

It was on a Thursday, as Chase was taking a solitary walk along the Seine, that his long-dormant phone came to life again. He never turned it off, even now.

Are you ready to work?

He read the silent challenge twice. Chase walked on and after fifteen minutes of trying to control the anger he felt inside, he responded back.

Not sure. I need a face-to-face.

He had never, in his twenty-plus years of service, demanded to meet his superior officer. The few times they had met had not been his choice. This request represented uncharted waters, and he felt oddly isolated the moment he sent his reply. A few minutes later, his phone buzzed again with another message from Control.

Saturday, Picasso Museum, 14:00, alone.

When Chase got back to the apartment, Samantha greeted him with a joyful smile and a warm kiss. "Let's go out today," she gushed. "The weather is so nice, and I need to walk with you again in the sunshine. I know a nice restaurant on the edge of the park—it has great foie gras—and the walk through the woods will do us both some good."

Chase looked at her for a few seconds, and then he blurted out without emotion, "They want me to come back to work."

Sam turned to face him with such speed and ferocity that it surprised him. "What?" She shouted this one word in disbelief. "Are you crazy or just still in shock? Those great spy-masters of yours almost got you killed. You can't possibly consider going back to that. No, no, and no! This will not do."

Then she turned her back on him and stood looking out the window with both arms crossed over her chest. She began to cry, softly at first and after that in big, gulping sobs. In her heart, she understood that this was one of the possible pathways for their life together, but it was too soon. She was not ready to risk losing him again.

Chase waited for a long minute and came up behind her and gently put his arms around her arms and gave her a soft hug. She stiffened at first and then she relaxed a little and turned around to hug him in a wet embrace.

"Sam, we will make all decisions like this together. I promise you this. I need to meet someone from the Agency so that I can work through my own issues with the job I do. I'm not ready to accept another assignment. I need to hear the reasons why it's important that I continue to do what I do. Can you trust me with this?"

"Yes, I trust you, you goof. Until now, I never realized that people can get killed in your little shadow world. It all seemed so harmless before . . ."

At this point, Sam hesitated briefly, and her lower lip began to tremble. The tears began flowing again. "I simply can't bear the thought of losing you, Robert, not for any cause, any country, or any reason."

-37-

Musée Picasso in Paris

It was one of Chase and Samantha's favorite places to spend lazy Saturday afternoons looking, talking, and enjoying each other. Sometimes they also looked at the art. The venue was in the Marais district, in a converted seventeenth-century manor house. The museum held more than three thousand works of all types by Picasso, including, as well, his own personal art collection from the beginning of impressionism until his death. The halls of the Picasso covered every phase of the artist's long and productive career. The busy crowds of tourists and art lovers who visited this shrine also made it a convenient place to meet and have a quick, clandestine conversation. Currently, the museum was closed for extensive renovations. Chase was in no mood to look at paintings anyway.

Always cautious, Chase took the Métro and got off two stops away from the station closest the museum. He circled around to approach the building from a direction that only a pathetically lost tourist on foot would be likely to come. As he turned the last corner, he pulled up quickly and stopped in place. A tall man stood twenty yards away, and he was looking in Chase's direction. He wore a dark wool overcoat not much different than his own.

"I sort of thought you might come in from this direction, Robert," came a familiar deep voice. "You were never one to use the front door." It was Reynolds Merrill, and he was alone. "Thank you for coming to meet me today. I knew that you would, but I was really relieved when I saw you walk around that corner."

Chase waited as the older man approached him; then he turned, and they walked together like two old friends. Chase said nothing. Merrill began to speak again. "You know, Robert, what happened to you couldn't have been foreseen or prevented. We had no indication that the Iranians were about to sanction anyone. You and Samantha were caught in the middle of something terrible; however, we did not put you in the line of fire. The world we work in is getting more violent. Human life is considered cheap and there are too many people out there who simply don't care whom they kill."

Chase stopped walking for a few seconds to turn and look Merrill in the eye. There was nothing friendly to be read in his face, and his eyes were dark holes. Then he turned back, and they continued their slow pace along the deserted sidewalk.

"I don't blame you, Reynolds, and I don't blame the Agency. I came to work for you because the rules of the game were ones I could accept. If those have changed, I'm not sure I want to change with them. For the past twenty years, we were the better people. At least, we were better than the rest. We made sure that dangerous ones were taken off the streets. Rather than killing them for questionable political reasons, we put them away where they couldn't hurt anyone again. That was a role I believed in. Now I'm not sure where this will all lead."

Merrill did not speak at once. Then slowly he began in an instructive and warm tone. "Robert, what you are able to do is unique and more important now than ever. If people like you step aside because our adversaries have become more ruthless, how will we ever stop them? If governments simply resort to killing the bad elements, we will learn nothing, and we will end up creating new martyrs—new causes. You must believe me. What you do so well keeps minor disturbances from becoming major conflicts. The information we were able to extract from the banker is only one example. We stopped a reckless adventure by Iran that would have resulted in the loss of hundreds of thousands of lives. Had you or I been sacrificed to achieve this one success, we would have spent our lives well."

They walked together in silence for a few more blocks while Chase processed what he'd heard. The struggle had become more desperate and the stakes much higher than when he had been a young recruit. He wanted a more normal life. *Why can't it be like it was?* He knew the answer before he finished his own question. The opposition understood that mindless terror will eventually weaken the will to resist. The comfortable citizens of cozy democracies will opt for the uncomplicated solutions proposed by their governments. Trapped in a world they no longer understand or control, they will find it easier to let the military deal with this small army of malcontents. That, in turn, will open the door to the sorts of upheavals that military action seeks to prevent. This all made sense to Chase. *We can disrupt them in a thousand little ways today, or we can drop thousand-pound bombs on them later and on everyone else who happens to be nearby.*

-38-

Andreas Nilsen had spent the past forty-eight hours trying to breach the system he was now calling the layer cake. He was both frustrated and excited by the challenge. The system had a layered security system of a type that he had never seen before. It was not a commercial product and he was certain that it was guarding something important, something exceedingly valuable. Each time he penetrated a level of security, he was faced with an almost infinite number of new possibilities, and he had to start all over again. He was into the third of an unknown number of security levels and already he knew that this was a very special security blanket.

To get this far, he had used a large network of hijacked computers all over Europe. This was a most valuable asset to him, one he had carefully constructed over the past few months. Once used, many of the owners of these computers would quickly discover the unauthorized routine, and he would need to start over to find new ones. For the moment, though, he had enough computing power at his command to break any security algorithm or, if he wished, to send a rocket to the moon.

At the CIA computer center at Langley, the frantic defensive activity was like putting all available fingers in a seriously leaking dike. Eric Smith had his full team of analysts working on the attack. It was apparent that the hacker was making steady progress toward a complete breach of the security surrounding one of their systems. In all, there were five elements that made up the carefully constructed electronic hurdles protecting some of the most sensitive information the CIA possessed. Each layer was progressively more difficult to penetrate; however, it was now evident that the hacker possessed enough computing power to eventually win. The only remaining defenses Eric had to work with were to shut down the hacker's access to the system, one way or another, or find and neutralize him. Neither of these choices would be easy to implement.

Each time Eric attempted to end an unauthorized access the hacker would simply come back under a new IP address. Short of catching the guy and putting him in prison, the only surefire way to protect the system would be to deny it to everyone. Eric made the call to close down all access to the system until he could come up with a better solution. On the other side of the Atlantic, Andreas's screen went blank, as did a thousand other screens at Langley and in American embassies around the world.

Andreas pushed his chair back and savored some measure of victory. "They know I am getting close," he called out to Bekka. "When they start it up again, I will be waiting."

Eric put in a call to his superior, who in turn contacted DDI Merrill to give him the news. Effective right now, no one in the CIA could access any information about Asian operations or threats from that sector. They were blind, and a little shaken by what had happened. There were other much more sensitive files that this hacker might reach if he breached all security. This is what worried Merrill the most.

Eric had been in front of his monitors for the past thirty-six hours. The only breaks he had taken were to hit the snack machines in the employee lounge and to use the toilet. He knew that his body was seriously out of balance, after subsisting on chips, Dr Peppers, and candy bars. It was critical that he remain in the moment and not drift away. He was used to marathons like this, although at thirty-six years old, he wasn't sure how much longer his old body would step up to challenges like these. He was following yet another pathway for the attack when it ended in nothingness. "I can't take this anymore!" he screamed. Then he stood up, roared like a tiger, and kicked his chair halfway across the room. His team of systems analysts looked up and howled with laughter. Their average age was twenty-two. They loved this life. It was like gaming, except they got paid for it. They loved their fearless leader too, even more so when he ran into a brick wall, like they did all the time.

Andreas knew that the agency that owned this system could not stay dark forever. If they had protected it this carefully it must be critical to its mission. On the other hand, if it stayed dark too long he would begin to lose his network of captive computers as their owners recognized the signs of having been repurposed. It was all about timing. He needed to start recruiting another network or to buy one from one of the other PLL participants. The currency they used most often was stolen credit card information. Credit card numbers and codes were the easiest commodity to steal on the internet. Banks and online retailers constantly reassured consumers that their information was perfectly safe. Andreas knew the cold truth. Internet security was still in its caveman stage. It was so easy to crack most systems that accomplished hackers like Andreas had to show exceptional self-control to not break the whole financial system. It was a little like being a small parasite in a large living organism. Take only enough nutrition to thrive and multiply, but don't kill the host.

-39-

Chase left Merrill near the river and walked to a nearby Métro station and began to retrace his steps back to the safe apartment near the Bois de Boulogne. He did so carefully, to make sure he had no followers. To do it right would require twice the time it had taken him to get into central Paris. Eventually, after he had checked and rechecked his trail, he would slip out of the woods and into Sam's arms.

He had promised Sam that the future was theirs to decide together. Now, as he rode the train in silence, he wondered how that might work. He was sworn to a life of service, in silence and in the shadows. She was a vivacious and social person who wanted to be in the public view, who wanted to enjoy life in the sunlight. For their union to succeed, they would need to build a complicated structure in which they both were completely invested in the shadows, and in the sunlight. Chase was not sure he had the necessary training to pull this off.

When he arrived back at the little apartment, Samantha was waiting in a chair, looking out of a window toward the woods. She glanced at him and smiled, but there was no other display of affection. In his absence, Sam had also been thinking about their lives and future. They sat down together on the small sofa, and he began to tell her about his meeting.

"Reynolds assured me that what happened to us was unforeseen," he began in his very rational way of presenting things. "I told him that I wasn't sure I wanted to work in this new world of senseless violence. I believed him when he said that what I do is important. That means everything to me. You and I were caught in the middle of a grudge match between Iran and the banker. We were bystanders who got in the way. It could have been anyone. It just happened to be us."

He paused to see if she had already tuned him out. She was still looking in his direction, her eye movement like she was searching his face. "The project I worked on prevented a deadly attack and probably another war as well. That's why I do this. That's why I can't stop."

Samantha listened quietly, which slightly unnerved Chase. He was bracing himself for a counterattack that he might not be able to deflect. Although they loved each other dearly, this marriage thing was all new, and he was not quite sure what the rules of engagement were. She got up and walked toward the window. She hesitated a moment and then walked sensuously back toward him. She stopped, leaned over, and put both of her hands softly on his shoulders and spoke to him from a distance of six inches.

"Robert, I have been thinking about us all afternoon. You are truly the love of my life, but there is a part of your life that I don't figure into at all. I don't see how our relationship can work if I can't have all of you. I can't . . . no, I *won't* sit in a little apartment hoping that you will always come home to me, all safe and sound. If the situation was reversed, you wouldn't accept it either. I am no longer the girlfriend on the other side of the Atlantic. We are like a new molecule of water and not simple hydrogen and oxygen atoms. I need us to live like we are one."

Chase was a little slow on the uptake. He could see her mouth moving although he wasn't completely sure what he was hearing. He had led a solitary life. There were secrets he had sworn he would never divulge to anyone. *What is she asking me to do?* He stood up and backed away a few inches to lessen her advantage and put his hands on her waist to help maintain a safe distance.

"Sam, I love you dearly too. Believe it or not, you figure into every decision I make, even when you're not physically present. What else do you want me to do?" As the last word left his mouth, he finally understood he had been outmaneuvered. He was about to hear exactly what she wanted from him, and he had invited her to do so.

Sam did not wait for him to speak again. This was her time, and she didn't want to hear all the reasons why what she was about to propose couldn't work. She held up a hand in front of Chase's face as he was about to protest.

"All I ask is for us to do together what you've been doing alone all of these years. I want to be a resource to you and a second set of eyes and ears. I don't want you to stop trying to make a difference, but I need to do it *with* you. That is my bottom line."

Hearing this, he fell back onto the sofa. For a couple of minutes, Chase sat in silence as he reviewed his options. *Sam can never be accepted into the Agency to do what I do. For the sake of argument, I could involve her as a private contractor, like I do now with others. She can help in the nuts and bolts of the tactical operations. I am the real obstacle to this. Samantha is smart, resourceful, and international. She speaks other languages in addition to French. She's an EU citizen, so she can travel freely and unnoticed. It could work, I guess, but then I will have nothing that is mine and mine alone. On the other hand, how well could it possibly work? I don't always have the time to explain my plans to my boss, let alone get approval from Sam. She's going to want to talk about everything and see it from every angle. What if she objects to the target for emotional reasons?*

Samantha interrupted his private session with a less serious question. "Well, what do you think, big boy? Can we do a deal here, or what?"

Chase finally allowed a small smile to creep onto his face. He really loved this woman. His was a battle with himself and with his sense of duty. He recognized this, and once he did, his defenses melted.

"We can do a deal. I must warn you that you may not like how I live when I'm on the road. I'm not on vacation and I keep strange hours, and I'm messy, really messy. However, your help would be nice and being together would please me a lot."

She smiled that warm and wonderful smile back to him, and then she walked up and hugged his head to her chest. A half-hour later, as they both lay on the bed, contentedly looking up at the seventeenth-century beams, he softly kissed her shoulder. "This is going to be a fine, fast ride, Mrs. Chase. I hope you are ready."

-40-

Europe

Interpol and the FBI were trying desperately to build a profile of the hackers and to identify potential persons of interest. This was like looking for the proverbial needle in a haystack. These hackers were all anonymous. They almost never met in person, preferring the safety of the internet to physical contact. Some members of PLL were suspected criminals from the former Soviet Union countries and the more advanced nations in Asia. These were people who feigned support for a cause, but who were only interested in obtaining financial information for a quick, untraceable raid on a financial institution. They were parasites two times over. They used the combined skills of a network of socially concerned hackers to achieve a score on a bank for personal gain only. Every network had them, and it was considered a cost of doing business by the more dedicated revolutionaries. Over time, what goes around comes around.

Andreas was a true revolutionary. He and Bekka believed they could break the capitalist system completely if they had enough time and computing power. To gain what they wanted, they relied on a network of hackers that included Boris Gridenko, who used the name Sputnik2 for his online work. Andreas didn't much care what his fellow workers did with the information they extracted. However, he insisted that they post how they broke a security system on a well-used bulletin board so that all the knowledge could be shared. Boris, barbarian that he was, always complied by posting his conquests on the BigBoard for the whole community to see. His latest message read: broke the back of Commerzbank, details follow.

Boris had worked his way inside of deposit records belonging to more than twenty thousand mostly blue-collar workers at a major German auto manufacturer. He had come away with account numbers and passwords that allowed him to liberate at least a million euros. He didn't boast about how much he had stolen on the bulletin board posting. He simply provided details of the successful attack and how he had done it. This was all the hacker community wanted to know anyway.

Most of the modern intrusion-detection systems used a technique called signature detection to match known malware addresses with the address trying to access a system. The best systems could identify that an intrusion was under way and automatically reconfigure the security software to block the attempt. Really skilled hackers were adept at keeping the initial access attack far below the frequency threshold necessary to trigger an alarm, and thereby avoid whatever defensive measures the system was designed to activate. They used hijacked computers from all over the world to maintain a fresh supply of seemingly innocent IP addresses. The CIA system that Andreas was trying to breach had reactive measures that could detect when a password search was under way and then temporarily scramble all valid passwords to stay ahead of the attack. With massive computing power it could be outpaced, but this was difficult to achieve. Most garden-variety hackers worked with powerful software, but their computing power was limited. Andreas and the other professional-grade hackers did not limit themselves to the hardware they could buy themselves. They borrowed whatever power they needed from unsuspecting owners and could cobble together the capacity of a near-supercomputer almost anytime they needed to.

Eric Smith had helped to design the multilayered intrusion-detection software that was protecting the CIA's secrets. He employed two techniques to prevent intrusions. The first was meant to capture the casual hacker who used software to query sites until his computer hit on a live connection. Eric inserted a honeypot in all his software that would provide an easy and almost irresistible route for a would-be attacker who was only searching for excitement. It was a trap and would lure the unsuspecting person into a dead end, and one that would provide the IP address where it originated. These were the easy ones to catch. For the most skilled attackers, Eric had designed trace-back software that could, while sending packets to the intruding computer, slowly identify the sequence of routers being used, and if the flow lasted long enough, identify the IP address at the source. It worked well with the layered software because, to succeed, an intruder needed to receive multiple packets of information back at his host computer. If the session continued long enough, Eric would win most of these challenges.

While Andreas was meticulously careful, Boris Gridenko was not. The day after his conquest of Commerzbank, he boasted of his success on an obscure dark-web bulletin board that was run covertly by a CIA analyst. This site had been carefully designed to be genuine and uber-hip, and it was considered one of the places a top operator needed to be seen. The Agency never directly acted on what was posted there, no matter what the threat. It was used to massage the egos of the elite cyber-terrorist community. The CIA wanted users to feel completely secure—protected enough to talk about anything. It was used by a small group of hackers, and this exclusivity made all the worst characters want to be members. The board was hosted by none other than Ron Tolar, who was the only member of Merrill's counterintelligence team with both the intellect and ego to match the world's best.

-41-

Cyberspace

At times, Tolar operated in his own secret and independent world. Much of what he was doing on the internet was not reported in detail back to Director Merrill. Tolar had spent most of his recent free time building an elaborate, yet deceptively simple trap. With the nearly unlimited financial backing of the CIA, and Merrill's quiet support, he had created a bogus bank site with files containing debit card numbers and passwords that he intended to use to trap an elusive unnamed opponent. The files contained fifty thousand debit card records, with each account holding relatively small balances, generally no more than seven hundred dollars. It would be enough of a prize to attract interest. He rigged the file so that one out of every eight accounts would be impossible to access, and he did so with a simple algorithm that selected those files that would fail, to fail randomly. This way, his target would simply assume that the accounts did not contain enough money to allow the specified withdrawal, or that the password had been changed recently. In total, the setup would cost the CIA no more than three or four million dollars, and that was if the hacker could clean out all the accessible accounts. That was unlikely. Even at full price it would be a bargain. If they could catch a significant person, he or she would lead them to much, much more.

Tolar phoned in his weekly report to Reynolds Merrill. "Chief, the trap has been set and the bait looks nice and fresh. I have a person of interest in mind, and I'd like to give it a go."

"Nice work, Ron. Tell me more."

"Well, we think that a dude named Sputnik2 has been raiding a lot of piggy banks lately. He likes to hack and extract credit card data and then make a quick withdrawal. He always posts his victories on the BigBoard with details of how he broke the security. He also seems to be involved in some of the PLL hacks, so he may lead us to bigger fish, maybe even the one who is trying to slam our system. The PLL uses a lot of freelancers, and the group seems to be indifferent toward how dirty they are. I think I can capture an ID on Sputnik2 if he's greedy enough to spring the trap. I've set up the debit card file so that it looks like a slightly older system, like a smaller bank might still use. He will need to move the data in reduced packets and each time he does, I will get a little closer to him. If we get lucky, I might be able to locate his computer and maybe the man himself at the keyboard."

"Ron, for the sake of discussion, if we had a surveillance team at the ready in his city, say within ten or fifteen minutes of his location, do you really think we might be able to catch him at work?"

"Yes, sir, I think that might be possible. The man has some cash right now. Based on previous posts, he seems fond of showing off in the club district of Moscow and in Monaco. He doesn't mind blowing it all and starting over. These two locations seem to be favorites of his. However, he can work from anywhere. Hell, you might find him sitting next to you in a Starbucks in D.C., drinking an espresso while he loots the next bank."

"Ron, I trust you completely with the Agency's money." Reynolds laughed. "For the sake of safety, I want to have a few more locations covered. Where else does he travel?"

"He mentions those cities a lot, and Paris and London should be on the list too. Both host a lot of the Russian underworld, and I am betting that the name Sputnik2 is meaningful. He is a Russian, and he circles the globe as he wishes. He is not the type to fear getting caught. When you find him, he'll be right out in the public view."

Merrill hung up the phone and began to build a game plan. He had assets in each of the cities that Ron Tolar had mentioned, and a few more besides. *Why take unnecessary risks?* He decided to cover all four cities named by Tolar, plus Rome, Berlin, and New York. He dialed the man with no job description and outlined what he wanted done.

-42-

Paris

Chase received instructions only minutes before his morning run. The text was one short line.

Monaco—now.

He turned to Sam and said, "Game on, not here—in Monaco. I'll arrange flights to Nice. Can you be ready to leave within an hour?"

Samantha smiled and nodded. Chase immediately fired up his tablet and touched the Air France icon. They could easily make a flight leaving de Gaulle in three hours. He made the separate reservations and used two credit cards he used only sparingly. Paying for flights was the one exception to his cash-only policy. He had several credit cards issued in various names, each with a matching identity. He used them on occasion to avoid the extra security checks that cash buyers at the airport had to endure. For this trip, his name would be Bernard Jameson, a British subject residing in Paris. Passport, tickets, and credit card would all match. The passport was genuine, but the holder didn't exist. It had been a gift from Her Majesty's government to the CIA, a common courtesy between the two spy agencies. The downside would be that MI6 would know where he was. That might invite interference, as the curious British spies tried to find out what Uncle was doing. It was a game, but one he didn't want to play today. Samantha could travel under her own name and escape any surveillance. That was unless she was seen with him. He would make sure that this wouldn't happen.

Chase sat down with Sam to share with her the rules of the game. "For this project we need to be two independent travelers. You will be most useful if no one can attach you to me. I will be using a British identity, and someone may decide to tag along after me to see what's up. If we're careful, we can meet in the evenings in one room or the other, but in public, we will need to work separately."

Samantha frowned a bit when she heard the news. She was hoping for a real honeymoon on the Côte d'Azur. "So, what are we doing in Monaco?"

It was a fair question to which Chase had no ready answer. "I am being positioned there for a possible intervention, although I don't know yet who I'll be watching. Sometimes, nothing happens. Usually it means that the target has not yet been identified. My guess is that the Agency is still trying to discover who it is. When the instructions come, you will be the first to know. When that happens, we will need to move fast and sure."

Samantha took a cab alone to the Gare du Nord, one of the train stations where the Charles de Gaulle Airport train departed. She would sit by herself on the flight. Chase took the Métro down into old Paris and then walked up to a hotel and waited for a taxi. They both arrived at the airport about the same time, and alone. Chase was correct in his assumption that the MI6 would have a slight curiosity about why this special passport was now in use. A man from the British embassy snapped his photo with his phone on a signal from the agent at the Air France check-in counter. He then sent the image to his counterpart in Nice, walked out of the terminal, and went home. Jameson, whoever he was, would be met and followed upon arrival at the Côte d'Azur Airport. Neither of these lower-level operatives would have the slightest idea why. It was a job.

Chase figured that if Monaco was the destination, his target would be drawn to the Casino de Monte-Carlo, where big bets could be placed in private games. He picked a hotel not too far from the center of the action, which in tiny Monaco could mean almost anywhere. The Principality of Monaco was only about as large as a medium-sized Kansas wheat farm, though much more densely packed with people, and infinitely more valuable. He wanted to be able to reach the casino within a five-minute walking time, so he chose a three-star tourist stop where lots of people came in and out, and no one cared. He texted the reservation to Samantha and told her to take the express bus from the airport. He would come on the next bus. In the meantime, he wanted to see if he had a minder assigned to him.

Chase was skilled at making a watcher reveal himself. He had an hour to kill before the next bus to Monaco, so he did his usual rope-a-dope. First, he went into a bar, still on the concourse, and ordered a beer. As he barely sipped the drink, he made a mental note of everyone who entered after him. The airport was moderately busy at this time of day, and he counted twenty-seven new patrons after he entered. He memorized each of their faces. Then, after a suitable wait, he casually walked to the nearest newsstand and did the same thing. After a full forty-five minutes of this routine, he was pretty sure that he had a follower. To make certain, he walked briskly out of the secure area and stood by the now empty baggage carousel, as if his bag had simply not yet arrived. His minder was following him at flank speed, and when he burst into the arrivals hall he skidded to a stop and quickly looked up at the baggage claim monitor. It was the tall, ruddy chap with the ginger hair, as he had guessed in the bar. Chase did one of his inside smiles: better to know who your enemy is, and your friends. He looked in another direction and located the baggage office behind the carousel. When he emerged a few minutes later, he had his tail exactly where he wanted him. Chase walked outside to the bus marked CANNES and boarded.

Chase sat down in the first row, across the aisle from the driver. The agent tailing him also boarded and moved deeper into the interior, near the back of the almost-full bus. Chase leaned over to the driver and said a few words in French. Then he handed him some cash. None of this was observed by the watcher who was still seating himself. As the bus was ready to depart, the driver stood up and began to walk slowly toward the rear, checking tickets. He was a large man, and he filled the aisle. It took him a leisurely ten minutes to work his way back to where the British agent sat. By then, Chase had already descended unnoticed from the vehicle and was now seated in the bus to Monaco, which departed almost immediately. Chase knew that they would most likely reacquire him in time if they decided to widen their search. However, this little maneuver might give him enough freedom to complete his assignment without any unwelcome assistance.

-43-

Washington, D.C.

Reynolds Merrill was not the type to bet on only one horse in any race. He trusted and respected Tolar's abilities, but he also decided that it might be worth opening another pathway to see if he could speed up the process of identifying the hacker. Reynolds called an old adversary from the KGB who now worked in the security services of the new Russian Federation. Alexander Popov had reached the military rank of colonel before the Soviet Union suddenly disintegrated. At the time, he had been in command of internal security for the area that included Moscow, a prestigious posting for such a young officer. After the formation of the new Russia, he was appointed to build and lead the anticyber-terrorism department of the newly formed FSB, still his current position.

Merrill had Popov's cell phone number, and the two men talked every month or so, making trades with information. This time it was Merrill who needed a favor.

"Sasha, old friend, has winter finally arrived in Moscow?"

"Reynolds, it is nice to hear from you again, and so soon too. Yes, we are freezing our newly capitalist asses off here in Moscow. The winters were warmer when we were all communists. Or so they seemed. Perhaps it was only the cheap vodka the state provided. So, tell me, what new adventure is your president contemplating to make our simple lives more difficult?"

That question was an invitation for Merrill to make his request. He cautiously waded in. "Sasha, I think we have someone of value that you might want to acquire. He is presently in Thailand." He was referring to the recently captured big-league arms dealer whom the Kremlin badly wanted to bring in from the cold and keep imprisoned in a nice, secure dacha for the rest of his life. "I'm in the market for a hacker you might know something about. He goes by the name Sputnik2. It may be possible to make a trade."

Merrill had just offered Popov one of the crown jewels. The man he referred to was a former Soviet infantry officer who had subsequently built a multibillion-dollar business hawking aging Russian arms to the highest bidder. Mostly, this meant that the weapons went to help fuel the bloody revolutions, counterrevolutions, and never-ending tribal violence in Africa. The Russians wanted this man back in their control above all others on earth. He knew secrets, too many secrets.

Popov didn't hesitate for even a second. The proffered exchange was inequitable and therefore, suspicious, but the prize was worth the risk to the Russian. "Reynolds, is this a serious offer? If so, there may be a way to make this work if we can move with some haste. You understand how quickly priorities can change. One minute a man is alive, the next he gets sick and dies. It happens all the time."

Reynolds understood perfectly well what Popov was saying. This most valuable of trading cards could have an accident in prison, and then he would have nothing to deal with. The Russians had been trying to reach this man and would not hesitate to kill him if that proved to be expedient. "Yes, Sasha, this should be considered a serious offer. We want to know who Sputnik2 knows. We don't plan to harm him. You can have him back after we talk to him if you wish."

"Thank you for the offer, Reynolds, but we know where to find him. It is better for us if he thinks he is free. Let him go after you are finished. When would you like to make the trade? You do understand that we must inspect the goods before anything happens."

"Sasha, I am going to need the identity and a photo of the hacker today. I can arrange the handoff of your package within twenty-four hours. I need you to trust me to deliver."

"Ah, my old friend, trust is a fragile and perishable substance. It has a short half-life, you know. It has never been found in abundance in the relations between our two countries." Popov let a moment of silence happen.

Then he continued, and now in a less serious tone. "I am toying with you, my friend. I will trust you because you, of all men, understand the prohibitive cost of mistrust. The man you seek goes by the name of Boris Gridenko. He'd been in Monaco for three days. I will send you a photo momentarily. I don't really care what happens to him, but please let me know if you toss him back into the pond. I will expect instructions for picking up our package before this time tomorrow. I know you will not disappoint me. And Reynolds, before you hang up, just out of curiosity, what has this man done that he has become so valuable to you?"

"It's not him we're after. It is someone we think he knows. That is all I can tell you."

Merrill hung up the phone and let the enormity of the price he'd agreed to sink in. The one satisfaction he had was that the Russians would never allow the arms dealer to leave the country again. In a certain sense, one prison was as good as another. The man was a bargaining chip, nothing more. He phoned Director William Hughes to explain the deal he'd made. Then he called the man with no job description and told him to set one hound loose.

-44-

Monaco

Chase received his new marching orders in a brief text message.

Boris Gridenko, Russian national, photo attached. Likes
nightlife and high-stakes games. This is urgent.

Chase felt a surge of life returning to him, and his mind immediately went to work on a plan. *Unless this guy owns a villa here, he will be staying in one of only a few exclusive hotels.* On a hunch, he looked up the number of the Hermitage, a favorite of wealthy Russian visitors, and asked for Mr. Gridenko, first name Boris. The clerk took only a few seconds to respond. "I'm sorry, Mr. Gridenko is not accepting outside calls. You may leave a message, and I will make sure it is delivered to him."

Chase declined and thanked the young lady for her help. "I will be seeing Mr. Gridenko later today. What I have to say can wait."

Chase called Sam on her cell phone. "The game is on. I'm sending you some information right now." He forwarded the picture of Boris and asked her to walk over to the Hermitage and have a seat in the lobby.

"If you think you have been there too long, move into the bar and ask for a drink to be brought to you. Don't stay in any one place more than ten minutes. Look beautiful," he added. "Ring my phone twice if you see him leave. No message; ring the phone and leave after him. Don't try to follow him. Just walk away. I'll call later to set up our next steps."

Chase hurried over to the Hermitage and walked through the lobby to the pool area. He didn't look in Sam's direction. He didn't see Boris by the pool, so he walked outside and found a location in the shelter of the shade trees in the small park out front, from where he could discretely monitor the main entrance of the hotel. It was about four o'clock in the afternoon, and the warm early winter sun was about to put him to sleep.

As he was scanning the area in front of the hotel, he saw Boris walking arm-in-arm with a beautiful creature at least fifteen years younger than himself. She was wearing a closely fitting dress which revealed most of her substantial physical assets, and she was carrying a few bags from some of the most exclusive shops in Monaco. *Ah, the shopping day foreplay. Boris must be doing rather well if is spending that kind of money.* Each bag contained an item or a trinket with a price tag that probably exceeded ten thousand euros. He dialed Sam and asked her to walk out the door in about five seconds.

"Take a good look at both, but don't stare. Remember her face. Smile nicely at Boris, as though he's the most interesting man in the world. Then go to the café on the avenue on the far side of the casino, it's called the Café de Paris. I'll be nearby. I will text you."

For Samantha, this whole setup seemed a little overdone. Her husband, and lover, was sitting two tables away, facing so that she could only see one side of his head. She wanted so much to go over and hug him. She knew that she couldn't, so she nursed her flute of Prosecco and waited for him to contact her. Her phone vibrated, and she looked down to see a new message.

> You are in the clear. Casino night—I will come by your room in about an hour. I have a plan.

> So do I.

She sent back.

It was considerably less than an hour later when Chase carefully checked for traffic in the corridor outside his room and took the stairs up two floors to Sam's door. As soon as she let him in, he understood how hard it was going to be working together as a covert team. Sam pulled him through the door and pressed herself into him while kissing him as though this would be the last time they would ever make love. He did not resist. He could not resist. She owned him, and he was as happy in her arms as a new puppy.

Thirty minutes later they both lay glistening on the bed, enjoying the memory of the other. Chase's rational side had tuned out for a short while, and now it flipped back on. The casino scene did not really start until after eleven, and so they had time for another round. He rolled back over, partly astride her and kissed her softly.

They got up after the sun had set. It was still only seven-thirty, so he asked Sam to order room service. He didn't need much, but a little food would help him stay alert. She ordered grilled quail stuffed with risotto, a large salad, and a bottle of mineral water. It was a perfect meal for one. When the food arrived, it was Samantha who met the waiter and signed the check. Chase was nowhere in sight.

Chase moved into his micromanager mode as he outlined what he wanted to do that evening. He expected Boris to take his girl to bed, then to dinner, and finally to the casino, which would feed his deepest need. At that point, he might send her off on her own to play and he would concentrate on poker, the game he loved most. Boris certainly had some amount of money remaining from his last score, and if enough, it could take him to the private tables where Chase and Sam would not be allowed to follow. He counted out all his cash and divided it between himself and Sam. They each would have ten thousand euros to play with, and as much as that seemed right now, they would need to focus their bets carefully to make it look like they belonged at the big tables.

"Sam, you cover roulette and Baccarat Chemin de Fer. It's a game not much different than Blackjack or Twenty-one. If Boris sits down at a table to warm up and test his luck for the night, which a lot of gamblers do, then try to join the same table after anything that looks like a win for the Russian." She was to act clueless and carelessly rich. On the first hand she would bet a thousand euros and, if she lost, she would act as though that was nothing. Then she would play one more hand with the same bet and, win or lose, move to another table where Chase would already be playing. Chase asked that she smile at Boris as she departed, however repugnant that might be. There was little doubt he would follow, for at forty-two, Samantha was breathtakingly beautiful and sensual.

Sam looked at him and smiled. "That part will be easy, but what if he starts to ask questions. Who am I?"

"I will leave that back story to your imagination. Give him enough to want more. And . . . make it consistent. He is a careful man, even with the ladies."

Sam smiled at this last comment. Chase had only a fragmentary understanding of the episodes of her life that had brought them together. Stories were her domain and she knew how to spin one and keep the individual parts consistent. She also knew how to handle herself in heavy traffic. *One day, my love, I will need to tell you all.*

-45-

Monaco

Chase returned to his room. He was still a little nervous about the possibility that the British intelligence officers would reacquire him and muck up his assignment. He texted Control.

> Can you have the Brits stand down?
> I am very close to completion.

The reply came back in minutes:

> Consider it done.

Then he asked for the delivery point. It would be a private yacht that had only today arrived in the harbor. He called a local car-and-driver service and booked a small limo for the night. He told the dispatcher that he and his companions would be at the casino most of the night and would need to be at the yacht harbor in the early morning. The driver would need to be prepared to work until dawn. From the response he got, this was not an unusual request in Monaco.

As he dressed for the evening, he went over every detail of his plan. He had little doubt that Boris would end up in a high-stakes private poker game before the night was over. There were two possible extraction points and both involved Samantha. The first would be almost too easy and therefore less likely. Boris would follow Samantha to the Chemin de Fer table where Chase would be waiting. After a few draws, he would let slip that a group of wealthy players were gathering for a game on a private vessel. They would get into the car and that would be it. Even Chase thought that this would be too obvious; however, it was always difficult to read gamblers. They were an unpredictable lot, moving one way or another to follow their hunches and winning streaks. The second option was almost bulletproof. Boris would play poker in a private game at the casino, and after either winning or losing hundreds of thousands of euros, he would emerge before dawn and walk a hundred yards back to his hotel. If Samantha happened to be exiting the casino at the same time, he would be trapped like a bee on honey. Either way, Chase figured they would have him.

After dressing, he stuffed his large-denominated euro notes into his jacket pocket, along with two auto-injectors containing the powerful, short-acting sleep agent he always kept with him. Each one guaranteed one hour of undisturbed slumber. He carried them on all his assignments. There were times when he had been tempted to use one himself to overcome the persistent insomnia that came with his constant travels. However, these two were reserved for Boris and anyone else who happened to interfere with the snatch. It was now 11:55 P.M. and approaching showtime.

The Casino de Monte-Carlo is an exceptional place to visit, especially at night when the games are underway, and the glittering clientele are pushing tall stacks of chips across the tables. Everyone looks like they are rich, although only a few are. The men wear tuxedos or expensive suits, and the young women companions tend toward costly low-cut dresses that allow the croupiers and dealers otherwise unachievable views for a few fleeting seconds. These days the tourists come early and play the machines. The real players arrive after fashionably late dinners and come to play with larger stakes, after the German and British middle managers and their wives have gone to bed. A bit after midnight, the action is riveting. Fortunes are won and lost. This is when Chase and Samantha came to play with their small stakes.

They entered the casino separately and moved to their agreed upon positions. A bit after midnight plus thirty, Boris appeared alone. He may have tired of his young companion, or perhaps she of him. He was rumored to be a serious gambler, and that description said it all. He couldn't go to the big games with a near-teenager hanging onto his arm, even if she oozed sexual energy. It was important to have the right look. Unfortunately, Boris had the appearance of a city hood made rich. He couldn't shake the tough look of the streets no matter how elegant his clothing. Some people could never escape what they were. Boris was one of those. He was nice looking, even handsome, but with a cruel aspect to him that didn't encourage small talk, even if that were possible. He was a hard man and perhaps more dangerous-looking than Chase had expected. He was, after all, reported to be a computer hacker, not a hit man. Still, Chase felt warned and he took this to heart. Boris had the cold, dead eyes of a killer.

As Chase expected, Boris entered the room and looked over the expanse of tables, searching for a gathering of players that indicated some action. Not seeing much, he made his way to a Chemin de Fer table that held four players and a croupier. He pulled a stack of five-hundred-euro chips out of his jacket pocket and sat down to play. The seat to the right of the first player—who was the designated banker for the hand—was empty, and he claimed it. It would give him the opportunity to bet before anyone else, which was the position he always preferred. The player in the first position could absorb the full amount of any bet offered by the banker, thus turning the game into a two-person contest. At times this could be advantageous. Everyone else at the table would then become unwilling spectators until they were allowed to cover part of the banker's bet.

The croupier looked at each player and was given a slight nod that indicated they were all ready to play. He pushed the shoe to his right, to a rosy-faced Englishman wearing an overtly patriotic tie. He was now the banker for this hand. He could keep the honor if he wished. He pushed a thousand euros into the square reserved for the banker's bet. Boris pushed forward two chips and covered the bet completely. Four cards were carefully slid out of the shoe—facedown—two for each player. Boris flipped his cards over to reveal a seven and an ace, a natural eight. The banker started to perspire, only a few tiny beads showing on his temple. He demanded loudly, "Card," and then dealt himself one more, this time faceup. It was a four. A big smile lit up his round pink face as he turned up his hole cards, which were a king and another four. His total also came to eight, the face card being discarded in this game. It was a *coup*, a draw. The hand would be replayed.

Boris was already bored with this game and with the company at his table. His gaze wandered across the room to where Samantha was sitting radiantly at a roulette table. She wasn't looking his way, but he smiled anyway. *That is someone I must meet.* The banker dealt the cards again, with the two men playing the same bet. Boris looked at his hole cards, a jack and a three. He said politely, *"Une carte,"* and a six appeared in front of him. He watched the banker draw a two and then held with what he had. Both players flipped over their down cards. The banker had a total of seven to Boris's unbeatable nine. Boris collected his winnings from the shaken man to his left. He looked up in time to see Samantha take a seat two places to his right and give him a discreet, and beautiful smile. Players frequently moved around from table to table, trying to find one that looked luckier than theirs. Common wisdom was that it often paid to bet alongside winners.

The Brit took a more aggressive position and pushed two thousand euros across the table. Boris, in a gesture toward at least one of his fellow players, bet only five hundred. The man between Boris and Sam bet the same. Samantha pushed five two-hundred-euro chips to the space in front of her and smiled a thank-you to Boris. The cards were dealt. Once again, Boris had a natural eight and flipped the cards over as the game required. Samantha looked at her cards, a five and a three, and did the same. The banker now faced two naturals and could avoid a loss only with an eight or a nine. He spoke the obligatory "a card," again in English, and dealt himself a king. His hole cards were two threes, for a total of sixteen, less the now irrelevant ten gave him six points in total. He shoved the shoe roughly in front of Boris, muttered something unflattering about Russians ruining the Côte d'Azur, and stormed away from the table. Boris looked in his direction and said something more chilling in Russian in return. Samantha saw a brief flash in his eyes of something that frightened her. She shivered. Boris was now the dealer. It only took two hands for Samantha to give back her winnings plus another thousand euros. To achieve this, she had to throw away a winning hand with a theatrical sigh that fooled everyone at the table. On cue, she got up and walked past two empty tables to where Chase was now sitting, his gaze fixed on Boris. Boris didn't even notice him. His eyes were already elsewhere. He passed the shoe, excused himself, and followed Sam to the new game.

-46-

Back at Langley, Eric Smith was ready to restart his system. For the past twelve hours, he and his staff had done what they could in such a brief time to bolster the available defenses. It was the middle of the night in Europe, and he hoped that his opponent needed sleep as much as he did.

***

Andreas did not need sleep, but he was currently occupied with a new challenge. Even revolutionaries needed a little money to live on, so he was preparing to breach a bank system and steal some cash. He had received the information from Boris, one of the few hackers in his network he had met in person. The deal he struck with him was to split the loot fifty-fifty, and Boris would, from his share, pay the commission to the original source of the allegedly stolen information. That source was Ron Tolar and he hadn't stolen anything; he had invented it.

Andreas didn't expect to need help to break into the bank; however, he asked Rebekka to come with him, more for her company than for anything else. Bekka was extremely competent and creative. She could do virtually everything he could do, but she was not quite as ruthless. She would not be happy that he was taking time from important matters to extract account information from a bank, although she had a practical side too. Money bought anonymity and this, in turn, kept them safe and free.

To succeed quickly in this attack, they needed bandwidth, and Andreas preferred a computer that could not be traced back to where they lived, or places they frequented. They had an acquaintance who was a graduate student in software design at the Goethe University in Frankfurt. In truth, he was more interested in dating Bekka than in helping Andreas. He had access to a private neutral site with exceptional technology and complete anonymity. It was perfect for their needs. They planned to start work at two A.M. local time. Andreas figured it would take three hours, tops. They would be done and out of there before Europe woke up.

Bekka was the first through the firewall and into the system. "Andreas, I am inside and ready to begin moving data. As you promised, we have access to the accounts and to the files containing the passwords. It would be safer if we simply made as many cash transfers as we need right now. We don't need to try to extract all the data."

"You're right, Bekka. However, today we have a silent partner who provided us with all the information. My deal with him was that we would maximize the amount of money moved. If we spend our time making account-by-account withdrawals right now, I think we'll only get part of the money. If we copy the data without leaving any fingerprints, we can come back time and again, and do much more damage."

Across the Atlantic, Ron Tolar watched with fascination as his trap was easily tripped. *These guys are good!* He'd designed the databases so that only a thousand records at a time could be accessed and copied. It was a tactic intended to require multiple data movements, each one getting him a little closer to the perpetrator. Each new request carried information from the routers used to send the data to the requestor's location. He called Reynolds Merrill and told him the game was on.

"Ron, can you shut this down at any time before the money is actually moved?" he asked.

"Yes, sir, but why would we want to do that?"

"This is a little premature, but I think we may have found your Sputnik2 through another channel. I will know if we have him in custody within a short time. He's under surveillance right now, and he is definitely not using a computer to do anything."

"Sir, if my guy is not doing this, then we may have a chance to nab someone else in the network. I still think we should get what we need before we slam the door shut."

Reynolds thought for a second or two and then replied, "You're right, Ron. As soon as you learn as much as you can, shut it down and save the cash for another day."

Rebekka was about half-finished moving the data they needed. "This is an ancient system," she smirked. "I guess the old idea of security was to make the data transfer as slow and laborious as possible."

Andreas was in his private world now, reengaging with the CIA system that had gone dark halfway across the world. At first, what Bekka said did not register with him. It took about fifteen seconds for his threat sensors to come to life. "Bekka, shut it down immediately! Don't argue; turn off your computer now." He closed his laptop and stood up abruptly. "We need to get out of here." Bekka wanted to ask why, but in her rapidly beating heart, she knew that it was something bad. Together, they exited the building with haste.

Ron Tolar was enjoying watching his trap spring shut. It was the culmination of weeks of demanding work. Suddenly, he looked at his screen and yelled, "They know!" He looked on as his tracer data continued to flow in. By the time he was finished, he would know where they had been, but not where they were now.

-47-

Frankfurt

Bekka and Andreas walked briskly back toward their apartment across the river from the central train station. It was only about ten blocks, and they were making the trip in record time. After a few minutes of silence, Andreas was the first to speak.

"It was a trap. I should have been paying closer attention. I got distracted. That dirtbag Boris set us up. I will take care of him later."

She could see that Andreas was fuming inside. He was unfailingly in control, invariably right. She felt like such a lightweight. *How could I not have recognized what was happening?* The files were set up to maximize the number of transfers, making them far easier to trace than with a single movement. *Still, the best they will be able to do is pinpoint the university lab. Andreas will take care of any loose ends, and the trail will end there.*

As he walked in silence, Andreas was already planning what he needed to do next. The graduate student would need to disappear. It was unfortunate but necessary. He could identify them, and he wouldn't understand the need to protect that information. Andreas wouldn't do it himself, of course, but he knew who to call to erase this connection to himself and Bekka. Next, he would deal with that lowlife Boris. He would take care of him personally and with pleasure. He wouldn't need to use violence, only some information that Boris himself had provided. Boris would end up in a German prison where he could spend his next three years fending off unwanted sexual advances by the other inmates. *A very fitting punishment for such a creep,* he thought.

***

Tolar completed his tracking process and called Merrill. "Sir, we traced the attempt to the computer science department at Goethe University in Frankfurt. We won't find the hacker there, although we may be able to find some leads. He's going to start erasing his footprints as soon as possible. He's probably already doing it. If we wait until tomorrow, I'm afraid it will be too late. I'm sure he knew he was being observed. He stopped midtransfer. He broke off the connection. I recommend that we get someone there right now."

Merrill hung up and called the CIA station chief at the U.S. embassy in Berlin. He reached the duty officer and gave him clear and urgent instructions to wake the chief and give him a message. A special request must be made immediately to the German Federal Police for assistance on a matter of national security. They would cooperate fully without asking too many questions. By morning, a team of investigators would blanket the computer science department and interview everyone who had access during the evening hours. Now it would be a footrace between Andreas and the German police.

***

Back at their shabby apartment, Andreas opened his computer and began to plan his revenge. His most urgent need was to silence the graduate student who had let them use the university computer lab. It was unfortunate that he needed to disappear, but Andreas could see no other solution. He was still so angry over the apparent betrayal by Boris that he decided to take care of him first. This decision would save one person's life, but perhaps not that of another. Andreas kept a private file on each of the freelancers who assisted the PLL from time to time. Boris's file contained a detailed list of his electronic break-ins and thefts, including copies of his posts after the fact. He bundled this information into a new file, and then he added Boris's full name and picture. It would be easy for the Russian security services to find him, or Interpol if he was still coming to the West as often as he did not long ago. Once the package was completed, he posted it on several bulletin boards for the world to see. "That should take care of the Russian," he muttered.

Satisfied with his effort, Andreas was about to return to the matter of the hapless grad student when he received a reminder that the site that had gone dark was now back up. He couldn't resist the urge to play with it. "Bekka, the site is up. Come help me."

For the next two hours, they retraced his steps through the first three layers. He remembered it all as if it was the path he took to school as a kid. The only change Andreas noticed was the insertion of a new honeypot. He showed the trap to Bekka and discussed how to recognize when a security system was making one way look far too inviting. They set about breaking the fourth level. Andreas tasked his network of computers with a brute force effort to find a valid password. With the computing power he had at his fingertips, it took only about an hour. He was into a new layer and he secretly hoped that this would go on forever. Whoever designed this system was brilliant and this was the most fun he had experienced in years. Sooner or later he would get inside.

It was Rebekka who found the final key. The system was now theirs. Andreas opened a few files. He couldn't believe his luck. The site contained intelligence files, probably CIA, pure gold in his world. He leaned over and kissed Bekka. Then he began to extract as many files as he could before access was cut off. One file he took carried the unassuming name LINEBACKER. It held the classified service records and the mission reports of Robert Chase and his teammates. It was never intended for public viewing.

Eric Smith was called as soon as the new attack began. He reached the center just after the last security layer was breached. He saw immediately that the hacker was extracting information and he ordered all access terminated. This was the second time in two days that he'd had to shut down the system. He asked for a damage report and then called in the unauthorized breach to his supervisor.

Reynolds Merrill received the news of the data loss within minutes of Eric's call. He asked for the names of the files stolen, and only then did he realize how great the loss had been. He immediately called the director.

"Bill, I have unwelcome news. Our computer center was breached about a half-hour ago and we lost some vital information. I think we need to be prepared to withdraw or reposition some of our assets. The hacker got two files of high value. The first was a list of civilians in China who provide unclassified information to us. The Chinese probably already suspect who they are, so a possible embarrassment, but only a minor loss. I'm most worried about the second file. It was Linebacker."

Merrill could hear the director of the CIA gasp as he mentioned the second file. No one, not a single member of Congress, not even the president, had ever heard that name spoken before. Only he and Merrill knew it existed. "Reynolds, please remind me how much information about the team was contained in the file?"

"It contains a lot. It has twenty years of mission reports, including names, dates, and places. The news outlets will only be able to embarrass us with the information. A foreign intelligence agency may be able to use the file to unmask covert assets we have used or are still using. For some officers it will be life-threatening. Most at risk will be those who are running networks in Russia, China, and Iran. If the information gets posted on some bulletin board for the world to see, we will see people suddenly disappear."

Hughes thought for a moment. "Recall the remaining team members until we can sort out the damage. I know that this is going to hurt our counterterrorism work, but we need to protect our people."

-48-

Frankfurt

Andreas read some of the individual reports carefully; he could hardly contain his excitement. It contained detailed information about American-sponsored agents around the world who, in his opinion, had conducted illegal searches and kidnappings. The mission reports were written in a cryptic style that did not always make sense to him. He knew that there were more knowledgeable people around the globe who would be able to put names and places with the actions he was reading. He just needed to get this information into their hands. This was a true treasure.

He encrypted the entire file and put it in a password-protected holding pattern on BigBoard. He prepared a second file with extracts of some of the reports he had just read. He wanted to control access to this little pot of gold. He selected one news organization each in the U.K., Germany, and the United States and sent the password for the summarized reports to the editor of each, along with a brief description of his conquest. He signed each letter "Andreas" this time. It was the first time he had ever used his own name, rather than that of the PLL, to claim credit for a release of secrets. The editor of the *New York Times* was one of the recipients. He called in the team of writers who covered national government news and set them loose to verify the developing story. One of the writers called Reynolds Merrill. They had worked together in the past.

"Director Merrill, this is Bradley Jackson from the *New York Times*. Thanks for taking my call. A file was posted on a private bulletin board this afternoon. It appears to be a list of CIA operatives and their mission reports going back for years. I'm going to assume that other news outlets received the same information, so this story is going to come out whether I report it or not. The file is code-named 'Linebacker.' Excerpts were posted on BigBoard earlier today. Have you seen this, and do you have any comments?"

Merrill had been expecting a call like this. He was glad that it was Brad Jackson who reached him first. He was a straight shooter and he would be fair in his reporting.

"Bradley, what you are referring to appears to be a highly classified file that was stolen from one of our systems by an unauthorized intruder sometime early this morning." As he was speaking, he buzzed for his assistant to come in and handed him a handwritten note that read: "Call Tolar. Shut down BigBoard website by any means."

Then he returned to his caller. "Bradley, I know that you understand that any release of classified government documents, even if come by innocently, is a slippery slope. Setting aside the national security concerns, that file contains names of our officers and reports of top-secret diplomatic missions. If this information gets out, lives will be in danger and much of what we have been doing for the past ten years to counter terrorism will be compromised."

"Yes sir, I do understand that, but the information is, for all practical purposes, out there. My not reporting on it will not put the genie back into the bottle. Can you give me a statement? I assure you that my editor is aware of his responsibilities; however, he won't consent to being scooped by another paper, and he won't simply stuff the story."

Merrill knew that Brad Jackson was right. He spent the next twenty minutes explaining that the CIA did have a covert team of agents who tracked and otherwise assisted other governments in apprehending certain international terrorists and their supporters.

"Bradley, this group was highly effective in helping eliminate criminals who have eluded all other attempts at capture. Their methods were unconventional and highly successful. I really hate seeing their tactics exposed for all to see. It will certainly weaken future efforts."

"I can see how you might feel this way," said Brad Jackson, "but all you can do is share your side of the story. The information is no longer confidential. But you have been speaking in the past tense. Are you indicating that 'Linebacker' is no longer operational?"

Merrill proceeded to spin a story that, due to budgetary pressures, the Agency had reassigned the team members to other duties, and the group no longer existed in the form contained in the file. What they had been doing had been absorbed by the Department of Homeland Security. If the full text of those missions got into the wrong hands, there would be retribution against the foreign nationals who had assisted them. He ended by saying, "In a sense, their lives are in your hands."

The next morning, the *New York Times* led with the story. The headline was: BLACK BUDGET CIA TEAM BATTLES TERRORISTS. True to his word, Brad Jackson kept some of the classified details out of the paper. His editor refused to release the names of active agents and only allowed mention of some brief details of successful ops. Included in the list of those who had died in the service of their country was Robert W. Chase. In Libertyville, Illinois an old woman gasped when she saw her missing son's name in print.

Even before the story was approved for publication, Ron Tolar mounted a massive denial of service attack on BigBoard until the Justice Department could obtain agreement from the site that the stolen information would be removed. Damage control would still be needed. Extracts of the file remained in the possession of other newspapers in the U.S. and Europe. The information could come out at any time, but for the moment, most news outlets preferred to let the *New York Times* have the credit, and the blame, for the leaked information.

-49-

In the Casino de Monte-Carlo, the sting was progressing. Samantha had walked to a new table with Boris in tow, and he was now seated next to Chase. They played five quick hands, with Chase winning two, and Boris winning the same, with one *coup*. Chase had dealt the last hand, and as he passed the shoe to Boris he said, "These games are for children. I'm going to move on."

Boris heard him and responded in kind. "I agree, small bets and little excitement. Are you going to the private rooms?"

Chase leaned over and whispered confidentially to the man. "I know of a late-night game in the harbor, on a nice boat. They play only poker. The stakes are attractive, and the players have limited skill. It is a group of rich Arabs having a good time in Monaco. They expand their game when it suits them. I won almost a hundred thousand euros last night. I'm going back in a few minutes to relieve them of some more of their money. I have a car waiting."

Boris had heard two of his most favorite words: poker and winnings in the six-figure range. "If you can wait a few minutes, I may wish to join you. That is, if it is acceptable to you. I realize we have only just met, but I assure you that I will not embarrass you."

Chase took a long minute to look him over as though he was searching for a dent on a vintage Ferrari. "I think that it would be fine, but no guns or weapons of any kind. These men are careful, and everyone who comes on board must be searched by their security guards. If you are carrying anything, I too will be denied entrance."

Boris smiled and got up from the table. "I will be only ten minutes at the most." Next, he walked over to Samantha and whispered something in her ear. She nodded and looked at Chase and winked as Boris hurried from the table in the direction of the toilets. The thing that had made Boris move so quickly was that he had observed a certain rude English gambler making his way unsteadily toward the exit from the gaming room and into the main hall. Boris had something to settle before he left the casino.

When he entered the men's room, he saw the Englishman trying to steady himself in front of a urinal, and another man drying his hands. He waited for the one to leave and then walked up behind the teetering man. With sudden ferocity, Boris slammed a massive fist hard into the man's back, just above the right kidney. The man moaned and fell to his knees, hitting his chin on the urinal's edge with a loud crack. Boris glared into his pained face and then kicked him repeatedly and viciously in the stomach and head until he fell to the floor. He stopped his attack when a flow of blood carrying several fragments of tooth began to pour out of the now unconscious man's mouth. Boris wiped his shoe on the man's shirt and went over to the mirror to straighten his tie. He walked out without a second look at his handiwork. Chase had been right: this man was a killer.

He returned to the table and smiled. He asked Chase, "Do you mind if I bring someone with me?" He nodded across the table at Samantha.

Chase looked at Sam and slowly turned back to Boris. "No, I guess not. These Arabs like beautiful women too. You may need to be on your guard." Boris just smiled coldly. It was a smile devoid of humor or happiness.

Chase got up from the table and tipped the croupier generously, a two-hundred-euro chip. Boris observed this and then did the same. Samantha came around the table and the trio, with Sam on

Boris's arm, walked out the front entrance. They could have been tycoons from anywhere in Europe; however, Sam was the one that everyone would remember.

The hired car was parked in front of the casino with the driver waiting alongside. He helped the three passengers to seat themselves in the plush Mercedes and then closed the rear doors. Chase gave him an address in the harbor, one of the docks reserved for short-stay yachts, and the car gently moved away from the curb. Chase reached into his right jacket pocket and wrapped his fingers around an auto-injector containing a fast-acting sleep drug. He flicked the protective cap off with his thumb. Boris made his job easier by turning away from him to give his full attention to Samantha. Chase brought the injector up with his right hand and smacked it firmly against Boris's neck, right on top of the carotid artery. The big Russian turned in surprise and immediately sensed that he was also in danger as he felt the effect of the sedative. He started to resist, but it was already too late. Chase pinned both of Boris's hands tightly against his chest while he struggled feebly until the drug carried him into the twilight. Chase let go of the now still hands and entered a number on his phone, speaking instructions quietly and urgently.

When they arrived at the boat, a wheelchair and two attendants were waiting for them. As the men loaded Boris into the chair, they continued speaking to him as if he was alert. Chase paid the driver and told him that it was a little too much vodka. "You know how these Russians are." The driver shrugged, regarded the extra two hundred euros he received as a tip, and drove away.

Chase looked at Samantha and said, "I am truly sorry for that."

Samantha looked back, unsmiling but not angry either. "It goes with my new job. If we are done here let's go home."

-50-

Monaco and at sea off the Côte d'Azur

Boris was carried unconscious to the lower part of the boat and left securely bound, gagged, and blindfolded in a storage locker. The boat was a nice, steel-hulled Bering trawler with a length of nearly sixty feet. The CIA rented it from time to time from a British owner who rarely took it out of its home port of Cannes. It was perfect for the use they had in mind.

As Boris slowly regained consciousness, he was immediately aware of the throbbing diesel engines. His head rested against the steel hull, and he could smell the mix of diesel fumes and mildew so often found belowdecks of a seagoing vessel. At this point, he was convinced that he was on board a real ship, and that he might be about to die. It was one of the few times in his life when he had experienced real, undiluted fear. He began to think of who might be behind this, among the nations or powerful people he had offended during his life of crime. There were too many to even begin.

He was left in his little prison for about six hours while the boat slowly plowed through moderate seas. He was seasick, and he worried constantly that he would vomit into his duct-taped mouth and choke. He began to hyperventilate. He was perspiring like an athlete in a race. The door to his locker suddenly opened and bright light flooded in. A hand ripped the tape roughly from his lips. The door slammed shut before he could say anything, and he was once more in darkness, alone with his thoughts. He couldn't tell whether the brief gesture of concern was a good sign or not. *If they really intended to kill me, they probably wouldn't have done anything to make me more comfortable.*

The trawler was only about fifteen miles off the coast of Monaco, and the captain was doing everything possible to make the little vessel take the moderate seas in the worst imaginable way. Even the boat's crew and the CIA interrogators were growing queasy. It was part of the process of making Boris cooperative, so they endured it. They intended to circle in the Mediterranean for a full twelve hours before beginning their questioning. By then Boris would believe that he had been at sea for a day or more. It was all being done to make him feel isolated and vulnerable. Each of his interrogators had gone through a similar experience during training, and they could verify that the tactic worked almost too well.

Boris was finally brought to a stateroom after more than twelve hours as sea. He would remain blindfolded and bound during the interrogation. If he needed to urinate, he would have to soil himself. He wouldn't be allowed any comforts until he gave them what they wanted. This is the way it had to be.

The lead interrogator began in Russian, "Boris Borislav Gridenko, you are charged with theft and other criminal acts. Our orders are to question you thoroughly. If you provide the information we want, you will be released in time. If you fail, we have orders to dump you into the sea. It's entirely your choice."

For Boris, the interrogation was not starting well. This last threat was especially frightening to him because he couldn't swim and often had nightmares of drowning.

"You have no authority to hold me or to question me," he protested. "I am an innocent man. Who are you people? I demand to be released." He could see he was getting nowhere, but something inside him drove him to continue. "I refuse to answer any questions; I demand to see someone from my government." *If they were going to kill me,* he thought, *they would have done it by now. They want something from me, and this is my only bargaining chip.*

"Boris, if you wish to be miserable for even longer, keep up what you are doing. We know about your involvement with the PLL and your other criminal acts. Your own people have betrayed you. We didn't have to catch you. Your friends pushed you into our net. A complete list of your crimes has been posted on an online bulletin board, along with your own boasts about how you did them. The entire world now knows what you have done. Even your friends have deserted you."

"I demand to speak to someone from the Russian embassy. It is my right!" he shouted out.

"Boris, I thought you were smarter than this. Your own government doesn't want you either. They gave us your name. They told us where to find you. We have permission to do whatever we wish with you. Don't you see? You have no friends. You have no country. We are your only hope, and to please us, you must speak now."

Boris was confused by this flurry of additional information. It is probably true, he realized. I've been trapped because someone I know has identified me. It wasn't an accident at all. It had to have been that little weasel Andreas. He knows everything about me, and he has the sort of contacts that could cause me considerable harm. I will pay him back in kind, but first I need to be free.

"What exactly do you want to know?" he asked more softly.

The interrogators used a rotating pattern, partly to keep the subject off balance, and to keep him in the dark as to the real objective of the questioning. If Boris were to understand what the interrogators really wanted, it could become a much more difficult and time-consuming process. He wasn't a dummy. Questions came from all angles, but from the interrogators' perspective, they all led back to identifying the leader of the PLL and where he or she could be found. The breakthrough came four hours into the first session. Boris, with a little coaching from his captors, was now determined to get even with Andreas, and to do so he needed to be free. He spilled everything he knew about him, but nothing that would implicate Boris himself. His questioners did not seem to care about this omission, though it was noted in their report.

When Boris finished talking, the interrogators left the room for what seemed like hours. When they returned, they asked him a few more questions and then stopped abruptly.

"If you are a good boy you will be released in a few hours. You may use the head to refresh yourself, and then you will be blindfolded again. We will not handcuff you for the return trip if you behave yourself. Your guards are well-trained and have orders to subdue you with any necessary force if you resist. I suggest you sit in a chair and relax until we reach the port. Do you understand this, and do you agree to this condition?"

Boris nodded his acceptance. He would do anything to be able to deal with Andreas himself.

-51-

Merrill ordered the remaining seven members of "Linebacker" to stand down and seek cover. This left him with only Chase in the field. Robert Chase was officially a dead man, and no one bothered to look for dead officers. He was now the perfect instrument for what Merrill had in mind.

Boris had given his captors the name of Andreas, and described his "little friend" Rebekka, though he didn't know her by name. He would have preferred not to have talked, but he understood that his freedom was at risk. He believed he could locate Andreas and deal with him long before these people, whomever they were, could find them. To throw them off the scent, he told the inquisitors that the pair was now in hiding in Berlin. What he didn't understand was that the city of Frankfurt had already been implicated, and Chase was on his way there to find the hacker.

Samantha was anticipating a holiday with Chase. Here they were in Monaco with time, money, and each other. She didn't understand yet how the river of his life flowed. Sometimes he had no time to himself for several months at a stretch. Then, just as quickly, he could be idle for the same length of time. It was not the ideal profession for carrying on a serious personal relationship, one reason why he'd never had one before he met Sam.

In the early morning hours, not so long after delivering Boris to his interrogators, Chase's cell phone chirped twice. Chase and Sam were lying under a thin duvet and deep in dreamland. It took Chase a few minutes to realize what had awakened him. He quietly slipped out of the bed and carried his phone into the bathroom. He had a new text.

You are needed in Frankfurt. We need to talk first.
Situation has degraded. Call home.

This was an unusual request. He dialed a highly classified number in Paris and was rerouted to another phone in Virginia. It was Reynolds Merrill who answered on the second ring.

"Let's not use any names," he began. "I'm not completely sure about this line. "We've had to shut down our business operations temporarily. Someone in Frankfurt posted some of our most sensitive trade secrets on a bulletin board. You are covered, but everyone else is taking a forced break. We will recover from this, but right now is a delicate time. We need you to contact the person of interest. Your Russian friend gave us a lot, and still, you'll need to do some quick work of your own. The Russian will be released sometime early tomorrow. It's not much of a head start, but it's the best we can do. He is almost certain to be looking for the same person."

"I understand," said Chase, "I'll leave immediately. And if my friend should happen to show up and start looking around?"

"Have a little talk with him. If you can use whatever he turns up, do so. Then find a place for him to chill for a while. Do not let him create a scene. Is this clear?"

"Yes, I understand completely. I will need some information to start with. Will that be forthcoming?"

"Yes, you'll have it by the time you reach Frankfurt. Be careful. This gambler friend of yours is not safe. Your hands are untied if he becomes a danger to you or the operation. Good luck!"

Chase clicked off the phone and immediately walked into the bedroom and turned on a light. Sam turned her head with a sleepy look, as if to say, "What's up?"

"We need to leave right now. There's no danger. We need to be in Frankfurt as soon as possible. I'm going to check flights while you get ready. How much time do you need?" He didn't wait for her answer.

Sam had awakened from a nice dream and was not fully alert when Chase flipped on the light. She woke up about halfway through his monologue and was alarmed. "I don't understand. What's going on?"

Chase sat down on the bed next to her and spent the next five minutes recounting his conversation with Merrill, including the information about Boris. Sam didn't look pleased. The first words out of her mouth were, "Robert, I can't face that pig again. What will we do if he shows up in Frankfurt?"

"Don't worry, Sam, I'll make sure he doesn't bother you ever again, even if I have to stop him myself. I promise."

-52-

Frankfurt

Andreas was angrier than Bekka had ever seen him. When he wasn't working at his computer, he was pacing erratically around the apartment and muttering to himself. Finally, he looked at her and said, "We need to hurt the establishment in a big way. I have an idea."

For the next hour, he talked about a way to bring serious financial pain to the parasitic international banks and their complicit governments. "We could hack into a couple major currency firms—you know, big traders—and leave them holding losses that will bring them down. Maybe we can cause the national governments so much harm that their central banks will fail too."

All foreign-currency trading houses can create shadow transactions, which are used to test their systems for speed and accuracy. It's exceedingly rare for one of these test packs to escape into the flow of real transactions, but Andreas had read that it had happened a few times before, with real gains and losses resulting from the errors. The test system and the live system were mirror images of one another, so every effort was made to keep the two apart. Once released into the transaction stream, even a test sale or purchase would look genuine.

Andreas felt that it would be possible to create, store, and then release on command a file of bogus currency transactions that could move the market enough to create huge unearned gains and losses for the traders and their banks. He didn't need to carry on the charade for more than a couple of minutes because of the incredible speed at which electronic transactions were settled. If he could move the market for even one minute, billions of dollars would be lost. In five minutes, he could shake the entire world. He didn't really care who gained or lost from his little demonstration. The point was to show the world that he could disrupt their precious banking system anytime he chose to. It was classic PLL.

Although Andreas wasn't an expert in currency markets, he was willing to bet that the greed motive was so strong that thousands of traders, mostly from the large international banks, would jump on board any moving train in milliseconds. They didn't care which direction the market moved. All had computerized trading platforms that were programmed to recognize emerging trends in narrowly defined markets and to issue buy or sell orders without the involvement of a human being. But the big bets weren't always made by computers. They were sometimes made by people who thought they were just as smart. These mighty managers might get caught in the feeding frenzy and add to the mayhem by overriding their computers and failing to exit positions when the market suddenly turned against them.

This was a cyber-terrorist's dream. In a minute or two it was possible to create incredible financial carnage. The beauty of financial market transactions is that trades were always final. There's no referee to toss a yellow flag in the air and make everyone do the play over. There are no red cards or penalty kicks. All trades are final. It was the foundation of the international market system. Andreas was about to use their own rule against them.

For their targets, Andreas and Bekka chose the venerable Swiss banking giant UBB, and a private trading partnership in the U.K. that went by the innocuous name of Broadway. Both firms were major league traders in everything from coffee to currencies. On a good day, UBB would log trades of all kinds that might equal nearly a trillion U.S. dollars. Broadway was privately held, bought out by a U.S. hedge fund a year earlier, and their currency trading business alone was rumored to involve hundreds of billions of euros and U.S. dollars each trading day.

Andreas went to work on UBB and assigned Bekka to Broadway. They first needed to see how difficult it would be to get past security and into the test systems. Andreas had visited UBB before, but for a different reason. He was confident he could slip back inside without much trouble. In their planning, they reasoned that the test system wouldn't have the same level of protection as the live production software. This was a good guess. Bekka broke through first and began searching through the files she would need. There was a firewall between the two systems; however, it did not resist her attempt to enter from the test system side. "Andreas, I'm through. Come see."

Andreas left his workstation and leaned over her shoulder, smelling her hair as he did so. Bekka was a very desirable woman, and he nuzzled his nose and mouth below her right ear as he moved in close for a look at her screen. "Not now, Andreas!" she said sternly. "Later!"

"Bekka, we have several options here. Open some files and let's see how they have been structured. See, there is the test system and it has no other security around it. There . . . go there."

Bekka pushed him off her shoulder both for space and to make a point. "I can do this work myself, Andreas. Stop crowding me. Why don't you spend some time on your own system?" He mumbled for a few seconds and then turned back to his own computer screen.

-53-

Frankfurt

The German Federal Police identified their hacking suspect shortly after eight A.M. local time. The graduate computer lab had a card entry system that maintained a record of whose card had been used to grant access in the hours before the attack. It was a doctoral student by the name of Daniel Greipel, who had no record, no history of any kind to suggest he was anything except a student. Daniel was taken into custody within an hour, and the police interrogators began questioning him about the incident. The lab security system also provided some grainy photos of Andreas and Rebekka that the police intended to use in their questioning. Copies were sent to their dispatcher, who forwarded them to the Berlin station chief for the CIA and to Interpol. It was a common courtesy between the agencies. Merrill received them and sent them on to Chase's controller. The entire transfer took only a few minutes.

Daniel willingly confessed that he'd provided access to the lab to two young students he met some months ago at a *gasthof*—a casual drinking house. He had no desire to encourage the interest being shown in him by the Federal Police. This was partly for himself, but mostly for the sake of his live-in Ukrainian girlfriend who was now illegally in Germany since her visa expired some months ago. He didn't know where the two hackers lived, but he told the police that he did know some of the places they frequented. He didn't realize they were hackers, only that they appeared to be serious software designers. He had allowed them access to the lab because they said they were working on a project. Always cautious, the police decided to hold Daniel for more questioning for at least another twenty-four hours. They were under instructions from Berlin to keep this young man out of circulation, and that was that. He could go free the next morning.

About the same time, Andreas had called Daniel's cell phone to ask another favor. "Hey man, by any chance has anyone contacted you about last night? It's not a big deal. There are some people I would rather not know. Call me as soon as you can. It's important we talk today." Andreas knew the computer lab was untouchable now, but he thought that perhaps Daniel would have another safe location they could use. He didn't know that the Federal Police had obtained a warrant to track activity on Daniel's cell phone and computer.

Those who knew Andreas well, and this was a very small group, did not consider him especially malicious or dangerous. Hackers were generally "live and let live" sorts of people. Andreas came across as a dedicated cyber-revolutionary who believed in his cause maybe a little more than most of his comrades. Still, he was a computer nerd and not a gangster, although the distinction was becoming increasingly difficult to make.

Deep in his thoughts, he was considering the risk of working with Daniel again, as well as the even greater risk that Daniel could identify him if their work last night had been traced. After a few more minutes of reflection, Andreas made a call to a man he had used a couple of times before. It was not a moral decision; it was simply business.

"Hans, this is Andreas. I need you to tidy up something for me, the same arrangement as before. Scrub the floor well." For the next two minutes, he provided the man named Hans with the essential information and address of Daniel Greipel. He had no way of knowing that his conversation was also being recorded.

The transcript of the phone call took about an hour to process and arrive on the desk of an investigator. As soon as he read it, the investigator mumbled to himself, "This looks like a hit. I know that voice—no one else talks like that." Another detective asked what he was muttering about.

"You remember that guy Hans Stumpf? He's been missing in action since the school bus incident, but I think I may have just heard him agreeing to another murder, this time here in Frankfurt." Stumpf was currently on the front page of Interpol's most-wanted persons report. He was a dedicated white nationalist who lived occasionally in Munich, although he had been born in the eastern sector of Germany. He hired himself out from time to time to revolutionary groups to do the nasty jobs that few other men or women were willing to do. Hans was a professional terrorist. He didn't care about the cause, only the pay. He was notorious for having loaded explosives on a school bus holding forty Muslim children in Kosovo in 1999, and then detonating it in front of a group of NATO negotiators, killing all aboard. He was rumored to have participated in genocides in Africa as well. He was alleged to be ruthless and without moral constraints.

After the call, Stumpf immediately made plans to leave the small village near Munich where he was currently living and travel to Frankfurt. He calculated that he could be there in less than three hours using the autobahn. Hans never used public transportation—too many security cameras in most European terminals. He was well-known and recognizable.

-54-

Frankfurt

Chase and Samantha departed Nice on a seven A.M. flight and landed in Frankfurt an hour and twenty minutes later. As before, they traveled separately, she in first class and he in coach. Samantha caught the first S-Bahn train to the central Frankfurt train station—the Hauptbahnhof, and Chase followed fifteen minutes later, after he had worked his sweep routine to see if he had anyone tagging along. He also bought a new cell phone and tossed his old one into the restroom trash can after removing and flushing the SIM card down a toilet. He paid cash.

As soon as she arrived in the city center, Sam went to the hotel that Chase had chosen and checked in. He did the same about twenty-five minutes later. He flipped on his tablet and received the email containing the pictures of Andreas and an unidentified woman taken at the computer lab. He also received a summary of the interrogation of Boris, including Andreas's cell phone number, places he frequented, and the general area in which he most likely lived. Boris had never met Andreas in his apartment; however, he was smart enough to have concluded that he lived within the vicinity of the several meeting places he frequently used. He reviewed the information for a few minutes and then called Sam using the new phone.

"Hi there! Take note of my new number. I'll be using it while we are in town. I have the details of our trip. How about a cup of coffee?"

Samantha responded, "I'm in room three-twelve in case you get lonely. I'm sitting here in my bare necessities thinking of you in a most intimate way. Any chance we can have nap time later?"

"That's my deepest desire," he replied with a private smile. "First, we have a little planning to do. There's a little café down the street from the hotel. Turn left and go about two blocks. It's on the corner of Konigstrasse. Take a table near mine, and not directly looking at my face. I'll text you."

Samantha frowned as she ended the call. She didn't understand his meeting style and liked it not one bit. Still, she trusted Chase completely, and if he thought this was important, she would accept it for now. She got dressed and took the stairs down to the street level. It was a chilly day in Frankfurt, and she wrapped a warm scarf around her neck and headed out into the brisk early winter air.

The little café was charming in the old German style. They served individual pots of coffee or tea and offered some tasty-looking pastries to accompany the beverages. Sam selected tea and a nice-looking slice of strudel topped with densely whipped cream. She sat back and waited for Chase to call her. He was seated two tables away and she noticed that he was talking in a much too friendly way with the young *fräulein* who was taking his order. She clenched her teeth and then immediately relaxed. It was all for public viewing. Chase was her guy and she knew this in a place deeper inside than she had ever known existed.

In about thirty seconds, her phone buzzed with the first text.

> The host country can listen in—in many ways. Here is safer than our rooms. No names please. I've received instructions to visit our new friend. He has a girlfriend as well. You might enjoy meeting her. Sending you a photo.

Chase sent her the security camera photos, plus a list of the places the couple might be found. She studied them for a few minutes and then sent a reply.

> I think a stroll would be nice. I'll catch up with you later. I'll let you know if I find any real bargains. If I find something nice, can I have it?

Chase was about to text "no," when he had a second thought.

Have fun but call me if you see something we both
might like. I'll join you. Have a good afternoon.

Chase left the café shortly thereafter and began the chilly walk to the university. Samantha finished her treats and left about ten minutes later. He would spend some time watching the computer lab just in case Andreas decided to make a return trip. She was going to try and locate Bekka.

After an hour or so of observing the computer lab at the university, Chase decided it was probably a dead end. *Andreas is too smart to use this place twice.* As he turned and began walking from the building that housed the computer sciences department, he was suddenly aware of someone. It was a grim man who was going in the opposite direction. He knew this face, but he couldn't quite place him. Chase turned back for a second look, but on a different walkway across the grassy quadrangle. When he turned once more he was slowly merging with this man. The man walked with a pronounced and uncomfortable limp. It looked like a hip injury from the way the man used his bad leg. His knee flexed, and on the return step the leg swung to the side as though the effort of moving straight north and south was too painful. Chase took out his Agency phone and selected the camera. He brought the phone to his cheek and then walked directly at the man, while carrying on an imaginary conversation in quiet German. He snapped a series of pictures, with the phone never leaving his cheek and moved past the man without a glance. He kept going and stopped at a bench where several pathways converged. He forwarded the photos to Control with a message.

I know this guy from somewhere. Who is he?

***

In the South of France, the boat carrying Boris Gridenko docked at the port of Marseille, where he was escorted ashore by two no-nonsense Corsicans of considerable size. He was not permitted to see the vessel, which promptly departed the port. The two guards released his arms and walked away with agility and speed. Boris decided not to follow. All that mattered to him now was that he was free.

Boris was not in a good humor. He had spent the entire return trip plotting how he was going to kill Andreas and his bitch. First, he needed to get back to Monaco to retrieve his belongings. He took a taxi to the rail station and boarded the next train east. Three hours later Boris arrived in Monaco. He went immediately to his hotel and checked out. His girl had already left, taking her presents and some cash he hadn't locked in the safe. By now he was not simply angry, he was enraged. He called a taxi and took the long and expensive ride to the Nice Côte d'Azur Airport.

***

Chase received a message that Boris was observed boarding a plane for Frankfurt, just moments before the response to his inquiry on the strange man came back. The report arrived soon after.

> Very dangerous man—repeat very dangerous—Hans
> Stumpf. Top of Interpol most wanted list. Be careful.

The message was followed by a document listing the many crimes and alleged offenses by this man Stumpf. The list was impressive in a sick and distorted sort of way. Stumpf was merciless and without conscience. His crimes went beyond senseless because he cared not at all for the cause that paid him. His presence in Frankfurt and on this campus was a most troubling thing. Chase watched him enter the same building he had been observing, and then come out again a few minutes later, showing visible irritation. He stopped and used his cell phone. Then he again walked past Chase and off the campus the same way he had come. On a hunch, Chase decided to follow him. This simply couldn't be coincidence. He texted his controller:

I may need help and a holding pen.

Control immediately sent back a phone number. His agency kept black-budget people and facilities all over Europe.

-55-

Sachsenhausen-a neighborhood of Frankfurt

Samantha had spent the afternoon poking her head into every café and bar on the list that Boris had provided during his interrogation. She did a little shopping and then repeated the search, location by location. It was already four P.M. and both the afternoon and the promise of a little romp with Chase were fast fading away. In the second-to-last café on the list, she finally saw the young woman. She was much more beautiful in person than the photo indicated. She was dressed grunge; however, her shabby-chic clothing could not hide how attractive she was. *She could be a model. What is she doing in an intrigue like this?*

Bekka was alone at a table reading a book. Every male who walked by her—and there were more than a few—looked in her direction and tried to gain her attention. She was having none of that. She was into her book and perhaps waiting for someone. Samantha took a table next to hers and ordered a small pilsner beer. She took out her phone and texted Chase.

Bingo—found the girl.

Chase was still across the river from Sachsenhausen, trailing Stumpf as the little man marched with determination toward the Hauptbahnhof. He had pulled a big woolen hat over his head that hid his facial features remarkably well. For a limping man, Stumpf could move fast. As they walked on parallel paths, Chase fired off a response to Sam.

You're on your own for now.
I can't break away quite yet.

When he reached the station, Stumpf stopped and turned to see if he was being followed. The end of the business day for the financial sector was in full flow, so Chase had the benefit of crowds of commuters to camouflage him. It was a good thing. Just as he reacquired Stumpf in the main terminal, he turned and took another careful look at the crowd behind him. Satisfied that he was not being followed, he walked over to a stand-up food provider where he met a young man. Chase suspected right away that this must be Andreas. The two men talked for about ten minutes, with Stumpf becoming more agitated as the conversation progressed. It ended in an argument. Andreas turned and walked away. Stumpf stood there fuming. Finally, he searched the faces around him one more time and then headed for the south exit from the station.

As soon as Chase saw the two men meet, he dialed the phone number given to him by Control. He requested a pickup near the Hauptbahnhof immediately. The man on the other end of the call said it would take at least fifteen minutes. Chase responded, "It needs to be much sooner than that. I will be in motion and not in a stationary position. When I have the right opportunity, I need to take this man down. Be there!" Chase could follow either of the two men, but he decided that Hans was the more dangerous.

Samantha has the young woman in in her sights; she will lead her to where Andreas lives. Right now, I need to get this killer off the street. Why does Andreas have any reason to have business with Stumpf? Can't answer that.

Chase trailed Stumpf to an exit and out onto the busy street. From his affect and his jerky motions, it looked like Hans had not yet decided which way to go. *Something has interfered with his plans and he is still figuring out what to do next.* Chase had to make a guess as to which direction he might head or be left standing alone and visible. He gathered himself into a large group waiting to cross the busy street heading toward the river Main. Stumpf made his decision and queued up behind and to the left of Chase. As the pedestrian tide moved across the street, Chase slipped back in the crowd and alerted his recovery crew of the direction he was now moving. It was still too crowded with pedestrians to attempt a snatch in daylight.

The tide of people began to thin out at each intersection, and by the time they reached the first bridge over the river, it was only the two of them and one other couple. Stumpf had forged ahead of Chase and appeared to be deep into his own thoughts. He wasn't paying attention to anything around him, which to Chase was unexpected. Stumpf was reportedly careful to a fault. He was obviously working through something important. Chase urged the snatch car into position behind him and waited to see if they could lose the couple walking fifty meters ahead of Stumpf. It wasn't going to work. Hans was quickly gaining on the couple, and once he passed them it would complicate what Chase had in mind. He called the chase car and quietly said, "Now!"

As the recovery car slowly approached the target from the rear, Chase increased his speed and overtook Stumpf on his right side, with several feet of separation and looking straight ahead, so as not to be perceived as a threat. Once he had gained a slight lead of three feet, Chase turned suddenly to intercept Hans, with the idea of quickly immobilizing him. Hans reacted quickly to the move by kicking his good leg toward Chase's midsection. He easily intercepted the leg in midflight and lifted it high, effectively causing Stumpf to do a split standing up. Without waiting for the next swing, Chase kicked the bad leg out from under the terrorist and knocked him semiconscious with a quick smack to his left temple. The chase car skidded alongside, and a door opened. Strong hands pulled the man inside as though he was a puppy. That was it.

Chase looked around expecting multiple witnesses, but it had all happened so quickly that there were none who were close enough to matter. An elderly man about two hundred meters away squinted like he had seen some motion. He took off his glasses, cleaned them on his sweater, and kept walking without saying a word. Chase turned away and walked at a brisk pace in the opposite direction, across the bridge, and sent a message to Samantha.

On my way.

Samantha had taken a long time before she dared to speak to Bekka. She waited for an opportunity. A slightly drunk man came up to the young woman's table and tried to engage her in conversation. Bekka ignored him for about a minute and then looked up with an icy stare and a sideways shake of her head. The man persisted until Sam spoke to him in German with the firmness of a more experienced woman, "Go away, she doesn't want to talk to you, quickly now."

As the red-faced youth retreated, Bekka looked over at Sam and gave a faint smile of thanks. Sam replied, again in German, "We need to stick together." That was all that happened for the next fifteen minutes.

Chase entered the café and saw that Sam was in a good position and needed no help from him. He went up to the bar and ordered a half-liter of beer and then turned around to survey the room. It was filled with mostly younger people, post-university and pre-employment from the looks of them. Almost every table was filled with intensely interacting men and women. There was a lot of energy in the room, and it was refreshing for him after his recent encounter with the sick killer Hans. He saw Sam lean over to Bekka and say a few words. She leaned back, and Bekka said a few words of her own. It was amazing for Chase to watch Sam at work. She was cool yet engaging. She was a natural. Another exchange happened before Andreas entered the room. Bekka said a few more words and then turned back to greet her lover.

"Who's that?" he demanded.

"She is no one. She helped me dust off an annoying man. That's all. I don't know her."

"Don't talk to anyone. Things are seriously screwed up right now. I can't find Daniel. We need to finish our work on the banking thing. Let's get out of here."

-56-

Along the River Main

Hans Stumpf had been sedated and moved to an unused riverfront warehouse on the outskirts of Frankfurt. The team that Chase had called in was prepared to put this man through their standard interrogation process, but the leader was a little unsure of why they had this criminal and what he could offer in the way of information. His only instructions were to hold him until told otherwise. Chase communicated back to Control.

> Stumpf is dangerous and a threat to current op. He
> must not be released. Ask about his relationship with
> Andreas. Then put him in jail forever.

He also requested that they not contact Interpol yet. There was a link between Stumpf and Andreas that needed further exploration.

Unless a prisoner was a trained intelligence officer, the CIA interrogation technique was always the same. They first isolated the individual and created enough sensory discord to warp the sense of time that most people depended on to remain oriented. Once time had been compromised, the next step was to create a feeling of complete helplessness and betrayal. This was always easier if comrades the subject trusted could be accused of treachery. The desire for revenge and the hope that it might still be achieved were strong motivators. Everyone, it seemed, liked to get even.

Hans was left wearing only a thin shirt and trousers, and was bound and gagged in a cold, damp cellar below the waterline of the river Main, twenty feet away. He could smell the acrid air, reeking of industrial chemicals and smoke. He was shivering in the 53-degree air as he leaned against a moldy wall. "I'm so fucking cold," he screamed out more than once. The team took this to be a good sign. Once the interrogation team had learned of his alleged crimes, they suspected that he might be a tougher case that most. They left him in his damp prison for twenty-four hours. By the end of that time, he would be soiled, hypothermic, and hopefully cooperative.

Late the next day, Hans was pulled roughly out of the cold into a warmer room where he was seated on a chair and bound with thick, rough straps. As soon as he was seated he immediately began to abuse his captors. "You have no right to do this," he screamed, "I will hunt you down, I will kill you and your families. Let me *out*."

He was still hooded and couldn't see anything, and he wasn't in much of a position to gain anything by attacking. Even so, it was in his nature to do so. He'd been raised in the eastern sector of Germany during the communist rule. His limp, he would later tell his captors, had been the result of a severe beating, more of a boot kicking, administered by the East German police after he was caught trying to rob an arms depot. He said he'd escaped before being sentenced for the crime. Since then he had been an international fugitive with a steadily increasing rap sheet. He was surly, cagey, and very strong.

"To hell with you all," he screamed as the hood was removed. "You can do anything you want to me, and I still won't tell you what you want to know. In the end, you will pay me for my secrets."

The lead interrogator allowed Hans to go on like this for about four hours without responding. In fact, all except one member of the team left the room and had a snack and a nap. When it began to look like Hans was running out of steam, they tried again.

"Hans Stumpf," the man began in German. "This can be difficult or easy. The choice is yours. You are nothing to us. We don't care if you live or die. Neither do the people who gave you to us. We want to know what you know about certain people." This was a nearly foolproof approach. "We don't want you; we want someone you know."

Hans opened his mouth, ready to fire an invective-laced tirade back at the interrogator. But just before he spoke, his self-defense mechanism, possibly triggered by extreme fatigue, finally began to function.

"Who do you want to know about?" he asked. "If I tell you what you want, will you set me free?"

The interrogating team knew that the front door was now open, although they still had a long way to go. For the next six hours, they grilled Hans on various alleged crimes, adding in Andreas's name from time to time to gauge his response. Hans seemed to stiffen when Andreas's name was mentioned, but he admitted nothing. Hans was allowed a drink of water and a five-minute break from the action, but he was not released from his chair. A new lead interrogator, a young woman, had the next turn at bat. Her questioning was more direct with respect to Andreas. She used a deliberately annoying tone, and she was not at all sympathetic to Stumpf's complaints or requests.

"Hans, we know you have had some business dealings with Andreas. Tell me, what exactly does Andreas do?"

Hans hesitated just long enough to betray his connection to Andreas. "Andreas is a computer hacker," he admitted. "He's a shit. I don't know specifically what he does. It's internet stuff. Other than that, I know nothing."

"Hans, this much we already know. Perhaps I need to be more direct. What do you and Andreas do together?"

Again, Hans hesitated as though he was deciding how to play for the greatest leverage. His face revealed much more than his words were communicating. "I can't answer that question without some guarantees. If it's Andreas you are after, then I can give him to you. I want all recorders off now, and I want to see your faces."

The interrogator considered taking a break to let Stumpf crumble a little more, but on instinct decided to press ahead.

"I don't think you are in a position to demand anything, Hans. If it helps you get comfortable, none of this is being recorded. We don't work that way. Just as you leave no evidence, we don't either."

Stumpf was quiet for a moment. He understood the implied threat in the last statement. These people couldn't be the police, or at least not any police that he had ever encountered before. He guessed they were criminals just like him. *Andreas must be making some bad enemies.*

He spoke again, "I tidy up loose ends for him. You know . . . threatening people, warning them to move on and not bother Andreas. That's about it."

"Then tell me, what are you doing here in Frankfurt?"

Hans was trying not to incriminate himself, but he realized that if he couldn't give a credible answer, he wouldn't gain his release. It was a tightrope he had walked before.

"He asked me to talk with a colleague; to warn him not to answer questions if the authorities came around. There's no law against that."

"Hans, we know you were looking for Daniel Greipel at the university. Let's make this easy. Were you asked to remove him?"

This was the question he'd been trying to sidestep for the past how many hours. He had "removed" two other individuals at Andreas's request over the past three years. Daniel would have been number three. Hans knew how to make people go away forever. He knew that Andreas was unusually paranoid and quick to rid himself of anyone he feared could compromise his projects. Hans couldn't answer this question directly and still walk away a free man. These inquisitors might be the Federal Police after all. He couldn't be sure.

"My job was to talk to him, nothing more."

"If this is true, tell me the names of others you have 'talked to' at Andreas's request." This was the final piece of the trap. Any name given now would implicate Hans in the disappearance of one of Andreas's past enemies. *If I tell them this I will never get out of prison.*

"I can tell you nothing more," Hans finally admitted with a much softer voice. Then he blinked. "I have heard that Andreas may have disappeared a couple of competitors in 2011, computer types. I was not involved in that. It's all hearsay. I can confirm nothing."

This was the end to the interview. Hans was given another sedative injection and was left bound on the floor of the warm room. The team leader would need additional instructions on his disposition. He would have no more dealings with the man. The team members wiped the room clean and left one by one.

-57-

Frankfurt

Chase received a text that Hans was still on ice and that additional instructions on what to do with the terrorist were being considered. Right now, he had a bigger problem. He had just seen Boris Gridenko walking down a street in Sachsenhausen.

Boris had arrived in Frankfurt the day before and had been searching for Andreas since then. He tried calling his cell phone several times without leaving messages. This alerted Andreas to his presence and made him more than normally cautious.

Chase understood that this would complicate the search and it was likely to cause Andreas to remain hidden. He would want to know why Boris was looking for him. The only edge that Chase now had was the tiny connection that Samantha had been able to make with Bekka. If Andreas stayed underground, she would be his only link to the outside.

After Boris arrived in Frankfurt, his first stop was a visit to a little bookshop not far from the Hauptbahnhof, in a somewhat shabby industrial area that bordered the tracks leading from the city to the rest of Europe. A moderately stooped and balding shopkeeper of about sixty had been his source for arms for a long, long time. The man greeted Boris by last name and then put a closed sign in the window and locked the front door. He led Boris into the back of the shop and down a hidden stairway to his little weapons arsenal.

Boris was looking for two items: an untraceable Glock 9mm automatic, and a sharp hunting knife, the type used for skinning animals. He didn't have hunting in mind, but he was thinking of skinning something. The Glock was unused with no visible serial numbers. He selected a fifteen-round magazine and a box of cartridges with soft points. He picked up the knife, and it easily sliced through a sheet of paper he found on the worktable.

Boris smiled and replied, "These will do fine. How much do you ask for everything?"

The shopkeeper shrewdly measured Boris for a few seconds and replied, "Six thousand euros. The gun has never been used in a crime and cannot be traced. It was stolen from the police in Austria two years ago, and I have had it here since it came out of its box. There are no numbers on the gun. You can resell it on the street and get all of your money back anytime you want."

Boris inserted five rounds into the clip while the shopkeeper looked on nervously. Then he stepped up to the counter facing the narrow underground firing range and put on a pair of ear protectors. He picked out a target with a human profile and calmly fired all five bullets through the little white heart. He smiled thinly and stepped back to reload the clip, this time completely full.

"Yes, this will do quite nicely. Five thousand you said?"

The arms dealer barely squeaked out a "Yes" in response and began to edge toward the door.

Without further hesitation, Boris quickly counted out twenty-five used two-hundred-euro notes and dropped them on the table. He placed the now loaded weapon and the knife into his shoulder bag and walked back upstairs. He gave the shopkeeper another mirthless smile before walking out the door into the street without saying another word. He was certain that he would eventually find Andreas somewhere in the tangle of streets and alleyways across the river. When he did, he planned to teach him about pain in a fearful way, and then kill him and his woman. *Maybe I will skin her first, just to practice. He will watch.* In Boris's world, this would be considered completely justifiable given the betrayal that he had assumed on Andreas's part.

Unknown to Boris, Chase was following him discretely and at a distance. Boris may not be able to recall Chase, but he was certain to recognize Samantha if he were to encounter her again. This would be a problem. An encounter like this was likely, given Sam's project to stay close to Bekka. Chase could see only sad things happening if that were to occur. He needed to know more about the Russian's business in Frankfurt. He texted the address of the shop Boris had entered a few minutes ago to Control, with a request for any information on what sort of activity went on there. Ten minutes later, as Boris entered his hotel on Neue Mainzer Strasse, Chase received his answer.

Arms of all kinds. Warning—keep clear.
There is surveillance.

The shop was a known pickup point for illegal weapons. The German Federal Police had a permanent hidden surveillance camera focused on the shop and everyone who entered the premises was photographed and logged into the police database.

Chase considered this new information for a minute. He was glad he hadn't walked by the shop out of curiosity and had his photo entered in the police log of possible perpetrators. That would have complicated his life. He wasn't supposed to exist. He tried to decide what level of threat this dangerous Russian presented. If Boris was now armed, and this was likely, he had plans to hurt someone. His interrogation report indicated that he thought Andreas had betrayed him. He was going to kill Andreas. There was no other way this could play out. Chase couldn't let this happen. It was more than a protective instinct for his operation and for Sam. He couldn't let harm come to another human being if it was in his power to prevent it. He moved down the street to a small café with a view of the hotel's front entrance. He sent another text to Control with an outline of a plan.

-58-

Sachsenhausen

Andreas and Bekka were now working furiously to complete their planned intrusion into the two banking systems. Andreas had learned that at least two important economic reports were to be released within three days, and the market was already on the edge. It was an exceptional opportunity. After the prolonged Greek monetary crisis, and the eventual default, most traders were expecting Italy and Spain to follow quickly in the same footsteps. The trading range of the euro had widened, and instability was in the air. Business news reports confirmed that more fiscal problems lay ahead. His plan could work if market players could be induced to believe that insiders were making trades on negative information that would be released soon. The stage seemed set for volatility.

Andreas devised a test scenario for the UBB system that commenced with sudden massive selling of the euro shortly after the European markets opened. This would be matched by equivalent buying of the Swiss franc. The test pack would show disintegrating support for the euro and the price, in dollars and francs, falling within seconds by more than 2 percent. This would be followed by a more precipitous dive of another 7 percent to simulate a market in free-fall. It would appear to be a sudden and decisive flight to safety by investors. A rout of this magnitude would cause automated trading systems worldwide to kick into action to protect existing currency positions, or to take advantage of the chaos by shorting the eurozone currency. If traders were already on edge and anticipating bad news, this rapid change in the value of key currencies would immediately trigger both speculation and damage control. It would be a perfect storm.

He was more right than he realized. Traders in European markets were primed for volatility this week. It was rumored that factory orders in both Germany and France had softened, while inflation in the eurozone was showing signs of spiraling up, due to an increase in the money supply by the European Central Bank. On the day Andreas planned to spring his little trap, monthly reports on both leading indicators were scheduled to be released a couple of hours after European markets opened. If these reports turned out to be more negative than expected, all markets would move decisively lower as investors sought safety. It might trigger an avalanche. Andreas could not have hoped for a better situation.

He was starting to feel almost giddy about the project. Bekka followed his lead inside the Broadway system, and he hoped that the two flows of false information would feed one another and the market's greed.

"Bekka, this is going to be our greatest victory yet. When we trigger our little surprise, hundreds of billions of euros, maybe even a trillion, will change hands in minutes. Banks will be ruined; governments will teeter. I can't believe how good I am."

Bekka frowned at this last statement. Andreas was conceited and proud and becoming more so. These were weak personal qualities that could get them caught. She was not happy with that prospect. She feared prison and the loss of her freedom even more than she feared death.

"Andreas, we need to be careful. We are going to hurt a lot of powerful people and not all of them play by the rules. Please, let's keep our names off this one. Just let the PLL take credit for what happens. I don't want to be involved in what might follow."

It was Andreas's turn to frown. The prospect of sharing any of the glory for this monumental disaster was not in his temperament. "Bekka, you are so weak. No one can hurt us now. We're anonymous, and none of the authorities have any idea who we are, or where we are. Besides, this is my biggest victory ever. How can I not boast about it?"

"But . . . what about Daniel? If the other night was a trap, someone can certainly trace everything we did back to the computer lab. He can implicate us. That's the weak part of your plan."

Bekka had just broken two important rules, one of which she didn't even know existed. She did understand that to question Andreas's plan, and to suggest that it had any flaws, was never done, ever, by anyone. The part she didn't understand was that mentioning Daniel was like digging open a fresh grave.

Andreas became uncharacteristically silent and looked away from her. "Don't worry about Daniel," he finally said coldly. "He's taken care of. He won't be able to hurt us."

Bekka turned quickly from what she was doing to stare directly at Andreas. "What do you mean by that?"

"Nothing! Daniel has gone away for a while. That's all. He'll come back when I tell him all is clear. Now, stop worrying about him and go to the store. We need some food and beer. I can't be seen out on the street right now, not until I hear from Daniel."

Bekka looked at him again, and this time with something more than curiosity; it felt to her like the beginning of fear. It made sense that Andreas wanted to remain out of sight until he could talk to Daniel, but she sensed something else was not quite right. What was he dragging her into now?

-59-

Frankfurt

It was almost dark when the Federal Police received word that a certain international fugitive could be found in an abandoned warehouse in Frankfurt. The police rolled several units to the location and found Hans Stumpf, bound and slightly groggy in the basement room where the CIA team had left him hours earlier. He reeked of his own waste and sweat. This was an important arrest for the German police. Stumpf was highly wanted by Interpol and at least three countries had outstanding claims on him. He was handcuffed and taken to the central jail facility in Frankfurt, where he was turned over to the custody of the state police for Hessen, the state where Frankfurt was located.

Instead of being immediately questioned and booked, Stumpf was stuffed into a crowded holding cell along with a crowd of petty criminals and intoxicated partygoers who were awaiting bail. It would be a colossal mistake. He wouldn't be found there in the morning. "In all likelihood," reported the public prosecutor's office the next day, "he was mistakenly released with a group of sports fans who had been detained for disorderly conduct after Frankfurt lost to Real Madrid in an exhibition soccer match at the stadium."

Once he was back on the street, Stumpf lost no time making his way back to the parking garage where he had left his car, and he departed Frankfurt in haste. He knew that he had overstayed his welcome. He blamed Andreas for his arrest and subsequent interrogation and swore to get even with him.

***

Bekka left the apartment and walked through the busy streets of Sachsenhausen toward a neighborhood market that she frequented. On the way, she decided to stop in her favorite *gasthof* for a small beer and some time to decompress after her verbal exchange with Andreas. He was becoming bossy and abusive, and she was not happy with this change. In Norway, where they both were raised, such behavior would have been unacceptable. She was angry and hurt.

As she entered the little drinking establishment, she saw Samantha at a corner table reading a book. She hesitated and then made her way to a table directly adjoining Sam's. Sam didn't look up at first, even though she had seen Bekka enter the little bar. Bekka ordered her drink and then, as if by accident, Sam looked up and acknowledged the younger woman with a brief nod and a smile before going back to her reading. She reached into her purse and thumbed a short text message to Chase. Her part of the game was now active.

After a few minutes of silence, Bekka leaned slightly toward Sam and began to speak. She had a pleasant, melodic voice and her German, while excellent, carried the singsong accent of some other northern country.

"My friend, the one you saw me with the other night, he's very complicated. I apologize for his rudeness."

Sam turned toward the young woman. "I really took no offense. He seemed nice enough, and so much like one of those brilliant and high-strung guys who are always trying to change the world. I understand the type. My boyfriend is the same way. I come here for a little break and for some sanity. Sometimes being apart makes being together better."

"Yes . . . yes, I feel the same way. Sometimes, I like him more when I see him less. I feel better already. Do you come here often?"

"From time to time. When I come, it is usually late in the afternoon, like today. I don't stay long . . . only until I clear my head."

Bekka finished her beer and got up to leave. Before she did, she leaned over and said, "I am Bekka. It's nice to meet you. Maybe we will see each other again."

Sam responded, "My name is Angelica. It's also a pleasure to meet you. It would be nice to talk again. I would enjoy that. Have a pleasant evening."

With that, Bekka left the *gasthof,* turning once near the door to give Samantha a small wave. *This is one lonely and burdened young woman,* thought Sam, as Bekka went through the door with a smile on her face.

Fifteen minutes earlier, Chase had received Sam's message indicating that she had contacted the girl again. Boris was not his primary target, although he had a strong personal interest in keeping track of him. He left his self-appointed post and took a taxi from the front of the hotel to a corner about a block from the place where Sam and Bekka were having their first conversation. Chase saw Bekka as she departed the *gasthof* and casually followed her to a small neighborhood market a few streets away. He entered the store after her, picked up a basket, and proceeded to shop for a few items. He left before she did and took up a position across the street. He knew it would be easy to follow the young woman, so he didn't press to keep up with her. He crossed the street several times and allowed small groups of pedestrians to buffer the distance between the two of them. When she finally turned into a doorway of a three-story residence, he paused about a hundred meters from the building. He watched her go through the front door and waited to see if the lights came on in the one dark apartment. They didn't. This meant that Andreas was probably already at home. They lived either on the first or second floor, since the ground floor was still dark. Locating the correct apartment would be easy.

Chase watched for a few more minutes and then walked back to meet Sam. He sent an update to Control.

> Have the location of our IT guy. I need final
> instructions.

***

Samantha was still inside the *gasthof*, so he entered and sat at the table recently vacated by Bekka. He gave Sam a small smile as he sat down. He sent her a text.

> Nice work! I know where they live.

She responded immediately.

> Can we meet in my room . . . twenty minutes?

After all, she was still on her honeymoon. Chase looked up with a smile of amusement and nodded his head.

***

Andreas was annoyed when Bekka came in. She had been gone too long for his liking, and he missed having his audience present while he worked. "That was a long time for a trip to the store, Bekka."

Bekka stiffened immediately and quietly replied, "I stopped for a small beer on the way. I needed some time to myself. Here are the things you asked for." She dumped the bag on the table with a thump and began to walk into the bedroom.

Normally, Andreas would have questioned her more about her detour, but he was proud of himself for coming up with a way to profit from the upcoming financial turmoil. He had decided to buy Swiss franc currency contracts as the market opened on Wednesday and then to liquidate them as soon as the market convulsed. The franc was one of the few places of safety when the euro was under pressure. He could make a small fortune in a few minutes without risking much. He explained this to Bekka.

"Not only will I shake up their precious markets, I will also get to rub their noses in their own shit. When it's over, let's take a trip somewhere warm to be sure there will be no blowback from what's going to happen. We need a vacation."

"Andreas, please be careful. Every move we make will leave some footprints. What if the authorities start checking all trades just before the system fails? I've heard that they do such things. They could come looking for us."

"You worry too much. Enjoy my triumph and leave the details to me. I know how to move the funds so that the trail will lead nowhere. We can spend the winter on the Côte d'Azur and some bank, somewhere, will be paying for it. Isn't it delicious?"

Bekka looked back at him with concern. So far, they had been able to avoid being personally identified with any of the actions of the PLL. This anonymity suited Bekka. She was part of this group mostly because she liked him. Now he seemed to be putting them both at risk for bad reasons. She wasn't at all happy with this latest version of Andreas.

-60-

Andreas was bursting with nervous energy and needed to be back online doing something new. He browsed several bulletin boards and ended up on the site that Ron Tolar ran in his spare time. Boris had recently left a message asking Andreas to contact him. Andreas had no information to suggest that anything had changed in his relationship with Boris. True, he had anonymously posted Boris's crimes for the world to see, but he knew nothing about his capture and subsequent interrogation. He was a little concerned that Boris had called his cell phone several times without leaving a message; however, there was no apparent reason to think that anything had changed. The perception was completely different to Boris. He was hunting Andreas with bad intentions. In his view of the world, Andreas had betrayed him and there could be only one acceptable outcome.

Boris also was full of energy, and prior to continuing his physical search for Andreas, had decided to search for him online. He visited several sites as well, and finally returned to Ron Tolar's site to post a message. After an hour more of searching, he closed his laptop and decided to hit the streets.

***

Back at Langley, Tolar had the website on one of his screens, and he noticed almost immediately that Sputnik2 had resurfaced after several days of silence. He looked at his post for a few minutes, trying to decide who he was trying to contact. Finally, he called Merrill to report that Boris was back in the pond.

"Sir, this is Tolar. Our friend Sputnik2 is back in circulation. He's putting out feelers to someone special. I think it might be our friend Andreas. No one has responded to his post yet. I thought you should know."

Merrill thought about his comments for a few seconds and then responded. "Ron, here is some current information. We brought Sputnik2 into custody and interrogated him for a couple of days. He got roughed up a bit, I'm afraid. We came away with a lot of useful information. Then we turned him loose to see where he might lead us. Does this help you interpret his post?"

Tolar was silent as he processed this new data. "This is only a guess, but he's probably looking for someone to punish. It could be Andreas, and it also could be whomever else he blames for his capture. He's not a kind soul. He has violence in his bloodline. If he'd wanted to disappear safely after your little talk with him, he could have gone back to Russia where he'd be protected. The fact that he's still somewhere in Western Europe worries me greatly."

"It worries me too, Ron. Thanks for your thoughts. Please let me know if anything new comes up."

With that, Merrill ended the call and immediately entered the number for the controller of Robert Chase's group. He gave him two sets of instructions. "His primary mission is still to bring Andreas in from the cold before Boris finds him. If he can't do this quickly and safely, he has authority to take down Boris again and keep him in storage. Once Andreas is out of the picture, Boris will return home to Moscow where his own government can keep an eye on him."

"But what if this Boris refuses to disengage?"

"Chase may use extreme measures to protect himself and Andreas. Is that clear?" Merrill said this knowing that Chase had never killed a man during his entire career. He had other ways of dealing with difficult people.

The only response to these orders was, "I'll see what I can do."

320 Genesis

***

Boris spent the middle part of the evening stopping at the places he had met or seen Andreas before. He did a quick sweep of the Sachsenhausen clubs and bars, and then repeated his search until past eleven at night. He concluded that if he wasn't out by now, he probably wasn't clubbing tonight. It was unfortunate, but certainly not fatal. Sooner or later Andreas would have to come up for air. He would be waiting for him when he did.

Boris had just exited another wine bar when he saw the girl. He instinctively turned to intercept her. It was not Bekka he had sighted. It was Samantha.

-61-

Sachsenhausen

Samantha had met Bekka for a drink and was heading back to reconnect with Chase. After the two women met earlier in the day, Sam suggested a late evening rendezvous in a neighboring wine bar, near the one Boris had recently left. Her objective was to get the younger woman to talk a little more. It should not have been a dangerous encounter.

Bekka was visibly nervous and stressed when she arrived. She began speaking first, and more rapidly than normal. "I'm so sorry to be late. My boyfriend is so jealous, and I had to walk out finally; he was getting so angry. I don't know what to do."

"I'm glad to see you, Bekka. Men can be strange sometimes. Is he having other problems, like at work, or money issues? Those frustrations can trigger a lot of irrational behavior in guys."

Bekka looked at Sam for a few long seconds. She was trying to decide if Sam was trustworthy enough to share any of what was spinning in her head. She finally began speaking again, and this time more deliberately and fighting for emotional control.

"Angelica, you must never repeat this to anyone." Sam nodded her head in the affirmative. "My friend's activities worry me sometimes. He's very smart, and often nice to me. He knows how to do things with computers that most people can't even imagine are possible. This can get him into dangerous places, with unsafe people, if you understand what I mean. I'm so worried that he's into something now that may hurt him and perhaps me as well."

Samantha was slow to reply as if she was hesitant to provide advice to someone she didn't know well. It was a planned response, it had been her idea, and Chase had readily agreed with it. She didn't wish to give this vulnerable young woman any reason to mistrust her. Whatever steps she eventually agreed to would need to be her own ideas.

"Bekka, I'm not in a position to make any value judgments. If you feel that your own safety might be at risk, maybe you should consider creating some space between you and your friend. I used to be a lawyer, and I know how difficult prison can be for young women. I wouldn't recommend it to anyone."

Bekka looked at Sam with surprise and a new respect. "Why is it that you are not still an advocate?"

"I guess I grew to mistrust the system. A lot of barely guilty people ended up being convicted, while the real criminals, you know, the bankers and the politicians, were rarely touched. I couldn't go on acting like it was fair. I finally quit the law, and now I edit other peoples' writing and do freelance work of my own. I'm much happier now."

Bekka smiled and visibly relaxed several degrees. "Thank you for telling me this. It helps. I think that Andreas—that is my friend's name—is taking unnecessary risks. He also dislikes the unfairness in the world, as do I, but I realize that doing some things to certain people can create unwanted trouble. I don't want him to get hurt."

Sam smiled back at Bekka. She already liked this young woman and hoped she could protect her from some of the landslide of pain that was about to fall on her if she continued to partner with Andreas.

"Bekka, I have a good friend who protects people. He's skilled at helping people escape their circumstances and restart their lives. I think he could help you too, and even Andreas if this is what you both want. This friend of mine is safe. I would vouch for him with my life."

Bekka was in conflict. In her heart, she wanted an escape hatch, but she wasn't sure that Andreas would agree. "I will think about what you've said. Can I meet you here again tomorrow?"

Samantha nodded and offered a small, and genuinely warm smile. "I will be here tomorrow, and then I'll need to leave for Paris the day after on business. I may be gone for a week." Sam understood that she needed to give the young woman a reason to decide sooner rather than later.

They spent a little more time in small talk, and then Bekka left the little bar first and walked briskly home. Sam lingered for a couple of minutes while she sent a text to Chase.

> Please retrieve me and take me home.
> We have a lot to discuss.

-62-

Sachsenhausen

It was when Samantha exited the wine bar that Boris first sighted her. He remembered immediately who she was. Samantha was many things, but she was not forgettable. *She's the one who tricked me in Monaco,* he fumed. He stopped thinking and went into a reactive mode, as he had so many times before in his life. He changed direction to follow her just as Chase emerged from an alleyway. Chase saw Boris a split second before he recognized Sam. He went into protective overdrive and moved rapidly to physically separate Boris from Sam, no matter the risk to himself.

Boris was about fifty meters behind Sam and closing quickly. Chase was about the same distance from the imaginary line between the two, and merging at an angle that would allow him to intercept Boris before he could get closer than ten meters to Sam. He didn't dare shout out to Samantha, though he desperately wanted to. If she stopped walking, even for a few seconds, Boris might reach her before Chase could cut him off. Her safety now depended on his timing, and the hope that Boris would not start to run toward her.

As Boris walked, he calmly reached inside his bag for the knife. He would take her down any way he could, but certainly with cruelty and pain. This was about more than simple revenge. Then he would have his fun before cutting her deeply and watching her hopes and dreams drain into the gutter. It was not a rational thing to do on a still-busy street in a major city. However, he wasn't exactly a reasonable man in this moment. Chase saw the glint of a blade emerge from the bag, and without realizing it, broke into a run. Boris heard rapid footsteps to his right, and turned as Chase emerged from the darkness, three meters away. Chase hit Boris squarely in the chest with the force of a linebacker, and both men fell dazed to the pavement, only an arm's reach apart. Chase was the first to his feet, and he quickly delivered a hard kick to Boris's midsection, followed by another harder blow to his head. Boris was out.

Only now did Chase feel a sharp pain in his side and looked down at a deep crimson stain spreading across his jacket. Boris had stuck him below his rib cage a split-second before Chase tackled him. It was a bad wound, and Chase knew it right away. He looked at Samantha to see she was safe, and then leaned against a nearby lamppost while he quickly punched in a phone number and gave urgent instructions.

Sam had been shocked by the speed and ferocity of the attack. It had been a blur of movement and a violent collision. She didn't recognize that it was Boris crumpled onto the ground until she rushed to Chase's side. He was already in distress. He tore open his jacket and shirt and asked her to put pressure on his wound with her bare hand. It was a sucking wound, and she could feel it on her palm as his injured lung struggled for air. "Help is on the way," he wheezed. He slipped to the pavement. There was already blood on his lips and his breathing was growing more labored.

-63-

Sachsenhausen

Help was not far away, but the distance was now measured in heartbeats. An unmarked white van pulled up within five minutes, and both Chase and the unconscious Boris were pulled into the vehicle. Samantha got into the front seat and immediately looked behind her, over the seat at Chase. He was very pale, but still conscious. One of the men in back was holding a dressing to the wound and talking urgently in German on a cell phone. Another held an automatic pistol aloft from Boris's bag.

The van sped into the heart of the city toward the University Hospital, which was part of Goethe University, a few blocks north of the main train station. The ride took ten long minutes. Upon arrival, an emergency team met the van, and Chase was wheeled at double-time into the emergency room with Sam only steps behind. The van, with Boris still unconscious inside, left immediately.

This hospital was experienced in dealing with extreme, life-threatening wounds. Chase was in good hands, but he was not in good condition. The ER staff could tell that his lung had been punctured, and that it was in danger of collapse from the building pressure within the chest cavity. The knife wound was clean, and the external bleeding had already slowed. He wasn't going to bleed to death anytime soon. The wound in the lung might close without surgery; however, the pooling blood inside his chest needed to be removed, and fast. The ER doc tore open a surgical kit and quickly poked a new hole into his chest, through his left side, and inserted a thin tube. Chase barely registered any pain from the penetration. Immediately a small pump began to gently suction blood into a collection bag. His breathing eased, and he began to relax.

The attending physician believed that the lung itself would probably heal on its own without further intervention. A subsequent scan of the chest showed only a small quantity of blood in the lung itself, and the decision was made to hold him for observation until morning. The exterior wound was stitched up with four small sutures. Chase was awake and alert throughout all of this. He felt little pain and insisted on having no anesthesia other than a local for the needlework.

Samantha was at his side the moment he was wheeled out of the treatment room. Chase smiled at her and winked. "It wasn't much more than a poke in the side. I'll be able to leave by morning."

At that, Sam released all her emotional tension in one big set of sobs. "Twice are too many times, Robert! There was so much blood. I thought I had lost you."

Chase smiled again and gently said, "My entire career and not a bruise. I meet a gorgeous redhead, and suddenly everyone is trying to kill me."

At that, Sam blinked her tears away and grabbed his hand and kissed it. "I need you, Mr. Chase."

Robert looked back at her and said, "I need you more."

-64-

Frankfurt

When Boris awakened, he found himself in unfamiliar and unpleasant surroundings. There was only a single guard present, and he had little interest in the man in his custody. Boris had been bound and lightly gagged to muffle his voice, and he was still blindfolded. He was in a small chilly room in the basement of another of the grimy industrial buildings along the river in Frankfurt. The CIA had a network of these single-use cells in just about all major cities of the world. This time there was no need for interrogation. The CIA had no more use for Boris Gridenko. The Russians didn't seem to want him either. He was here to await a final disposition. No one was inclined to set him free again. He had demonstrated how dangerous he was, and there was little doubt that he would kill, or try to kill again. The German Federal Police would gladly take him for his illegal Internet exploits, but even if proven in court, those would net him only a couple of years of soft prison time. He would be back in circulation in no time, and he would certainly resume his hunt for Andreas, and for Samantha and Chase. He spent a long and uncomfortable night. He raved and cursed his captors, but no one was listening.

***

In another part of the city, Chase was checked by the physician on duty early in the morning and reluctantly pronounced stable enough for release. The doctor was being pressured by the police to move this patient and to eliminate any record that he was ever here. There would be no official medical chart maintained in the hospital for the treatment of anyone named Robert Chase. He was admitted and discharged under the German equivalent of "John Doe" and the paperwork was immediately sealed and handed to an impatient man from the U.S. embassy. The file referenced "Linebacker," and that was it. The entire folder was on its way to Langley where it would be buried forever.

Sam had spent the night by Chase's side. She was more than glad to take her man from the hospital and back under her control. The two of them took a bus to their hotel. Chase wore an ill-fitting jacket from the found-items bin at the hospital. His wound hurt more than he was willing to admit. She held tightly onto his arm and buried her face into his shoulder. After a few minutes she asked about Boris. "Where is he now? Can he hurt us again?"

Chase whispered back to her. "He's in custody; we can deal with him later. He won't be released anytime soon, at least that's what I've been promised. Now we need to get back on top of our mission. If Andreas is planning something big, he won't wait long to spring it. We may be too late already."

Chase shifted uncomfortably in the seat and realized that he was not completely operational. This was a cause for concern. He depended on his physical quickness and strength to keep them safe. He would need to ask for help.

Back at the small apartment in Sachsenhausen, Andreas was completing his last programming task. He had been editing the kill-switch software that both UBB and Broadway used to stop malware or any runaway program from doing more than minimal damage. He reasoned that once the string of false transactions was released to the production stream, someone would notice the aberration and move to stop it, at least until it could be verified that the transactions were legitimate. Both trading houses used the same commercial security software, and Andreas had been successful in violating similar fail-safe switches before. For this hack, as soon as the kill switch was activated, a new routine he was about to insert would cause the safeguard to begin a nearly-endless loop that would disappear after five minutes, when his code would automatically remove itself and shut down the system. There would be confusion, and while this was going on, he planned to erase the rest of his footprints. Minutes after the euro began to collapse everyone would be scratching their heads and wondering exactly what had happened. It was nearly perfect.

Bekka had been at work as well on the Broadway system, but she allowed Andreas to make the final changes. Tomorrow morning, fifteen minutes after the European markets opened, both UBB and Broadway would begin spewing out a stream of false currency trades that would get everyone's attention. As they were wrapping up the last details, Bekka noticed that she had a text message from Angelica on her phone. She waited until Andreas went to the tiny kitchen to grab a beer, and then she looked at it.

Can you meet my friend today, say 4:00?

She thought about this for a moment and then deleted the message. She felt a little funny, sort of like she was cheating on Andreas, but that was silly she thought. This was a friend, and right now she needed a friend more than ever.

Andreas came back with two beers. They had been up all night, and soon he would need to sleep. First, he would want sex, and then he would sleep until evening. Bekka saw that this would provide her the opportunity to meet Angelica. It would be a small price to pay. Besides, she still liked Andreas. She just didn't trust him anymore.

-65-

Frankfurt

Samantha and Chase went back to her hotel room to make plans for Andreas and to find a way to remove Bekka from the line of fire. Chase knew something was imminent, but how close he could only guess. His sole source was Samantha, so the two of them began to dissect the information Bekka had been willing to share. It was not much to work with.

"Okay," he began. "We do know that Andreas is one of the best, and that his trademark, at least until now, has been breaking into classified sites and putting out the information he finds for everyone to see. He and the PLL are dedicated to the goal of making it impossible for anyone to keep secrets. He likes to embarrass governments and big multinational companies, although he doesn't seem to be in it for personal gain. The same cannot be said for some of his acquaintances, like Boris."

Sam made a face when Boris's name was mentioned. The man made her flesh crawl. She feared him and hated him more than anyone she had ever met. She shook it off and began to speak.

"I could see fear in Bekka's face yesterday. Whatever Andreas is doing, I think it is big, dangerous, and maybe not consistent with her understanding of whatever mission they used to share. She made it clear that she feared the consequences for them both. I think she might grab a lifeline if we can offer one. Whatever we say, we can't tell her that Andreas might go to prison. We will need to save him too."

Chase looked at Sam with a new appreciation for her insight and her grasp of how people learned to deal with the inconsistencies in their own lives. She was good at this.

"That's a tall order. I think for Andreas to be rescued too, we are going to need to understand what he's planning, and whether it can be stopped. If he does too much damage, it might be difficult to protect him. My boss is more than a little angry with him. He put a lot of good people at risk, and that won't be easily forgiven."

Samantha picked up the thread. "I think Bekka trusts me. If we can promise to protect Andreas too, I'm sure she will meet with you, and we might be able to defuse this whole thing. Can you manage to do that, Robert?"

One wonderful thing about his job was that the rules of engagement were always flexible. The mission objectives trumped all other considerations and promises made toward that end were invariably honored by Langley. The CIA wanted Andreas to cease his attacks on all their systems. There was no interest in him personally, and for all they were concerned, he could knock himself out trying to make the world a better place. He needed to leave the CIA alone. Homeland Security might have different wishes, but the Agency didn't much care what those pencil heads wanted. They could do their own fieldwork. If Andreas could be redirected to other causes, Chase had considerable latitude in how he approached him. He could even recruit him. He might turn out to be useful in the future. The CIA was not in the business of law enforcement. The Agency was a firewall against the truly dangerous enemies of the United States. Chase did not see Andreas as being one of those.

"I think he can be protected if he agrees to change his ways. We don't really want him, but others might. See what you can do with the girl. Whatever you agree to I will support."

With that, Sam and Chase began to work through how she might approach Bekka. During this discussion, Bekka texted back a "Yes" to Sam's earlier question. They would meet this afternoon.

-66-

Sachsenhausen

Bekka slipped quietly out the door of the apartment a little before four in the afternoon. Andreas was still asleep, and this made it much easier for her to keep her appointment with Angelica. It was a short walk to the little *gasthof* where she and Angelica had first met. She was nervous and shivered more than usual in the cool afternoon air. She tried to organize her thoughts; however, the emotions of the moment kept causing her thoughts to wander in a hundred "what if" directions. Her objective, if it could even be called that, was to keep them both safe. She had no intention of trying to stop Andreas from disrupting the financial markets tomorrow morning. To her, it was not a crime, it was a political statement.

As she entered the little establishment, she saw Angelica seated with a pleasant-looking man of about forty years, maybe a bit younger. He looked friendly and warm. Even so, she was immediately on her guard. She greeted Angelica with a firm handshake and did the same to Chase after she was introduced to him. She looked him straight in his eyes, and he looked back, honestly, and without any apparent guile. Only a few words of introduction had been spoken and already Bekka felt safer.

"Bekka, this is my friend Robert. I've told him a little of what you told me yesterday, and he thinks he can help you and your friend Andreas." At this, Bekka allowed herself a tight, nervous smile, but she said nothing.

Chase didn't smile back, although his face remained friendly. He said, "Andreas is in considerable danger, and this means you are too." He could see the immediate impact of his words on this young woman. "There are at least two men, very violent men, who are looking for your friend. I don't know why they are looking for him, but when they find him, they will hurt him badly. I have seen them both here in Frankfurt."

Bekka looked frightened, although she had enough presence of mind to be wary as well. "Are you with the police? How do you know such things? You need to convince me that I should trust you."

Chase stared back at her for a long minute and was about to speak when Samantha broke the silence.

"Bekka, all I can tell you is that neither of us wishes to harm Andreas nor you. You told me that you were worried about what might happen to you because of what Andreas was doing. We are not the police, but we can offer you a way out. Here's the deal. We won't ask questions; you won't ask questions. We will take you to a safe place, and then you both will need to leave Germany and keep a low profile for a long time. That's the only condition. Can you do that?"

***

At the apartment, Andreas awoke and called lazily, "Bekka, where are you? Bring me a beer." He got out of the messy bed and walked naked from room to room looking for his lover. Assuming she had gone to the store, he dressed and lit up his computer. He had one more task to complete before tomorrow, and it was convenient that Bekka was not here to witness it. He wanted this to be a surprise.

Andreas kept several offshore bank accounts to finance his mission in life. Most contained few funds. One, however, was a Forex currency trading account domiciled in Gibraltar, where he had managed to stockpile a little more than two hundred thousand euros from years of hacking adventures.

The Forex market is a highly decentralized, international marketplace in all the major currencies. Money of all types may be bought and sold for reasons ranging from protecting a purchase or sale from currency fluctuations, to the most elaborate trading strategies designed to wring a tiny profit per unit from massive positions in almost any currency. For the traders in this market, information, preferably inside information, was the lifeblood of the business. The biggest risk to any trader was the unpredictable actions of the central banks themselves. One might have rightly discerned an unstoppable market trend in a currency, only to have the central bank of the country move into the market without warning to turn the tide. Huge fortunes could be made or lost, and the leverage used on these bets was massive. What intrigued Andreas the most was that the trade was all electronic and instantaneous. Each day, more than a trillion U.S. dollars of value in world currencies changed hands.

Andreas had created a scenario where, for five brief minutes, the currency market would perceive that the euro was selling off to a degree not seen before. The initial price quote versus the Swiss franc would drop almost 2 percent, followed by a more precipitous drop of 7 percent, confirming everyone's worst fears. Other currency pairs would follow. He expected it to be even worse once traders tripped over one another trying to gain an advantage. Although a drop like this was unprecedented, and on its face deserving of careful research, it would also be irresistible to traders waiting for anything interesting to happen. The fact that confirming orders would be coming from both London and Zurich would be enough to cause a brief feeding frenzy.

Andreas decided he wanted a little taste of the action. He logged into his Forex account and entered an order to be executed at the opening of the market the next day. He was purchasing, on margin, two hundred contracts selling the euro and buying Swiss francs. Once executed, Andreas would effectively own twenty million euros' worth of francs at the posted "bid" of 1.2000 franc per euro. If the price of the euro were to go down even a little, he would make a fortune. His investment, and his potential loss if it all went wrong, would be limited to his initial investment of two hundred thousand euros at the going margin rate of 1 percent. Because he understood that his deception would quickly be uncovered, he placed a "take profit order" that instructed the Forex broker to close out his position when the euro/franc bid reached 1.1469, which was a significant decline, but less than the bottom he thought the currency would reach. The net profit from this brief ownership of so many Swiss francs would be about a million euros. It would not be a bad return for creating five minutes of chaos. The kicker for Andreas would be the gotcha he could then claim. That would be priceless.

-67-

Elsewhere in Europe

Departing Frankfurt in great haste, Hans Stumpf had stopped only briefly at his apartment near Munich to retrieve his most valuable possessions. These included a small duffle of weapons, some cash he had saved, and his books. Within an hour, he was on his way out of Germany by car. Someone, or some agency, already knew too much about him. This was reason enough to disappear. He had friends in Serbia who appreciated his past contributions to their war of independence. He could stay in a safe apartment in Belgrade while he considered his next steps. Everywhere in Europe, right-wing and nationalistic causes were emerging. He felt at home in this environment. He felt sure that he could find employment somewhere.

The eurozone was in turmoil. At the insistence of the European Central Bank and the International Monetary Fund, the weak governments of Greece, Italy, and Spain had enacted austerity programs that were defunding the jobs of hundreds of thousands of public employees almost overnight. Every week, strikes were being called in the major cities, and the middle class was growing fearful. The social contract between the people and their governments, in place since shortly after World War II, was being undone. Immigrants from former colonies in Africa were becoming a growing burden on welfare states, and this observation was not lost on those native Europeans without jobs. Most of the continent was already simmering with discontent.

In the South of France, a new nationalistic political party was gaining power. It was centered in the teeming city of Marseille.

It was called the New National Party for French Independence, PNIF in the native language. They wanted to fill the jails with criminals, and empty the country of all immigrants, especially the Islamists. They would not mind if France regained control over Algeria either. It was time to return to the good old days, and back to the French franc.

-68-

Sachsenhausen

It took Bekka more than two hours to feel comfortable with Chase's plan to relocate her and Andreas. What made the difference in her interest level was Chase's description of Boris and his interrupted plan to visit great physical harm on the young couple. She promised that she would talk to Andreas this evening and that the two of them would meet Chase and Sam in this same *gasthof* in the morning. Chase was not convinced that this would happen; however, he kept this to himself until Bekka left.

"Sam, what do you think she's going to do?" he asked as soon as the young woman went out the door.

Samantha took a deep breath and let it out with a sigh. "I think she will do her best, but she will not be able to convince Andreas. He's not nearly as nice as she thinks. His connections with Boris and Hans are so troubling. I think he will disappear as soon as she says anything about this meeting. We can't let that happen, can we?"

"We could, but not if we care what happens to them. Either Boris or Hans will find them eventually. They are young and careless. They think that they make no mistakes. Everyone makes mistakes. Everyone leaves a trail. If we don't stop them, we will regret it."

Samantha smiled warmly at her friend and lover. "You have a soft heart, you know."

"Yeah, I've always suspected that I did. I can live with that. Let's round up this pair before someone else does." Chase took out his phone and gave detailed instructions to attentive ears on the other end.

Before they left, Chase pulled out his Agency phone and noticed a text message that he had ignored while they were pleading with Bekka. It was from Control:

> Could not hold Boris any longer—his countrymen had a change of heart and want him home. Be careful!

This was a complication Chase didn't need right now. Boris would be disarmed, although still dangerous. Worst case, he could have acquired another weapon on short notice. His first thought was to keep Samantha at a safe distance. It would put his mind at ease and allow him to focus on the details of the operation. He called the backup car with additional instructions. Sam would watch the operation from the car. In his present condition, Chase would need some physical assistance. He asked for the young man named Rolf, whose strong hands had pulled him to safety after the stabbing by Boris. Chase could tell that this man had the right disposition, and the ability to do whatever was necessary to complete the mission.

As the two left the *gasthof,* Chase leaned close to Sam and said, "I need you to ride in the car for this one. One of the guys will go in with me. I need someone physical to watch my back."

Sam started to protest, but Chase gave her one of those looks that meant "it has to be this way." She took a deep breath and let it out with a sigh. "Okay, but please let the other guy go in first. No more hospital visits, right?"

Chase smiled at her as the car pulled up to the curb. Sam relaxed when she saw the same crew that had rescued them less than twenty-four hours ago. "This will be all right," she whispered to herself. Then she deposited Boris's gun from the other night in Chase's left coat pocket. He looked into her eyes, but she could see he wasn't surprised.

-69-

Sachsenhausen

As the two men ascended to the top floor of the small apartment building, the sounds of a desperate struggle, and then screaming, emerged from the door ahead. Rolf bolted the remained steps onto the landing and pressed himself against the wall to the left of the door, his sidearm drawn. Chase made it to the other side of the doorway a split second later, and in extreme pain. Rolf dropped low with his weapon aimed into the apartment. He could see only broken furniture, and a young woman pressed up against the wall of a small kitchen area.

He motioned Chase to follow and then moved himself, scanning the now visible spaces with his gun and his eyes moving as one. Two men were rolling across the floor, one with a frying pan that he repeatedly bashed into the other man's head. Chase didn't wait for another signal from Rolf. He sprinted across the room and delivered a heavy kick to the aggressor's ribs. He followed with a knee to the chin as the man tried to rise and another to the man's midsection. This fight was over. Chase slumped over his own knees in obvious pain.

Boris lay on the floor covered with the blood from several wounds on Andreas's head. He was semiconscious. Chase pulled out a small auto-injector and slapped it against the man's upper arm. Boris was finally safe. Andreas was leaning against an overturned chair, thick red blood oozing from two especially deep scalp wounds on the right side of his head. He was dazed, almost unconscious. Chase motioned to Bekka to come closer. "Get a clean towel and hold it firmly against the bleeding," he gently ordered her. "He will be fine."

Chase called the car and asked that Sam and one other agent come up quickly. When Sam arrived, she only had eyes for Chase. She assured herself that he was unharmed and then asked what she could do to help.

"Take Bekka to the car. Andreas will be coming with you too. I need to stay here to tidy up, but I will meet you back at the hotel in about an hour."

Sam, Bekka, the other agent, and Andreas walked slowly down the stairs to the waiting car. Rolf and Chase remained behind. Rolf gathered up two laptops from a table, scanned the room for anything else of interest, and then looked at Chase. Rolf turned to leave with his loot. He stopped before the apartment door and looked again at Chase. "This next part never happened." Then he left the room and returned to the waiting car, which departed immediately.

During the entire time he had done clandestine work for the CIA, Chase had hoped that a situation like this would never arrive. It was the first time he had ever faced an adversary who was so obsessed with revenge that self-preservation didn't matter. Boris was pathological. He was like a mad dog leaping against a steel door until all its teeth lay splintered on the ground. Even then, it would not stop attacking the door that was its perceived enemy.

Chase went into the kitchen and grabbed a towel, wetted it, and began to clean off his shoe and his trousers. He methodically rubbed the spots of damp blood until few visible traces remained. All the while, he was thinking—carefully considering—whether he could cross a threshold that would forever lead in only one direction. He didn't hate Boris. He was a dangerous man and lacking self-control. He would do what he did tonight, and last night, as many times as he would feel necessary, until the day that someone stronger stopped him.

After cleaning himself of any blood residue, Chase dropped the towel on the floor and wiped his feet on it. Then he put it in the sink and rinsed it. He took the last remaining dry towel and wiped every surface that he, or anyone on his team, had touched. He took out his phone and sent a text to Control.

What do I do with Boris?

As he waited, Chase moved methodically through the small apartment looking for anything that should be removed before he left. After a few minutes of waiting, he received his final orders.

You know the house rules. We have no home for him.
Leave him and walk away.

Chase descended the stairs to the street a few minutes later and headed back in the direction of the river and the city center. His mind was clear and finally at peace. He could barely wait to rejoin Sam and hold her in his arms. As he walked across the long river bridge linking Frankfurt and Sachsenhausen, he reached inside his coat pocket with a tissue and removed a small automatic handgun. He stretched his hand over the railing and dropped it into the icy river below. It carried no identifying marks of any kind, and its magazine was full, less one round.

-70-

Elsewhere in Germany

The car containing the wounded Andreas was driven to a small clinic in a northern suburb of Frankfurt. It was already dark. A physician known to the Agency examined the young man and then stitched up three scalp wounds caused by the frying pan. Andreas appeared to have no permanent injuries, and the doctor recommended keeping him awake for the next twelve hours to observe for any signs of a concussion. The two agents who escorted him into the office laughed and assured the doctor that Andreas would not be sleeping for at least that long. The doctor shrugged indifferently and accepted some large-denomination bills for his services.

Andreas and Bekka were taken to a safe house in Hofheim, about a thirty-minute drive outside of the city, near the Taunus Mountains. It was a typical postwar cement block bungalow, covered with plaster and now gentled with mature cherry trees and a flower garden. In contrast with the usual locations used by this team, this one had heat, and the two young people were offered something to drink. Andreas was still hurting, and his head was swollen after the severe beating he had received from Boris. He would have to live with that for now. His hosts needed to know a great deal about his activities of the last few months. He and Bekka were separated, and the questioning began. The focus was on Andreas, but Bekka was also questioned to determine the extent of her involvement, and whether Andreas was telling the truth.

The interrogation had been going on for about four hours and Andreas, true to his nature, was happy to boast about limited details of his exploits. He was vague about any personal involvement with the CIA break-in, but he made a point of telling his interrogators how he had forced the big companies to admit their deceptions. The agents put up with this. What they were really after was what, if anything, might be about to happen next. Their orders were to protect the Agency. The rest of the world would have to defend itself.

"Andreas, we're going to give you an opportunity to go free. You and your friend can return to Norway, or the United States, or anywhere else you want to go. We will always be watching you. First, tell us what mischief you have been up to in the last few days."

Andreas was not frightened in the least, but he reasoned that victory is only sweet if your opponent knows he has been beaten. "Watch the markets tomorrow. What I have done will be obvious."

"I suppose you can stop it if you want to?"

"No, nothing can stop it. Relax! No one is going to die. It's only money."

With that, Andreas ceased talking. In his mind, the interview was over.

Aftermath

As Andreas had predicted, the financial markets in London and Frankfurt opened without much activity as everyone awaited the midmorning release of two significant reports of French and German economic output. At precisely fifteen minutes after nine Paris time, the automated currency trading systems at UBB in Zurich, and Broadway in London, released a flurry of trades involving the EUR/CHF currency pair. Someone with significant resources or superior knowledge was selling the euro and buying Swiss francs in great volume. The exchange rate immediately fell more than 2 percent and then trading systems across the globe kicked in, to either protect or improve predetermined positions relative to both currencies.

To their credit, both institutions attempted to kill the transaction flow until their experts could verify what was going on. Both attempts failed. The activation of the kill switch in each trading system triggered a second release of transactions, these at rapidly declining prices for the euro that indicated either a massive intervention by a hedge fund or a national bank, or that negative news on the major euro-economies was imminent. Whatever the cause, a great deal of money was moving out of the euro and into the safety of the franc.

By 9:19, the EUR/CHF bid stood at 1.1395. At this point, Andreas's sell-order should already have been executed. However, he had not foreseen the paralysis of pending orders that would occur. His stop-loss order was frozen with a million others and was never executed. He lost everything he had bet.

Then, as it always does postconvulsion, the market finally made a swing back toward the starting point of the day. If one had not been involved in currency trading, it would have appeared that nothing had happened. However, something momentous *had* happened.

At 9:21, the European Central Bank halted all trading in the euro, but its action was already too late. In five short minutes, more than seven hundred billion euros had changed hands, and losses in the tens of billions had been incurred by banks and trading houses. It would only take Broadway a few minutes to understand what had happened to their system. It had been designed to protect against external threats, not those from inside the company. The firewall between test and production systems was considered foolproof. That was unless some fool found a way to break it. One had, and now others would try.

On a fast train somewhere near the German/Swiss border, Andreas watched the market convulse as the news on his phone streamed in. He smiled over at Bekka and said, "It happened just like we planned." Then he turned his attention back to the news. He knew that shortly a prerecorded message would announce that the PLL had once again infiltrated one of the most secure systems in the world. It would read, "We know where you keep your money—we know where you live—next time we will come for you."

At the next stop, while Andreas was walking toward the bar car for a celebratory beer, Bekka grabbed her backpack and left the train. This ride was over. She smiled as the train pulled away, and she began a new life.

***

Sam and Chase left Frankfurt by train as well. A few hours later they were walking out of the Gare de l'Est into the brisk winter air of Paris. They had talked only a little during the ride, preferring to lean on one another and doze. Chase was still in some pain from the wound he had received from Boris. Neither of them mentioned the madman. Samantha understood that the door on this topic had been permanently locked. She decided that she could live with that. In all honesty, the only thing she cared about was that Boris would never bother her man again. She could accept that. It was good enough.

Made in the USA
Middletown, DE
17 January 2021